What's New in Visual FoxPro 7.0

Tamar E. Granor
Doug Hennig
Kevin McNeish

Hentzenwerke Publishing

Published by:
Hentzenwerke Publishing
980 East Circle Drive
Whitefish Bay WI 53217 USA

Hentzenwerke Publishing books are available through booksellers and directly from the
publisher. Contact Hentzenwerke Publishing at:
414.332.9876
414.332.9463 (fax)
www.hentzenwerke.com
books@hentzenwerke.com

What's New in Visual FoxPro 7.0
    By Tamar E. Granor, Doug Hennig & Kevin McNeish
    Technical Editor: Alex Wieder
    Copy Editor: Farion Grove

ISBN: 1-930919-06-9

Manufactured in the United States of America.

Our Contract with You, The Reader

In which we, the folks who make up Hentzenwerke Publishing, describe what you, the reader, can expect from this book and from us.

Hi there!

I've been writing professionally (in other words, eventually getting a paycheck for my scribbles) since 1974, and writing about software development since 1992. As an author, I've worked with a half-dozen different publishers and corresponded with thousands of readers over the years. As a software developer and all-around geek, I've also acquired a library of more than 100 computer and software-related books.

Thus, when I donned the publisher's cap four years ago to produce the *1997 Developer's Guide,* I had some pretty good ideas of what I liked (and didn't like) from publishers, what readers liked and didn't like, and what I, as a reader, liked and didn't like.

Now, with our new titles for 2001, we're entering our fourth season. (For those who are keeping track, the '97 DevGuide was our first, albeit abbreviated, season, the batch of six "Essentials" for Visual FoxPro 6.0 in 1999 was our second, and, in keeping with the sports analogy, the books we published in 2000 comprised our third.)

John Wooden, the famed UCLA basketball coach, posited that teams aren't consistent; they're always getting better—or worse. We'd like to get better…

One of my goals for this season is to build a closer relationship with you, the reader. In order for us to do this, you've got to know what you should expect from us.

- You have the right to expect that your order will be processed quickly and correctly, and that your book will be delivered to you in new condition.

- You have the right to expect that the content of your book is technically accurate and up-to-date, that the explanations are clear, and that the layout is easy to read and follow without a lot of fluff or nonsense.

- You have the right to expect access to source code, errata, FAQs, and other information that's relevant to the book via our Web site.

- You have the right to expect an electronic version of your printed book to be available via our Web site.

- You have the right to expect that, if you report errors to us, your report will be responded to promptly, and that the appropriate notice will be included in the errata and/or FAQs for the book.

Naturally, there are some limits that we bump up against. There are humans involved, and they make mistakes. A book of 500 pages contains, on average, 150,000 words and several megabytes of source code. It's not possible to edit and re-edit multiple times to catch every last misspelling and typo, nor is it possible to test the source code on every permutation of development environment and operating system—and still price the book affordably.

Once printed, bindings break, ink gets smeared, signatures get missed during binding. On the delivery side, Web sites go down, packages get lost in the mail.

Nonetheless, we'll make our best effort to correct these problems—once you let us know about them.

In return, when you have a question or run into a problem, we ask that you first consult the errata and/or FAQs for your book on our Web site. If you don't find the answer there, please e-mail us at **books@hentzenwerke.com** with as much information and detail as possible, including 1) the steps to reproduce the problem, 2) what happened, and 3) what you expected to happen, together with 4) any other relevant information.

I'd like to stress that we need you to communicate questions and problems clearly. For example…

- "Your downloads don't work" isn't enough information for us to help you. "I get a 404 error when I click on the **Download Source Code** link on **http://www.hentzenwerke.com/book/downloads.html**" is something we can help you with.

- "The code in Chapter 10 caused an error" again isn't enough information. "I performed the following steps to run the source code program DisplayTest.PRG in Chapter 10, and I received an error that said 'Variable m.liCounter not found'" is something we can help you with.

We'll do our best to get back to you within a couple of days, either with an answer or at least an acknowledgement that we've received your inquiry and that we're working on it.

On behalf of the authors, technical editors, copy editors, layout artists, graphical artists, indexers, and all the other folks who have worked to put this book in your hands, I'd like to thank you for purchasing this book, and I hope that it will prove to be a valuable addition to your technical library. Please let us know what you think about this book—we're looking forward to hearing from you.

As Groucho Marx once observed, "Outside of a dog, a book is a man's best friend. Inside of a dog, it's too dark to read."

Whil Hentzen
Hentzenwerke Publishing
July 2001

List of Chapters

Table of Contents

Chapter 3: New and Better Tools   43

Chapter 12: Building World-Class COM Servers in VFP 7   161

Chapter 15: Working with Web Services 225

Acknowledgements

No technical book of any significance springs fully formed from the fingers of its authors onto the page. Other people always provide inspiration, technical information, clarification, and support. We hope this book is significant, and there are a number of others we need to thank.

First, as always, the Visual FoxPro team at Microsoft deserves our kudos and yours. With VFP 7, they've made our lives as developers easier and made it possible for us to build even better applications. In addition to the team as a whole, a few members deserve special recognition for providing help above and beyond the call of duty. Product Manager Randy Brown answered tons of questions about this new version. Beta newsgroup sysops Jim Saunders and Brad Peterson checked our bug reports, let us know when we were right, and clarified things when we misunderstood. Program Manager Gene Goldhammer also helped us to understand some of the new features.

Some of our fellow beta testers also helped us to get it. We won't name names for fear of omitting someone, but you know who you are.

David Frankenbach deserves credit for the technique shown in Chapter 6 for making a form circular.

Our technical editor, Alex Wieder, caught us when we were unclear or sloppy or just plain wrong, and made this a better book.

Finally, our common expression of appreciation must include our friend and publisher, Whil Hentzen, who took a huge risk a few years back in order to ensure the availability of VFP books.

Of course, we each have individual thanks to offer as well.

Working with Doug and Kevin has been a pleasure. The whole process of writing this book went more smoothly than any other I've worked on, and managed not to engulf my whole life.

My family continues to support my writing habit, in ways large and small. Grateful thanks to my husband Marshal, and our sons, Nathaniel and Solomon, all of whom appreciate that writing is something I just have to do.

—Tamar

My thanks must start with Whil, who doggedly insisted for over a year that I write this book, and found a sly way to get me to do it. Working with Tamar again was a treat, and I enjoyed working with Kevin and Alex for the first and hopefully not the last time. My wife Peggy and son Nicholas are the sunshine in my life; their love and support made it possible for me to take time away from them to work on this project. Finally, I'd like to thank Kevin for propelling my sex-symbol status into the stratosphere!

—Doug

Thanks to Whil, Doug, and Tamar for twisting my arm into writing the chapters on COM—it was a lot of work, but also a lot of fun. Thanks to my wife Nicole for her copy editing skills, patience, and support throughout the whole process. Also thanks to my sons Jordan, Timothy, and Alexander who had to give up some "Daddy time" on nights and weekends.

—*Kevin*

About the Authors

Tamar E. Granor

Tamar E. Granor, Ph.D., works with other developers through consulting and subcontracting. Editor of *FoxPro Advisor* magazine from 1994 to 2000, she is currently Technical Editor and co-author of the popular "Advisor Answers" column. Tamar is co-author of several books, including the award-winning *Hacker's Guide to Visual FoxPro 6.0*. She is Technical Editor of *Visual FoxPro Certification Exams Study Guide*. Her books are available from Hentzenwerke Publishing (**www.hentzenwerke.com**). Tamar, a Microsoft Certified Professional and Microsoft Support Most Valuable Professional, speaks frequently about Visual FoxPro at conferences and user groups. E-mail: tamar_granor@compuserve.com.

Doug Hennig

Doug Hennig is a partner with Stonefield Systems Group Inc. He is the author of the award-winning Stonefield Database Toolkit and author of *The Visual FoxPro Data Dictionary* in Pinnacle Publishing's *The Pros Talk Visual FoxPro* series. He writes the monthly "Reusable Tools" column in *FoxTalk*. Doug has spoken at every Microsoft FoxPro Developers Conference (DevCon) since 1997 and at user groups and developer conferences all over North America. He is a Microsoft Most Valuable Professional (MVP) and Certified Professional (MCP). Web: **www.stonefield.com**, e-mail: dhennig@stonefield.com.

Kevin McNeish

Kevin McNeish is President of Oak Leaf Enterprises—a company that specializes in object-oriented custom software, training, and developer tools. He is the creator of The Mere Mortals Framework and has spoken at many Visual FoxPro conferences and user groups in North America and Europe. He has also written articles for *FoxPro Advisor* and *FoxTalk* magazines. Kevin mentors and trains many software companies to build flexible, component-based applications that scale from the desktop to the Internet. He is a Microsoft Certified Developer and has created many enterprise-wide applications for a wide variety of vertical markets using Visual FoxPro as the primary development tool. Phone: 804-979-2417, Web: **www.oakleafsd.com**, e-mail: kevinm@oakleafsd.com.

Alex Wieder

Alex Wieder is the principal of Tasmanian Traders, an independent consulting firm specializing in object-oriented development using Visual FoxPro. Originally from Venezuela, he has been developing software since the late 1970s and currently concentrates on workflow, document management, and barcoding applications. He has written several articles for *FoxPro Advisor*.

How to Download the Files

Hentzenwerke Publishing generally provides two sets of files to accompany its books. The first is the source code referenced throughout the text. Note that some books do not have source code; in those cases, a placeholder file is provided in lieu of the source code in order to alert you of the fact. The second is the e-book version (or versions) of the book. Depending on the book, we provide e-books in either the compiled HTML Help (.CHM) format, Adobe Acrobat (.PDF) format, or both. Here's how to get them.

Both the source code and e-book file(s) are available for download from the Hentzenwerke Web site. In order to obtain them, follow these instructions:

1. Point your Web browser to **http://www.hentzenwerke.com**.

2. Look for the link that says "Download"

3. A page describing the download process will appear. This page has two sections:

- **Section 1:** If you were issued a username/password directly from Hentzenwerke Publishing, you can enter them into this page.

- **Section 2:** If you did not receive a username/password from Hentzenwerke Publishing, don't worry! Just enter your e-mail alias and look for the question about your book. Note that you'll need your physical book when you answer the question.

4. A page that lists the hyperlinks for the appropriate downloads will appear.

Note that the e-book file(s) are covered by the same copyright laws as the printed book. Reproduction and/or distribution of these files is against the law.

If you have questions or problems, the fastest way to get a response is to e-mail us at **books@hentzenwerke.com**.

Foreword

An internal combustion engine designer knows a great deal about how a car engine works, but that doesn't mean that he's a good driver. He understands all the necessary nitty-gritty details of air-fuel mixtures, compression ratios, and such, but he may not know how to drive to the local computer store. Likewise, a piano technician/tuner knows how to rebuild and tune a piano, but she's often not the best choice for dinner music.

As the lead developer on the Visual FoxPro team, I've had many opportunities over the years to design and implement lots of cool new features to the product. I understand things like how a VFP form or index works and how early binding is implemented, but I don't have much recent experience designing full-blown vertical market applications that meet the business needs of customers.

In my prior life as a FoxPro developer for many years developing vertical market apps for customers, I knew what it was like to have a client call and say, "The sales tax law changes tomorrow: It is now being applied to customer rentals. Can you make the changes to the program please? Now?!?" or "I want you to make your program work with Foobar customers. Foobars are exactly the same as normal customers..." (yeah, right).

I know that Doug, Tamar, and Kevin have received numerous requests from clients to make apps sing and dance much more recently than I have. They've had to struggle through deciding when it's best to use local views vs. cursors, table buffering vs. transactions, or forms vs. classes. Their cumulative years of experience in making such decisions add a wealth of insight to explaining the new features of Visual FoxPro in this book.

Having Doug, Tamar, and Kevin explain and expound on these features is like reading a how-to book on getting from here to there written by great race car drivers like Mario Andretti, Al Unser, and Dale Earnhardt, or having Wolfgang Mozart or Ludwig van Beethoven guiding your fingers on the keys.

Calvin Hsia
Senior Software Design Engineer
Microsoft Visual FoxPro Team

Introduction

Why a book on the new features of VFP 7?

Back in the old days, whenever a new version of FoxPro came along, we'd read the manuals from cover to cover. It was a great way to get up to speed on the new material and get a refresher course on the rest of the product.

Alas, life isn't so simple now. First, VFP no longer comes with paper manuals, and reading vast amounts of documentation in front of a computer just has no appeal. More importantly, we have no doubt that if you printed out the VFP documentation, it would amount to thousands of pages. We don't have time to read all that and we doubt you do, either.

But why not just rely on the Help sections that talk about new features and functionality? There are two reasons. First, because it's not that easy to find them all. Although the FoxPro documentation gets better with every version, a hyperlinked document is not the best way to get all the information available about a topic. Second, because sometimes the documentation tells you what, but doesn't tell you why.

Enter this book. It's designed to be a concise guide to all the new features, language elements, and functionality in VFP 7, including the items that have changed since VFP 6. It puts all of that information in one place, organized in what we hope you find is a logical way. We've also tried to give you an idea why you'd want to use each new feature. Unlike the *Hacker's Guide to Visual FoxPro* (also available from Hentzenwerke Publishing), this book isn't intended to be an exhaustive look at the new features, but instead to give you an idea why it was added or what you might use it for.

Organization

This book has three major sections. Chapters 1 through 4 cover changes in the IDE, the development environment you use to create applications. They also cover changes that affect the run-time environment, and language items introduced or modified to support the IDE changes. So, for example, you'll find the _CODESENSE variable in Chapter 1, "IntelliSense," because it supports IntelliSense.

Chapters 5 through 10 cover new and modified language features, other than those that support IDE changes and those related to COM development. Each chapter covers changes relating to one part of the language (except for Chapter 10, "Bits and Pieces," which covers everything that didn't fit into the other chapters).

The final five chapters cover COM-related changes—anything that makes it easier to develop and use component technology in VFP. Because we believe that component development is still new to most VFP developers, this section of the book takes a somewhat different approach. Rather than just covering the new items and showing their uses, it provides more background. In fact, Chapter 11 doesn't cover any new features at all—instead, it introduces component development and explains how it fits into the development picture.

Since many new and changed items could logically fit into more than one place in the book, we've tried to be liberal with cross-references, pointing you to other sections or chapters where a topic is discussed more fully.

Get the picture

We're not sure that a picture is worth a *thousand* words, but certainly, pictures can say some things more concisely than words. You'll find a few icons used in this book. Here's your key to them.

 This symbol is your clue that there's example code available. All the code for this book can be downloaded from **www.hentzenwerke.com**. *See page xxi for details.*

Some items just need to be pointed out or don't fit very well into the flow of the text. This icon identifies notes of that sort.

In some places, you'll see text that looks like this: dialog text. That font indicates that the text is a caption in a dialog or form.

What about the code?

The code for the first 10 chapters of this book is organized by chapter, with a separate ZIP file for each chapter that has code. Each ZIP file should be self-contained, with everything you need to run it. For the COM section of the book, there's a single ZIP file, containing all the COM-related samples.

Go to it

We think VFP 7 is a fantastic upgrade to an already solid product. We hope that, once you've read this book and spent a little time with the product, you'll agree.

Section 1
Developer Productivity

Chapter 1
IntelliSense

One thing VFP developers have long envied in other Microsoft development environments is IntelliSense. In VFP 7, this great productivity enhancement is finally available.

One of the most obvious differences between VFP 6 and other Microsoft development environments is IntelliSense. Type a statement such as "Dim SomeVariable As" in Visual Basic and a list of all of the types a variable can be defined as (data types as well as objects) immediately pops up. This is a great productivity booster for several reasons: You can quickly pick the one you want from the list, it avoids spelling mistakes, and you don't have to always head for the manual or Help file to figure out the syntax for a little-used command. VFP developers have felt shortchanged ever since IntelliSense was introduced.

Fret no more! VFP 7 introduces IntelliSense to VFP developers, and makes up for the long wait by providing a better version of IntelliSense than other products have. Once you start appreciating how much more productive IntelliSense makes you, you'll wonder how you ever coded without it.

What IntelliSense offers

IntelliSense is only one word, but it encompasses several behaviors, including:

- Automatic keyword completion
- Command and function syntax tips
- Lists of members, values, and most recently used files

Automatic keyword completion

Xbase descendents such as FoxPro have always supported two ways to enter keywords, such as command and functions: using the full, official keyword (such as Browse) or using the first four or more characters (such as Brow). However, veteran developers will tell you that while it's fine to use "Repl" in the Command Window, you really should use the full "Replace" in code for clarity.

VFP 7 provides the best of both worlds: You can now type just enough of a keyword to make it distinct, and then press Space or Enter in the case of a command or "(" in the case of a function, and VFP completes the keyword for you. For example, if you type "modi" and press Space, VFP replaces it with "MODIFY". Because some keywords start with the same set of characters, be sure to type enough to distinguish the keyword from any others. If you want to use the MessageBox() function, you can't just type "mess("; VFP expands that to "MESSAGE(".

Some commands actually consist of more than one keyword; examples include Alter Table, Report Form, and Open Database. Since the first keyword must always be followed by the second, VFP automatically adds that keyword as well. This can take a little getting used to; for a while, you'll probably find yourself typing "OPEN DATABASE DATABASE MyData" because you didn't notice that VFP automatically inserted "DATABASE" as soon as you pressed Space after typing "open".

"Set" is the first keyword in a long list of Set commands. When you type "set" and press Space, IntelliSense displays a list of each of the keywords that can follow "set", such as "deleted" and "exact" (see **Figure 1**). Some commands include the word "to", such as Set Classlib To; as you'll see later in this chapter, you can choose whether IntelliSense automatically inserts the "to" or not.

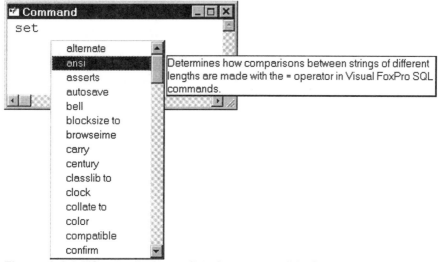

Figure 1. IntelliSense displays a list of every possible Set command.

VFP doesn't complete keywords in the middle of a statement. For example, if you type the While clause of a Replace command as "whil", that's how it stays; VFP won't expand it to "WHILE".

Notice the case VFP uses; even if you type the entire word "modify", VFP replaces it with "MODIFY". This probably won't bother long-time Xbase developers, who expect keywords to be in uppercase, but this is very disconcerting to those who prefer lowercase or even "camel" case (such as "TableUpdate()"). Fortunately, you can control the case used for keyword expansion through the IntelliSense Manager, which is discussed in the "Configuring IntelliSense" section of this chapter.

There may be times when you don't want VFP to expand a keyword. Pressing Ctrl-Space rather than Space at the end of a command suppresses expansion for the command. To undo an expansion, press Ctrl-Z twice (the first removes the replacement and the second restores the original keyword, leaving it selected), and then press End to move the cursor to the end of the keyword.

Command and function syntax tips

After typing "repl" and pressing Space, you may notice something besides the keyword completion: a tip window showing the complete syntax of the Replace command (see **Figure 2**). This feature, which Microsoft calls "Quick Info," is a great productivity booster; how many times do you find yourself bringing up the VFP Help file because you can't quite remember the exact syntax for Alter Table or whether the string to search is the first or second parameter in At()?

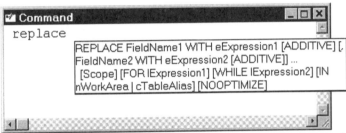

Figure 2. Quick Info saves you a trip to the Help file by displaying the complete syntax for commands and functions.

The tip window stays on-screen as you continue to type the rest of a command or enter the parameters of a function, method, or event, only disappearing when you complete the function with ")", move to another line (such as pressing Enter), or press Backspace (in that case, it reappears when you move the cursor to the next element of the command). You can manually hide it by pressing Esc and manually display it with Ctrl-I or the Edit | Quick Info menu item. It's especially useful for functions, methods, and events: The parameter you're currently typing appears in bold (see **Figure 3**).

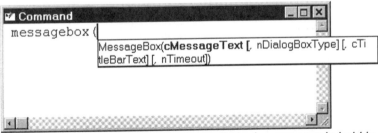

Figure 3. The parameter you're currently typing appears in bold in the Quick Info tip window.

For some functions, the tip window displays information about the values for a specific parameter. For example, the second parameter for MessageBox() is an additive value for the buttons and icon for the dialog. As you can see in **Figure 4**, IntelliSense shows the complete list of valid values for this parameter. Other functions accept only one of a list of predefined values for some parameters. For instance, the second parameter in DBGetProp() specifies the type of data object (connection, database, field, table, or view), and the list of values for the third parameter, the property, varies with the type of object (for example, DefaultValue is only available for fields). For the type parameter, IntelliSense displays a list of the object types; choose the desired type from the list and IntelliSense inserts it, complete with quotes, in the command line. The list of values displayed for the property parameter includes only those applicable to the selected type; again, you can choose the property from the list to add it to the command line.

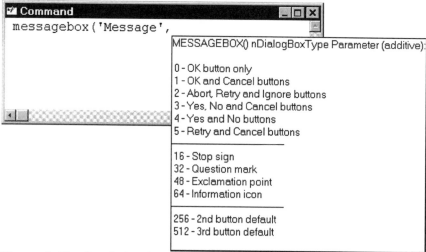

Figure 4. The tip window for some functions shows detailed information about the current parameter.

The SYS() function is a special case of this. Although there's only one keyword, it really consists of a large number of functions, with the specific function determined by the first parameter. As **Figure 5** shows, IntelliSense displays a list for this parameter showing not only the numeric values but also the meaning for each one. Once you've selected which one you want, the tip window shows the syntax for the rest of the function call.

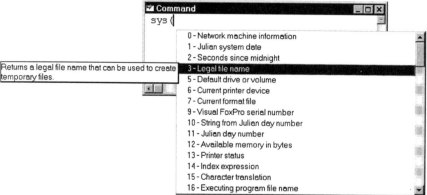

Figure 5. IntelliSense makes it easy to figure out which value to pass SYS() for which function.

List of members

In today's object-oriented code, the IntelliSense List Members feature does more to save you typing than any other. When you enter the name of an object and press ".", VFP displays a list of all members (properties, methods, events, and contained members) of the object; an icon indicates what type of member it is. **Figure 6** shows an example, displaying the members of a newly instantiated Custom object.

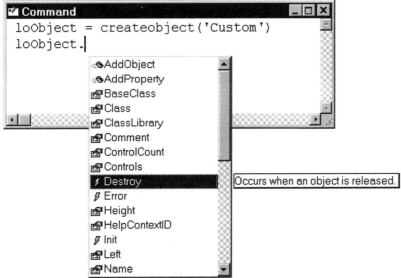

Figure 6. IntelliSense's List Members feature displays the members of an object.

You can navigate through the list using the up and down arrow keys, the Page Up and Page Down keys, or using incremental searching by typing the first few letters of a member's name (the letters you type also appear after the period in the command line). As you do so, a ToolTip box shows the description of each member, once again saving you a trip to the Help file.

IntelliSense adds the selected member's name to the command line and hides the list if you press Tab (the cursor appears right behind the member name), Enter (the cursor moves to the next line), or some non-alphabetical character such as Space, ".", "=", or "(" (the character is added at the end of the member name). Pressing Home, End, Esc, or the left or right arrow (if they move the cursor before the period or past the end of what's already typed) hides the list without adding the member's name to the command line. You can manually display the list by pressing Ctrl-J or choosing the Edit | List Member menu item.

List Members works in object hierarchies too. Imagine how much you'd have to type to programmatically change the Caption of the header in the third column of a grid on page 2 of a page frame in a form:

```
Thisform.PageFrame1.Page2.Grid.Column3.Header.Caption = 'some value'
```

Oops, the name of the grid is actually grdCustomers, so when you run this code, it'll bomb. List Members saves you from both making a spelling mistake and having to type all that code; after you type the period following Thisform, you can select PageFrame1 from the member list and press "." to display the member list for the page frame, choose Page2 and press "." to display the member list for that page, and so on until finally you choose Caption for the header and press "=" to close the list.

List Members doesn't just work with native VFP objects; it works with any instantiated object, such as a TreeView ActiveX control you've added to a form or a COM object you've instantiated with CreateObject(). Unlike Visual Basic's IntelliSense, VFP's version supports member lists for objects in collections (such as Excel's Cells collection) rather than stopping at the collection itself. Even better, it can work with objects you haven't instantiated yet. That leads to the next topic.

Early binding

VFP is a late-binding client of COM objects. That means during development (in the editor and at compile time), VFP has no idea what kind of object you're instantiating in a call to CreateObject(). Only when that code is actually executed does VFP figure out what the properties, events, and methods (PEMs) are for the object. It does that by reading the type library for the object; for a discussion of type libraries, see Chapter 12, "Building World-Class COM Servers in VFP 7." Early-binding clients, such as Visual Basic, read the type library at development time instead. This provides several benefits, but the one related to IntelliSense is the ability to display the members of the COM object in the editor. Say, that sounds just like the List Members feature of VFP 7. The problem is that since VFP doesn't know you've instantiated an Excel object in your code, how can it display Excel's members?

To solve this problem, Microsoft added the As clause to the Local and Public commands (it's also available in Parameters, LParameters, Function, and Procedure declarations, but that's for a different purpose; see the "Strong typing" section of Chapter 12, "Building World-Class COM Servers in VFP 7"). This clause allows you to specify the class of object a variable will contain at run time. When you type the variable name followed by a period in the VFP editor, IntelliSense sees that the variable has been "typed" as a class, gets the members for that class (reading the type library in the case of a COM object), and displays them in the List Members list. **Figure 7** shows the members of the variable loExcel, which has been declared as being an Excel.Application object. Notice there's no CreateObject() statement in this code, so it won't actually work at run time. The As clause doesn't instantiate the object—you still have to do that in code—it just tells IntelliSense how to treat a variable in the editor.

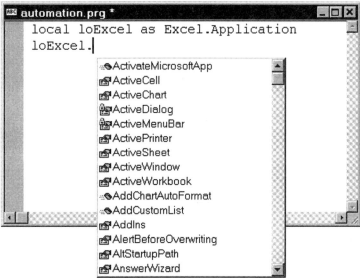

Figure 7. IntelliSense can show COM members if you declare a variable "as" the COM object.

After you type the As keyword and press Space, a list of types appears. This list includes VFP data types (such as Integer and Numeric), base classes (including Form and Custom), registered type libraries (for example, ADODB and Excel), your own classes, and Web Services. As with many things in VFP, the list of types is defined in a table, so you can add type libraries, classes, Web Services, and other types. This is discussed in detail later in this chapter in the "Configuring IntelliSense" section.

There's one slight consequence of this cool new feature: Spaces are no longer supported between variable names in Local and Public statements, such as:

```
local MyVar1 MyVar2
```

Since most people didn't know you could separate variables with spaces (the Help file has always shown the correct syntax using commas), this likely won't break too much code.

Values list

Some object properties accept only a small range of values. For example, Form.AutoCenter is Logical, so the only acceptable values are True and False. Object.BackColor accepts a fairly wide range of numeric values, but these values each represent a color, of which there is a relatively small number of commonly used ones. Unfortunately, figuring out which number to use for the desired color isn't easy. IntelliSense makes it easy to select the correct value for properties like these. When you type "=" after some property names, IntelliSense displays a list of the valid values for those properties; see **Figure 8** for an example.

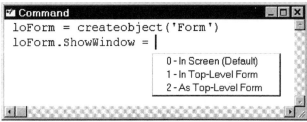

Figure 8. *The List Values feature makes it easy to select the correct value for a property.*

Logical properties like AutoCenter and AlwaysOnTop have a list with True and False displayed. Those numeric properties that have an enumerated list of values, like BorderStyle, ScrollBars, and WindowType, display the possible values and their meanings. For properties with more complex values, IntelliSense displays an appropriate dialog, such as a color picker for properties representing colors (such as BackColor, FillColor, and ForeColor) and an Open Picture dialog for properties containing image file names (such as Icon and Picture). As with the List Members feature, List Values supports COM objects as well as native ones; IntelliSense displays a list of values for those properties with enumerations defined in the type library. **Figure 9** shows how useful this feature is with an ADO RecordSet, which uses enumerated values for many properties. Notice the line of code above the one showing the list; IntelliSense not only inserted the value but a comment showing the enumerator name for the value, making your code much easier to follow.

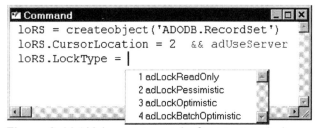

Figure 9. *List Values even works for enumerated properties of COM objects.*

Some properties that you may think should have a values list or dialog don't. For example, although they contain image file names, IntelliSense doesn't display an Open Picture dialog for DragIcon, MouseIcon, and OLEDragPicture. You may be surprised to not see a font dialog for the FontName property. You'll see later in this chapter how you can script IntelliSense so you could add this functionality if you wish.

The List Values feature doesn't have its own menu item or hot key; the List Members item and hot key (Ctrl-J) serve the same function.

Most recently used file list

Some VFP commands open or process files. Examples include all the Modify commands (such as Modify Program), Open Database, and Report Form. IntelliSense presents a most recently used (MRU) list for these commands, making it easy to use a file you previously worked with. **Figure 10** shows this list in action. You also get an MRU list of directories with the CD command. Note that this feature is only supported in the Command Window. See the "Auto MRU (Most Recently Used) Files" topic in the VFP Help file for a complete list of commands with MRU lists.

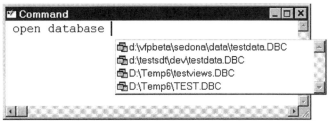

Figure 10. The MRU list IntelliSense displays makes it easy to select a file you used before.

The View page of VFP's Options dialog has a Most Recently Used list contains option that gives you control over how many items IntelliSense will display for you.

Table, field, and variable lists

IntelliSense extends the MRU list for the Use command: In addition to tables you've opened before, it lists the tables and views in the current database. The list has a value tip window showing the comment for the selected table or view. IntelliSense also extends the values list for the Replace, Modify Memo, and Modify General commands: If a cursor is open in the current work area, it displays a list of fields in that cursor. A value tip window shows the data type, size, caption, and comment for the selected field; see **Figure 11** for an example. If you type "m." in the Command Window, IntelliSense displays a list of declared variables. The value tip for each variable shows its current value. As with the MRU list, none of these features works in an editor window.

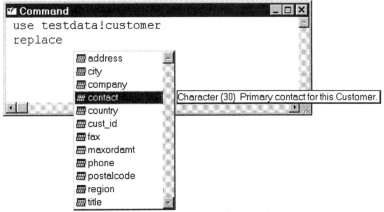

Figure 11. IntelliSense displays a list of fields in the current cursor for some commands.

Configuring IntelliSense

IntelliSense may not work exactly as you wish straight out of the box. For example, if you prefer that keywords appear in something other than uppercase, you'll be frustrated typing them in your desired case only to see VFP automatically change them to uppercase when you press Space or Enter. Similarly, you might prefer to type the "to" keyword yourself in a Set command such as Set Classlib to avoid inadvertently putting duplicates in the command. (If you type "to" without noticing that VFP inserted it for you, you end up with "Set Classlib To To"). Fortunately, the VFP team is smart and made IntelliSense data-driven. Most IntelliSense settings are stored in a table called FoxCode. The name and path for this table are stored in the new _FoxCode system variable; the default is FoxCode.DBF in your VFP "user" folder (something like C:\Documents and Settings\<user name>\Application Data\Microsoft\Visual FoxPro; as described in Chapter 8, "Resource Management," Home(7) will return the complete path to this folder). You can also change this setting in the File Locations page of the VFP Options dialog. This table is discussed in more detail in the "Scripting IntelliSense" section of this chapter.

IntelliSense Manager

VFP comes with a new tool called the IntelliSense Manager (available in the Tools menu) that you can use to configure the behavior of IntelliSense. Like many other tools in VFP, the IntelliSense Manager is a VFP application. The new _CodeSense system variable contains the name of the application; the default is FoxCode.APP in the VFP home directory. However, since the source code for FoxCode.APP is included with VFP (in the Tools\XSource\FoxCode directory of the VFP home directory), you can create your own version and change _CodeSense to point to your application instead. You can also change the IntelliSense Manager setting in the File Locations page of the Options dialog.

The first page of the IntelliSense Manager, shown in **Figure 12**, allows you to configure the behavior of the List Members, Quick Info, and keyword expansion features of IntelliSense. You can disable IntelliSense altogether by turning off the Enable IntelliSense option. You can configure both List Members (which includes List Values) and Quick Info to one of these choices:

- Automatic—the default setting

- Manual—you have to press the hot key or choose the item from the Edit menu to activate it

- Disabled

The combo boxes in the Capitalization / Expansion group control the case of expanded keywords. FoxCode default controls the default setting for all keywords; you can also change the settings for commands and functions individually. The case choices are uppercase, lowercase, proper case (first letter in uppercase and the rest in lowercase), mixed case (also known as camel case), no auto-expansion, and, in the case of the Functions and Commands combo boxes, use the FoxCode default and leave the current setting. If you check the Apply changes to Visual FoxPro language only check box, these settings will only be applied to VFP commands and functions, not other settings (such as custom shortcuts, which are discussed later). The Tips button brings up a window displaying syntax tips for the command or function entered in the Command Window or any editing window. The Browse button browses the FoxCode table.

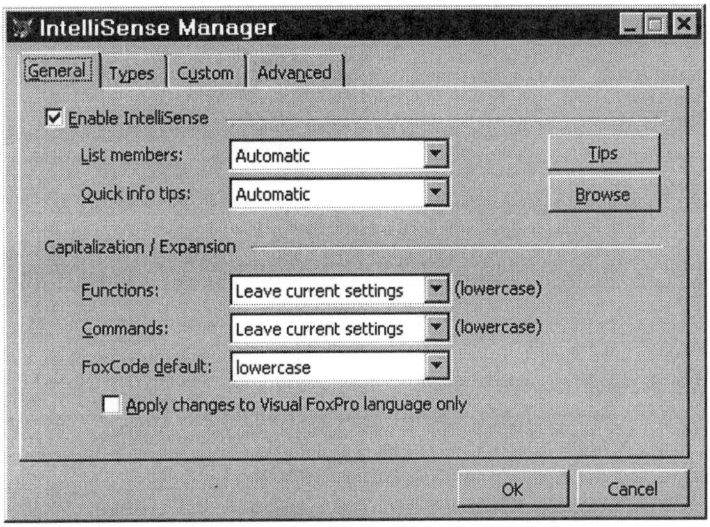

Figure 12*. You can configure the behavior of IntelliSense using the IntelliSense Manager.*

The Types page of the IntelliSense Manager (see **Figure 13**) allows you to define the types listed for the As clause of a Local, Public, LParameters, Parameters, Function, or Procedure declaration. By default, this list includes VFP data types and base classes, but you can add other things, such as your own classes, registered type libraries (for example, ADODB and Excel), and Web Services. You can sort the list by clicking on the appropriate column header. The third column in the list contains an asterisk if that item has script code associated with it; script code is discussed later in the "Scripting IntelliSense" section of this chapter. The check box in front of each item indicates whether that item appears in the values list for As; unchecking it actually deletes the record for that item in the FoxCode table. The Edit button displays the FoxCode record for the selected item in a Browse window; see the "Customizing IntelliSense Using FoxCode" topic in the VFP Help file for details on the structure of the FoxCode table. The Type Libraries button displays a list of all registered type libraries on your system so you can add any ones desired to the list; you can have it display COM servers, ActiveX controls, or both. In an editing window, if you type a Local declaration and select a type library from the values list for the As clause and press ".", a new list with the visible classes in that library appears. The Classes button allows you to select a class in a VCX to add it to the list. Use the Web Services button to add Web Services to the list; see Chapter 15, "Working with Web Services," for details.

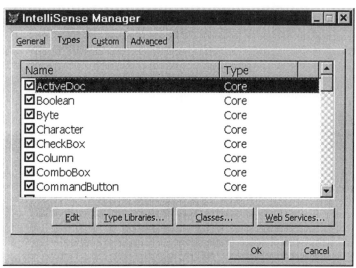

Figure 13. You can define new "types" in the IntelliSense Manager.

The Custom page allows you to define your own shortcuts. **Figure 14** shows a few custom shortcuts already defined. "mc", which expands to Modify Command, and "mf", which expands to Modify File, are simple examples that just expand a shortcut to a command. "dc" is a more complex shortcut; it expands to:

```
DEFINE CLASS classname AS Session OLEPUBLIC

PROCEDURE Init

ENDPROC

PROCEDURE Destroy

ENDPROC

PROCEDURE Error(nError, cMethod, nLine)

ENDPROC

ENDDEFINE
```

"Classname" is selected so you can enter the name of the class. This type of shortcut uses script code to define what it does; an asterisk in the third column of the list (not visible in the figure) indicates an item with script code.

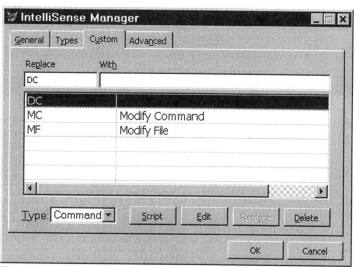

Figure 14. The Custom page allows you to define your own shortcuts.

To create a new shortcut, enter the abbreviation in the Replace text box, enter the expanded text in the With text box, and then click on the Add button. To edit a shortcut, double-click on it in the list or select it in the list and click on the Edit button; a Browse window appears with the FoxCode record for the item. Alternatively, you can change the text in the With text box and click on the Replace button. The Delete button deletes the selected item.

The Type combo box indicates the type of shortcut: Command and Function mean the shortcut expands to a command or function, Property is used for script code for an object property, Script is for script code called from other items, and Other is for other, user-defined types. Script code is discussed in the "Scripting IntelliSense" section of this chapter.

The Advanced page has two options: Custom Properties and Maintenance. Clicking the Edit Properties button displays the dialog shown in **Figure 15**. This dialog allows you to fine-tune the following IntelliSense behaviors:

- lEnableFullSetDisplay: This property determines whether a second keyword (such as "To") is included when Set commands are expanded.

- lHideScriptErrors: If this property is True, IntelliSense doesn't display information about errors in script code.

- lKeywordCapitalization: Set this property to True if you want IntelliSense to change the capitalization of keywords associated with a command (such as From and Where in the SQL Select command) to match the capitalization chosen for the command. Set it to False to leave keyword capitalization alone.

- lPropertyValueEditors: This property controls whether a values list or dialog appears for object properties.

- lExpandCOperators: IntelliSense provides several shortcuts matching operators in the C language. *variable++* expands to *variable = variable + 1*, *variable--* expands to *variable = variable - 1*, *variable+=* expands to *variable = variable +*, *variable-=* expands to *variable = variable -*, *variable*=* expands to *variable = variable **, and *variable/=* expands to *variable = variable /*.

- lAllowCustomDefScripts: If you set this property to True, IntelliSense will call scripts from within the default script handler. This is discussed in the "Scripting IntelliSense" section of this chapter.

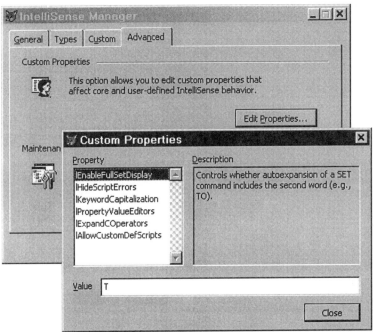

Figure 15*. The Custom Properties dialog fine-tunes IntelliSense behavior.*

Click the Cleanup button in the Advanced page to display the Cleanup and Maintenance dialog shown in **Figure 16**. The Restore FoxCode button restores the default settings for all records in FoxCode except the custom records you added. Cleanup FoxCode packs the table. Cleanup Lists removes MRU file entries that no longer exist, while Zap Lists removes all MRU entries.

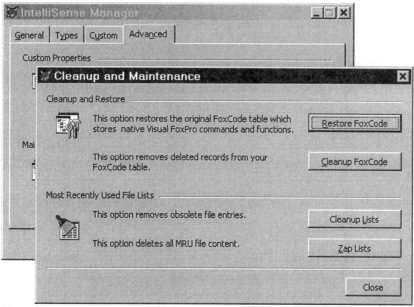

Figure 16. The Cleanup and Maintenance dialog performs maintenance tasks on the FoxCode table.

Configuring IntelliSense programmatically

You can configure some IntelliSense settings using the new EditorOptions property of the _VFP system variable. This property contains a string in which each character represents a setting; an empty string completely disables IntelliSense. Include "L" and "Q" in the string to enable Auto List Member and Auto Quick Info, or "l" and "q" to disable the automatic capability of these features but permit manual activation. "T" enables the tip window displayed in lists. "K" enables the display of hyperlinks in editor windows, and "W" enables drag and drop between words; see Chapter 2, "Editor Enhancements," for details on those new features.

Scripting IntelliSense

One of the incredibly cool things about how Microsoft implemented IntelliSense in VFP 7 is that it's extendible using VFP code. A couple of the ways you can extend IntelliSense are creating your own shortcuts and hooking into the default script fired when you press the Space key. For more tips on scripting IntelliSense, see the "Using Scripting in FoxCode.dbf" topic in the VFP Help file.

Creating your own shortcuts

Earlier in this chapter, the "dc" shortcut was mentioned. This shortcut expands to more than a simple piece of text; it gives a multi-line block of code (a programmatic class definition) and highlights the text "classname" automatically so you can type the desired class name. To see how that was done, examine the "dc" record in the FoxCode table:

```
use (_foxcode) again shared
locate for Abbrev = 'DC'
browse
```

Table 1 shows the contents of this record. See the "Customizing IntelliSense Using FoxCode" topic in the VFP Help file for a detailed description of the structure of the FoxCode table.

Table 1. The contents of the "dc" shortcut record in the FoxCode table (only fields of interest are shown).

Field	Value
Type	U (user-defined shortcut)
Abbrev	DC
Cmd	{}
Data	LPARAMETERS oFoxcode IF oFoxcode.Location #1 　RETURN "DC" ENDIF oFoxcode.valuetype = "V" TEXT TO myvar TEXTMERGE NOSHOW DEFINE CLASS ~classname~ AS Session OLEPUBLIC PROCEDURE Init ENDPROC PROCEDURE Destroy ENDPROC PROCEDURE Error(nError, cMethod, nLine) ENDPROC ENDDEFINE ENDTEXT RETURN myvar

The fields of interest in this record are Abbrev, Cmd, and Data. Abbrev specifies the shortcut that triggers the current script or command ("dc" in this case). Cmd specifies the script: A blank value means there's no script code, a value between curly braces (such as "{color}") specifies the Abbrev value of a script (type "S") record, and empty curly braces (as in the case of the "dc" shortcut) means the script is contained in this record. Data contains the script code.

Now let's analyze the script itself. The first line in the code shown in the Data field in Table 1 is an LParameters statement. All FoxCode script is passed a FoxCodeScript object.

IntelliSense creates this object, filling its properties with information about the FoxCode record, what you typed, and the current environment (see the "FoxCode Object Reference" topic in the VFP Help file for a description of each property of this object). The "dc" script code checks the value of the Location property and simply returns "DC" if it isn't 1. Location indicates where you were typing when the shortcut was invoked; a value of 1 means the PRG editor. So, if you type this shortcut anywhere but in a PRG, nothing appears to happen, which makes sense, because that's the only logical place for a class definition. The return value, which must be a string, is actually ignored, so a blank string could have been returned with the same results.

Next, the code sets the ValueType property to "V". This property specifies what happens after the script code is done; "V" means IntelliSense replaces the shortcut with the return value of the code (since it wasn't set earlier, IntelliSense ignored the previous "DC" return value). The code then uses the Text command to place several lines of text (in this case, the class definition code) into a variable and returns that variable. Note the "~" characters surrounding "classname" in the text. A single "~" tells IntelliSense where to place the cursor after replacing the shortcut with the text (without a "~", it places the cursor at the end of the text), while two of them specify text to highlight. This makes it easy for you to complete the text by entering more information (such as the class name in this case). If you'd rather use something other than "~", set the CursorLocChar property of the passed object to the desired character.

Here's another example of a useful shortcut implemented with scripting. One block of code you've probably written many times either selects a table if it's already open or opens it if not:

```
if used(some alias)
  select some alias
else
  select 0
  use some alias again shared
endif used(some alias)
```

Since the only thing varying in this code is the alias, it's possible to create a shortcut that asks you for the alias and then expands to this entire block of code. **Listing 1** shows the script code that does this.

***Listing 1**. Script code for the Use or Select shortcut.*

```
lparameters toFoxCode
local lcReturn, ;
  lcTable
if toFoxCode.Location <> 0
  lcTable = inputbox('Table/view name:')
  if not empty(lcTable)
    toFoxCode.ValueType = 'V'
    lcReturn = GetText(lcTable)
  endif not empty(lcTable)
endif toFoxCode.Location <> 0
return lcReturn

function GetText(tcTable)
local lcDelimiter, ;
```

```
    lcTable, ;
    lcText
lcDelimiter = iif(left(tcTable, 1) = '(', '', "'")
lcTable = iif(empty(lcDelimiter), strtran(strtran(tcTable, '('), ')'), ;
    lcDelimiter + tcTable + lcDelimiter)
text to lcText textmerge noshow
if used(<<lcTable>>)
    select <<tcTable>>
else
    select 0
    use <<tcTable>> again shared
endif used(<<lcTable>>)
endtext
return lcText
```

Like the "dc" script code, this script accepts a FoxCodeScript object parameter and checks where you typed the shortcut by examining the Location property. It doesn't make sense to expand this shortcut in the Command Window, so if Location contains 0, the rest of the code is skipped. Otherwise, the code prompts you for the name of a table or view. If you enter one, the code sets the ValueType property of the FoxCode to "V" and calls the GetText routine to place the desired block of code, with the name you entered inserted at the appropriate places, into the return value of the script. Note that you can either enter an alias, in which case the script places it in quotes in the "If Used" statement, or the name of a variable surrounded with parentheses (such as "(lcAlias)"); the latter will generate the following:

```
if used(lcAlias)
    select (lcAlias)
else
    select 0
    use (lcAlias) again shared
endif used(lcAlias)
```

To create this shortcut, bring up the IntelliSense Manager, select the Custom page, enter the shortcut code you want to use (such as "us" for "Use or Select") but leave the With text box blank, and click on the Add button. Click on the Script button and enter the code shown in Listing 1.

*The Developer Downloads at **www.hentzenwerke.com** include NewFoxCode.DBF, which contains the FoxCode records for this and the next example. You can simply open FoxCode.DBF (using the Use (_FoxCode) command) and Append From NewFoxCode to avoid typing in these scripts.*

Listing 2 shows another example: This code inserts program header comments. Like the code in Listing 1, it only works from a code editor, not the Command Window, it uses text merge to create the text to replace the abbreviation in the command line, and, with the "~" character, it tells IntelliSense to put the cursor in the "Purpose" comment line after the expansion is complete. It has a couple of interesting wrinkles, though. First, it reads your name, company name, and e-mail address from the Registry using the FoxPro Foundation Classes (FFC) Registry class so it can insert them into the header. Second, it uses WONTOP() to insert the name of the file being edited. As you can see, script code can be considerably more complex than simply outputting some text.

Listing 2*. Script code to insert a program header.*

```
lparameters toFoxCode
local lcReturn, ;
  lcTable
if toFoxCode.Location <> 0
  toFoxCode.ValueType = 'V'
  lcReturn = GetText()
endif toFoxCode.Location <> 0
return lcReturn

function GetText
local loRegistry, ;
  lcKey, ;
  lcCompany, ;
  lnResult, ;
  lcContact, ;
  lcAccount, ;
  lcEmail, ;
  lcText
loRegistry = newobject('Registry', home() + 'FFC\Registry.vcx')
lcKey      = iif('NT' $ os() or '5.0' $ os(), ;
  'Software\Microsoft\Windows NT\CurrentVersion', ;
  'Software\Microsoft\Windows\CurrentVersion')
lnResult   = loRegistry.GetRegKey('RegisteredOrganization', @lcCompany, ;
  lcKey, -2147483646)
if lnResult <> 0
  lcCompany = ''
endif lnResult <> 0
lnResult = loRegistry.GetRegKey('RegisteredOwner', @lcContact, lcKey, ;
  -2147483646)
if lnResult <> 0
  lcContact = ''
endif lnResult <> 0
lcKey    = 'Software\Microsoft\Internet Account Manager'
lnResult = loRegistry.GetRegKey('Default Mail Account', @lcAccount, lcKey, ;
  -2147483647)
if not empty(lcAccount)
  lcKey    = lcKey + '\Accounts\' + lcAccount
  lnResult = loRegistry.GetRegKey('SMTP Email Address', @lcEmail, lcKey, ;
    -2147483647)
endif not empty(lcAccount)
if lnResult <> 0 or empty(lcEmail)
  lcEmail = ''
else
  lcEmail = ', mailto:' + lcEmail
endif lnResult <> 0 ...
text to lcText textmerge noshow
*===========================================================================
* Program:          <<wontop()>>
* Purpose:          ~
* Author:           <<lcContact>><<lcEmail>>
* Copyright:        (c) <<year(date())>> <<lcCompany>>
* Last revision:    <<date()>>
```

```
* Parameters:
* Returns:
* Environment in:
* Environment out:
*=====================================================================

endtext
return lcText
```

Here's an example of the output of this shortcut:

```
*=====================================================================
* Program:          TESTPROGRAM.PRG
* Purpose:          the cursor is positioned here
* Author:           Doug Hennig, mailto:dhennig@stonefield.com
* Copyright:        (c) 2001 Stonefield Systems Group Inc.
* Last revision:    4/20/2001
* Parameters:
* Returns:
* Environment in:
* Environment out:
*=====================================================================
```

You can either add this to IntelliSense manually or append the record with the abbreviation "header" from the NewFoxCode table described earlier into your FoxCode table.

The Tools\XSource\VFPSource\FoxCode subdirectory of the VFP home directory (you must unzip XSource.ZIP in Tools\XSource to create this directory structure) contains a table called FoxPak1 that you can append to your FoxCode table. FoxPak1 contains a shortcut called "now" that has the following script code:

```
LPARAMETER oFoxCode
oFoxcode.ValueType = "L"
DIMENSION oFoxCode.items[3,2]
oFoxCode.items[1,1] = TRANS(DATETIME())
oFoxCode.items[2,1] = TRANS(DATE())
oFoxCode.items[3,1] = TRANS(TIME())
oFoxCode.itemscript = "now2"
RETURN oFoxcode.UserTyped
```

Here, ValueType is set to "L"; this tells IntelliSense to display a list box using the contents of the Items array as its values. This code puts variations of the current date and/or time into this array. It then sets ItemScript to "now2"; this property contains the Abbrev value for a script record containing code to execute after you select something from the list. Finally, it returns the UserTyped property (as you can guess, this contains what you typed) so the shortcut is replaced with itself.

You might think the script code in the "now2" record, executed after you select something from the values list, would simply return your selection to insert it into the text. Unfortunately, it's not that simple; since this code isn't fired directly for the shortcut, IntelliSense ignores its return value. Here's the script code:

```
LPARAMETER oFoxcode
LOCAL lcItem
```

```
lcItem = ALLTRIM(oFoxcode.menuitem)
IF EMPTY(lcItem)
  RETURN
ENDIF

IF FILE(_CODESENSE)
  LOCAL eRetVal, loFoxCodeLoader
  SET PROCEDURE TO (_CODESENSE) ADDITIVE
  loFoxCodeLoader = CreateObject("FoxCodeLoader")
  loFoxCodeLoader.cReplaceWord=lcItem
  eRetVal = loFoxCodeLoader.Start(m.oFoxCode)
  loFoxCodeLoader = NULL
  IF ATC(_CODESENSE,SET("PROC"))#0
    RELEASE PROCEDURE (_CODESENSE)
  ENDIF
  RETURN m.eRetVal
ENDIF

DEFINE CLASS FoxCodeLoader as FoxCodeScript
  cReplaceWord=""
  PROCEDURE Main
    THIS.ReplaceWord(THIS.cReplaceWord)
  ENDPROC
ENDDEFINE
```

The MenuItem property of the FoxCodeScript object contains the item you selected in the list. If you closed the list without making a selection (MenuItem is blank), this code just returns. If not, it needs access to the command line you were entering so it can replace the shortcut with the selected value. Fortunately, IntelliSense provides a way to do that: through the FoxCodeScript class. This class, which is defined in the IntelliSense Manager (hence the reference to _CodeSense, which contains the full path and name of the IntelliSense Manager, in this code), has a ReplaceWord() method that replaces the text you typed with the specified value. Call the Start() method first, passing it a reference to the object the script code was passed, so it can set itself up properly. Start() calls an abstract method called Main(), which can do the actual work required after setup. So, this code actually instantiates a subclass of FoxCodeScript called FoxCodeLoader, in which the Main() method calls ReplaceWord(). Here is an alternative way of doing this, without using a subclass:

```
loFoxCodeLoader = CreateObject("FoxCodeScript")
eRetVal = loFoxCodeLoader.Start(m.oFoxCode)
loFoxCodeLoader.ReplaceWord(lcItem)
```

If you want to dig into exactly how IntelliSense handles scripts, look at the source code for the IntelliSense Manager, provided in the Tools\XSource\FoxCode subdirectory of the VFP home directory. FoxCode.PRG has the class definition for FoxCodeScript, which does a lot of the work (the rest is internal to VFP itself).

Hooking into the default script

The lAllowCustomDefScripts custom property, discussed in the "IntelliSense Manager" section of this chapter, enables you to hook into the default script fired when you press the Space key.

The default script is contained in the FoxCode script record with an empty Abbrev field. Find that record and look at its script code:

```
use (_foxcode) again shared
locate for Type = 'S' and empty(Abbrev)
modify memo Data
```

The important code is near the end:

```
DEFINE CLASS FoxCodeLoader AS FoxCodeScript
  PROCEDURE Main()
    THIS.DefaultScript()
  ENDPROC
ENDDEFINE
```

As with the "now2" script examined earlier, this script subclasses the FoxCodeScript class. The subclass's Main() method calls the DefaultScript() method. You can examine the code for DefaultScript() (located in FoxCode.PRG) yourself, but here's how it handles hooking custom scripts:

- If the lAllowCustomDefScripts custom property is True, it calls the HandleCustomScripts() method.

- HandleCustomScripts() finds a record in FoxCode with Type containing Z and Abbrev containing "CustomDefaultScripts" and places each line of the Data memo into an array.

- For each row in the array, HandleCustomScripts() calls RunScript() to find the script record with the specified Abbrev value and execute it. If any script returns False, custom script execution is halted.

So, to hook into the default script, set the lAllowCustomDefScripts custom property to True and add the Abbrev values for the script records you want executed on their own rows in the Data memo of the CustomDefaultScripts record. Here's an example:

```
use (_foxcode) again shared
* Specify the custom scripts to execute when Space is pressed
locate for Type = 'Z' and Abbrev = 'CustomDefaultScripts'
replace Data with 'test1' + chr(13) + 'test2'
* Create the script records
insert into FoxCode (Type, Abbrev, Data) ;
  values ('S', 'test1', 'lparameters toFoxCode' + chr(13) + ;
  'wait window "Test1"')
insert into FoxCode (Type, Abbrev, Data) ;
  values ('S', 'test2', 'lparameters toFoxCode' + chr(13) + ;
  'wait window "Test2"')
```

Now when you press the Space key after typing any command in the Command Window, you'll see two Wait Window messages before the syntax tip window appears.

Let's look at a more practical example of this. Microsoft Office XP includes a technology called Smart Tags. If something you've typed is recognized, a dropdown menu of choices appears. One of the choices might be to insert the complete address for a customer (the recognized text might be the customer's name).

We can implement smart tags in VFP by hooking into the default script. To prepare for this, do the following:

```
use (_foxcode) again shared
append from NewFoxCode
locate for Type = 'Z' and Abbrev = 'CustomDefaultScripts'
replace Data with 'SmartActions'
use
```

FoxCode.DBF will now include a script record called SmartActions. The code for this script is:

```
lparameters toFoxCode
local loSmartTag, ;
  luReturn
set procedure to home() + 'Smart.APP' additive
loSmartTag = createobject('FoxSmart')
luReturn = loSmartTag.SearchMe(toFoxCode)
loSmartTag = .NULL.
if atc('SMART.APP', set('PROCEDURE')) <> 0
  release procedure home() + 'Smart.APP'
endif atc('SMART.APP', set('PROCEDURE')) <> 0
```

This code instantiates a class called FoxSmart, defined in Smart.APP in the VFP home directory, and then calls its SearchMe() method. Due to its complexity, this chapter won't discuss how Smart.APP works in detail. However, the source code is provided, so feel free to examine it yourself.

 *The Developer Downloads at **www.hentzenwerke.com** include Smart.APP, the source code files for this application, and the SmartTag table. Copy Smart.APP, SmartTag.DBF, and SmartTag.FPT to the VFP home directory so the example described in this chapter will work. Thanks to Randy Brown of Microsoft for providing the idea (and a large part of the source code, especially the hard stuff) for this example.*

Smart.APP is data-driven; it uses the SmartTag table to define what it does. SmartTag has three fields, all memos containing VFP code. The code in the Search field defines when the current record is used; here's the code in the sample record:

```
lparameters toCode
return upper(toCode.cLastWord) == 'DOUG'
```

toCode is a reference to a FoxCodeScript object, and its cLastWord property is the last word typed by the user. In this case, this record will be used when "Doug" is entered because this code returns True in that case.

The code in the Data memo is used to specify the list of actions. It's passed a reference to a SmartTag object. This object has an aItems array property that contains the list of items for the dropdown menu. The first column of the array is the prompt for the menu and the second is a keyword for that choice. The code in the sample record defines two actions: navigating to a Web site and sending an e-mail:

```
lparameters toSmartTag
with toSmartTag
   dimension .aItems[2, 2]
   .aItems[1, 1] = 'Check Web site'
   .aItems[1, 2] = 'WebSite'
   .aItems[2, 1] = 'Send email'
   .aItems[2, 2] = 'SendEmail'
endwith
```

The Script memo defines what to do when the user selects an item from the menu. It's passed two parameters: the keyword for the user's selection and a reference to a FoxCodeScript object. The code in the same record declares the Window API ShellExecute function, and then uses it to either send an e-mail or navigate to a Web site, depending on the keyword.

```
lparameters tcFunction, ;
   toCode
declare integer ShellExecute in SHELL32.DLL ;
   integer nWinHandle, ;
   string cOperation, ;
   string cFileName, ;
   string cParameters, ;
   string cDirectory, ;
   integer nShowWindow
do case
   case upper(tcFunction) = 'SENDEMAIL'
     ShellExecute(0, 'Open', 'mailto:dhennig@stonefield.com', '', '', 1)
   case upper(tcFunction) = 'WEBSITE'
     ShellExecute(0, 'Open', 'http://www.stonefield.com', '', '', 1)
   otherwise
     wait wind tcFunction + ' not implemented'
endcase
```

To see smart tags in action, type "Doug" in the Command Window and press Space. An icon will appear with a down arrow (see **Figure 17**). Click the down arrow and select one of the choices from the menu ("Cancel", which was added automatically, closes the smart tag).

Figure 17. This smart tag is displayed by typing "Doug" in the Command Window or any code editor.

Other IntelliSense-related items

VFP 7 includes the new ALanguage() function that fills an array with VFP keywords. The first parameter is the array to fill and the second is a numeric value indicating the type of keywords you want. Pass 1, 3, or 4 for a one-dimensional array of commands, base classes, or DBC events (see Chapter 5, "Data," for information about DBC events). Passing 2 results in a two-dimensional array of functions. The first column contains the function name and the second a string indicating the number of required parameters and, if the function has optional parameters, a dash and the total number of parameters. The string also contains an "M" if you have to type the entire function name rather than an abbreviation, such as with CreateObjectEx. This function could be useful in a developer utility that parses code for some purpose, such as outputting syntax-colored HTML.

There are two final IntelliSense-related items. First, the values list respects the List display count setting in the Editor page of the Options dialog (as do all list boxes and combo boxes in VFP itself). Second, tip and list windows respect your Windows font settings.

Summary

IntelliSense is a wonderful addition to the VFP development environment. It helps you avoid spelling mistakes, boost your productivity, cut down on trips to the Help file, make your bed in the morning, and end world hunger. (Editor's note: He's lying. IntelliSense won't end world hunger.) You'll find IntelliSense so compelling, you'll even find yourself firing up VFP 7 when you have to maintain VFP 6 applications!

Chapter 2
Editor Enhancements

While IntelliSense has gotten all the press, VFP 7 has many more developer-friendly changes to the code editor. Improvements range from matching of parentheses to a "dirty file" indicator to a better tool for finding particular code.

It seems that the tools for creating code get better in each new version of Visual FoxPro. In VFP 7, the most noticeable change is the addition of IntelliSense (see Chapter 1, "IntelliSense"). But there are a host of other changes that make it easier to get it right the first time, to make your code look good, and to test and fix code.

Writing code

IntelliSense is the big change that makes it easier than ever to write code in VFP 7. But there are a few other enhancements that increase your chances of getting it right the first time.

Parenthesis matching

Code editing windows now automatically match parentheses for you. That is, when you type a right parenthesis, VFP highlights everything from the corresponding left parenthesis through the right parenthesis you just typed. The highlight disappears as soon as you type another character. If nothing else is typed, it disappears after a period of time that you set in the Options dialog—the default is 1500 milliseconds. This feature also works with square brackets ("[" and "]").

Dirty file indicator

VFP 7 makes it easier to be sure your changes get saved. All windows where you can type any kind of text offer a "dirty file indicator." As soon as the contents change, an asterisk appears in the title bar next to the window caption. **Figure 1** shows a code window containing changes.

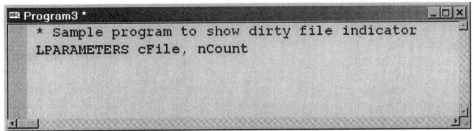

```
* Sample program to show dirty file indicator
LPARAMETERS cFile, nCount
```

Figure 1. The asterisk in the title bar shows that this window contains changes that haven't been saved yet.

Live hyperlinks

The final change that affects what you're writing is the ability to have hyperlinks enabled. That is, like other Microsoft products, you can set VFP to turn anything that looks like a hyperlink into an actual hyperlink. So, for example, your standard header comment might include your company Web site, and it can be a live link. **Figure 2** shows an example.

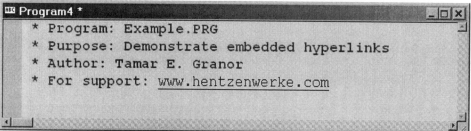

Figure 2. *You can embed hyperlinks in text. Fortunately, you can also turn off that ability.*

VFP recognizes anything with "www." as a hyperlink. In addition, you can include other kinds of links by prefacing them with the appropriate protocol information. This means that while the editor won't convert "billg@microsoft.com" to a hyperlink, it will convert "mailto:billg@microsoft.com".

Since you may not always want this automatic conversion, there are a number of ways to control it. The Editor page of the Options dialog (shown in **Figure 5** later in this chapter) controls this setting globally—check the Enable hyperlinks check box to allow hyperlinks to be enabled. When this setting is turned off, you can't enable hyperlinks anywhere.

If hyperlinks are allowed, you can use the Edit Properties dialog (**Figure 3**) to control them for an individual file—check the Embedded hyperlinks check box to enable hyperlinks. As always, you can apply your changes to the current file only or to all files of its type. The new IDE page of the Options dialog (see **Figure 6** later in this chapter) also lets you control hyperlink enabling by file type.

Enabling of hyperlinks can also be controlled programmatically. The new EditorOptions property of the _VFP application object controls several editing functions. Most apply only at development time. However, the ability to enable hyperlinks applies at development time and run time. (See Chapter 1, "IntelliSense," for explanations of the other elements of EditorOptions.)

To enable hyperlinks, include either "K" or "k" in the EditorOptions value. To disable hyperlinks, omit those characters. Including either string indicates that anything that looks like a hyperlink is to be treated as one. When the property includes "K", using Ctrl-Click on the hyperlink performs the appropriate action (opens the Browser to the specified page, starts an e-mail to the address indicated, and so forth). When the property includes "k", you only need a Click on the item to perform the action. You might choose the "K" setting at design time and the "k" setting for your users. The EditorOptions setting for hyperlinks corresponds to the Enable hyperlinks check box in the Options dialog—that is, it's a global setting.

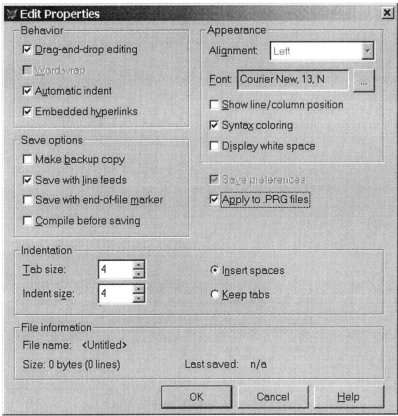

Figure 3. *The Edit Properties dialog, available on the context menu for editing windows, offers several new features, including control over hyperlinks.*

There are several things to be aware of with hyperlinks. First, for any given file, it's an all or nothing situation. Either links are enabled and any text that looks like a hyperlink becomes one, or links are disabled and no hyperlinks appear. If you check Embedded hyperlinks in the Edit Properties window, all text that can be a hyperlink is enabled immediately. This also means that VFP doesn't offer the ability that Word does to reverse the conversion of an individual string to a hyperlink by pressing Ctrl-Z. If it looks like a link, and hyperlinks are on, then it will be a link.

Second, hyperlinks can be enabled at run time as well as at design time. This means users can type hyperlink strings and have them converted to links. This feature applies only in editing windows like MODIFY MEMO, not inside controls.

Formatting code
Following a set of formatting rules makes your code easier to maintain. VFP 7 offers a number of changes that improve code-formatting options.

Tabs vs. spaces

The first change makes it easier to publish your code (whether in a book or on the Web), as well as to move it from one environment to another. You can set the Tab key to produce spaces in an editing window rather than an actual tab character. When you do so, indentation automatically inserted by pressing Enter at the end of an indented line also uses spaces. In addition, the same setting determines whether you get a tab or spaces when you highlight a block of code and indent it by pressing Tab.

The Edit Properties dialog shown in Figure 3 includes a set of option buttons to determine whether tabs or spaces are used. The Tab size spinner determines the amount of indentation produced by pressing Tab for a single line (and by the automatic indentation of subsequent new lines). The Indent size spinner indicates the amount of indentation for blocks of code that are highlighted and then indented with Tab.

As with embedded hyperlinks, the Edit Properties dialog controls these settings for individual files and types of files, while the IDE page of the Options dialog (discussed in "More options to set," later in this chapter) provides global settings for each file type.

Visible white space

Another item in the Edit Properties dialog controls whether "white space" in a file is visible. White space includes spaces, tabs, and, for files with word wrap turned on, returns. Turning it on makes it easy to see whether things are properly lined up and whether you've used tabs rather than spaces. **Figure 4** shows part of the GENDBC program with white space turned on.

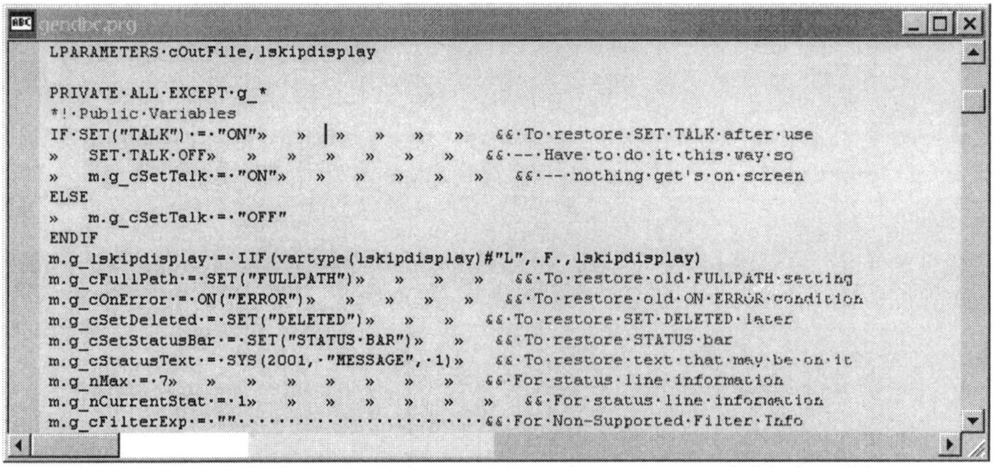

Figure 4. You can make spaces, tabs, and sometimes returns visible in editing windows by choosing the View White Space option from the Format menu. You can make this view the default for any kind of editing window by checking it in the Edit Properties dialog.

You can control the display of white space in three different places. As noted previously, the Edit Properties dialog has a check box for this feature. Using that dialog, you can choose a setting that applies to the current window or to all windows of its type. The IDE page of the

Options dialog (Tools | Options on the menu) lets you set this item for all editing windows. Settings in individual Edit Properties dialogs override the global setting. Finally, you can also set this option from the Format menu—the item View White Space is a toggle affecting the current file.

Turning on white space in an unnamed editing window turns it on for subsequent new windows of that type. That is, if you issue MODIFY COMMAND, and then turn on white space using either the Format menu or the Edit Properties dialog, new windows you create with MODIFY COMMAND will have white space turned on.

More options to set

We already mentioned several new settings in the Options dialog (available on the Tools menu), but there's actually been some major restructuring there.

The page labeled Syntax Coloring in VFP 5 and 6 is called Editor in VFP 7. That's because it now controls more than just syntax coloring (see **Figure 5**).

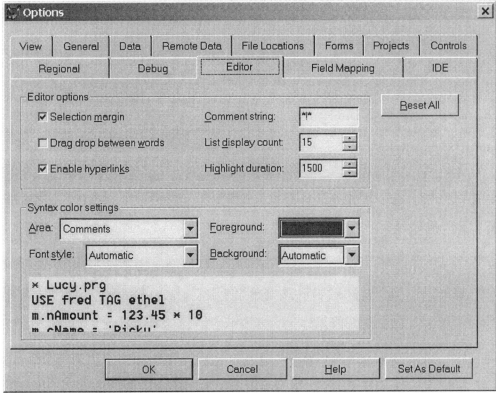

Figure 5. The "Syntax Coloring" page of the Options dialog is now called "Editor" and controls additional editing options.

The Editor options section of this page lets you specify some new items and some that existed in earlier versions, but were hard to manage. Selection margin determines whether code-editing windows have a border that shows breakpoints, bookmarks, and task list shortcuts. (See Chapter 3, "New and Better Tools," for a discussion of the task list, and "Marking points" later in this chapter for more on bookmarks and setting breakpoints.)

Enable hyperlinks is discussed in "Live hyperlinks," earlier in this chapter.

Drag drop between words determines what happens when you're dragging text with the mouse. When this item is checked, dropped text is always placed between words—you can't drop into the middle of a word. (Unlike the Microsoft Word version of this functionality, though, spaces are not added on either side of the dropped word.)

The ability to have text dropped only between words can also be controlled by the EditorOptions property of the _VFP application object. Add "W" to the EditorOptions string to turn this feature on, and omit it from the string to turn it off. Changing this option in the Options dialog changes the EditorOptions string and vice versa.

Comment string lets you specify the string used when you choose Comment from the Format or context menu. In earlier versions of VFP, you could set this item only by changing a Registry key.

List display count specifies the maximum number of items that appear at once in various IntelliSense lists and in combo boxes that are part of the VFP interface such as the dropdowns in the Property Sheet. See Chapter 1, "IntelliSense," for details on the IntelliSense aspects of this item.

As described in "Parenthesis matching" earlier in this chapter, Highlight duration determines how long matched parentheses are highlighted.

The IDE page in the Options dialog (see **Figure 6**) is new in VFP 7 and provides a global way of setting up the different kinds of editing windows. You indicate which type of file or window you're configuring using the Type dropdown. The Extensions text box lets you indicate which files are considered to be of that type, useful if you use custom file extensions. The set of items you can actually change varies with the file/window type—for the Desktop, the only configurable item is the font, accessed through the ellipsis button next to the Font text box.

The Override individual settings check box lets you indicate that the settings on this page should be used rather than the settings stored in the resource file (FoxUser.DBF). Overriding settings doesn't change what's stored for the file—it simply ignores it. When you uncheck the item, the file goes back to using its stored settings.

The remaining items on the IDE page have the same meanings as in the Edit Properties dialog (Figure 3). The new items are discussed elsewhere in this chapter.

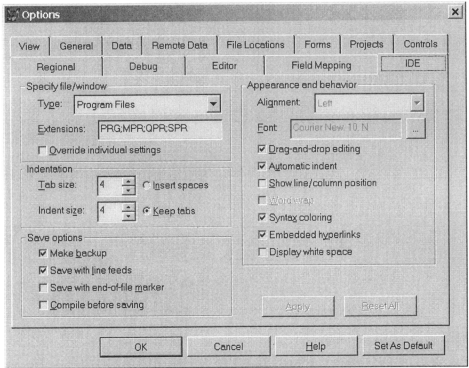

***Figure 6**. The new IDE page in the Options dialog lets you set up editing options globally. It also lets you override the settings stored for individual files.*

More menu items

There are a number of new menu items that apply to editing windows. While they're split between several popups on the system menu, they're also available on the context menu for editing windows. (**Figure 7** shows the updated context menu.)

In addition to the View White Space option discussed in the "Visible white space" section earlier in this chapter, the Format menu contains items to convert strings to uppercase and lowercase. These two items have menu shortcuts, as well—Ctrl-Shift-U for uppercase and Ctrl-U for lowercase.

The Format menu also has a Toggle Word Wrap item that's enabled in MODIFY FILE and MODIFY MEMO windows. (Note also that the shortcut menu omits code-related items in those windows.)

The Edit menu contains List Members and Quick Info items to provide access to IntelliSense functions. See Chapter 1, "IntelliSense," for details on these choices.

The Edit menu also contains a new Bookmarks item that allows you to turn task list shortcuts and bookmarks on and off and to navigate between bookmarks. (See Chapter 3, "New and Better Tools," for an explanation of the Task List. See "Marking points" later in this chapter for a discussion of bookmarks.)

Figure 7. *The context menu for code editing windows has several new items in VFP 7, including access to IntelliSense functions and commands to change text to uppercase or lowercase.*

Working with existing code

Most developers spend more time editing and debugging existing code than creating new code. Fortunately, VFP 7 includes improvements in that area as well.

Moving around in the editor

The first set of changes makes it easier to navigate in editing windows. The Ctrl-LeftArrow and Ctrl-RightArrow keys that navigate a word at a time are much smarter about deciding what constitutes a word. The changes are most noticeable when dealing with quoted strings and with comma-separated lists. In older versions, closing quotes and commas were considered to be part of the word they followed. VFP 7 understands that those are separate items and doesn't include them with the words that precede them.

Two new keyboard shortcuts have been added, as well. Ctrl-UpArrow and Ctrl-DnArrow allow you to scroll a window without moving the cursor position. They scroll one line at a time.

Marking points

VFP 7 offers several techniques for marking particular points in a block of code. The first, breakpoints, exist in earlier versions, but VFP 7 makes it easier to set them. By default, code editing windows have a selection bar running down the left-hand side. (You can control the presence of the selection bar through the Editor page of the Options dialog. See "More options to set" earlier in this chapter.) Double-click the selection bar next to a line of code to set a breakpoint on that line. You can also turn breakpoints on and off using the context menu for code windows (see Figure 7).

There are two new techniques for quickly identifying a given point in code: bookmarks and the Task List. **Figure 8** shows a code window with all three kinds of marks in the selection bar.

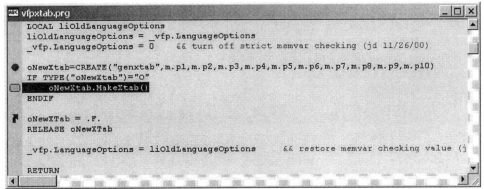

Figure 8. The new selection bar holds three kinds of markers. The circle indicates a breakpoint, the rounded rectangle is a bookmark, and the arrow is a task list shortcut.

Bookmarks in VFP let you find spots in a file within the editor. You can put as many bookmarks as you want into a file and then move among them using either the menu or a pair of menu shortcuts (F2 to move forward to the next bookmark, Shift-F2 to move backward to the previous bookmark—both wrap around at the top or bottom of the file).

There are several ways to set or remove a bookmark: Shift-DblClick in the selection bar, Toggle Bookmark on the context menu, Toggle Bookmark on the Edit menu's Bookmarks submenu, or Alt-Shift-F2. Bookmarks are saved during your VFP session, but are discarded when you close Visual FoxPro.

The Task List is a new tool designed to let you track items that need your attention. One way to add items to the Task List is to mark lines of code with Task List shortcuts. As with bookmarks, there are a variety of ways to set or clear a task list shortcut: Ctrl-DblClick in the selection bar, the Add Task List Shortcut item on the context menu (which changes to Remove Task List Shortcut for lines that contain shortcuts), the Toggle Task List Shortcut item on the Edit menu's Bookmarks submenu, or Alt-F2.

The Task List tool that lets you manage your shortcuts is covered in Chapter 3, "New and Better Tools."

Finding text

Searching for text in VFP's editing windows is significantly easier in VFP 7. In addition, it's possible to search in ways you never could before.

There are more ways of searching using only the keyboard. While Ctrl-F still opens the Find dialog and Ctrl-L is still the shortcut for Replace, both F3 and Ctrl-G can be used for Find again. (However, the Find Again item has been removed from the Edit menu.) In addition, Shift-F3 performs Find again, but moving toward the beginning of the file. It's like checking Search backward in the Find dialog. You don't need the Find dialog open to use Ctrl-G, F3, and Shift-F3.

Two new keystrokes let you search without opening the Find dialog in the first place. Ctrl-F3 searches forward (toward the end of the file) for the currently highlighted text. Ctrl-Shift-F3 searches backward for the highlighted text. Once you start the search with one of these, you can continue with Ctrl-G, F3, or Shift-F3. Be aware that using either of the "search backward" shortcuts checks the Search backward check box in the Find dialog.

The Find dialog supports wildcard searching, as well. There's a new Use wildcards check box—when it's checked, various characters in the search string are used for pattern matching rather than exact matches. **Table 1** shows the characters you can use and their meanings. **Figure 9** shows an example.

Table 1. Wildcard searching is now available. These characters let you build search strings for wildcard matches.

Character	Meaning
?	Match a single character.
*	Match a series of characters (0 or more).
#	Match a single digit.
<	Match the string only at the beginning of a word.
>	Match the string only at the end of a word.
[list of characters]	Match any of the specified characters. The list can include ranges separated with hyphens. For example, [0-9,B,C,D].
[! list of characters]	Match any character other than those listed. The list can include ranges separated with hyphens.
\	Treat the following character as the character itself rather than a wildcard.

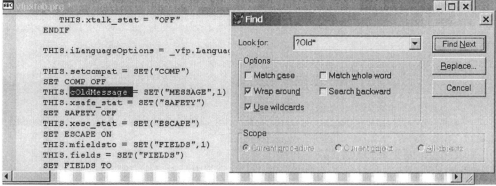

Figure 9. The new wildcard search makes it possible to find all strings that match a certain pattern.

Finding places

Bookmarks, the task list, and powerful searching all are helpful in finding what you're looking for in code, but VFP 7 offers even more. The new Document View tool (accessed through the Document View item on the Tools menu) provides you with a list of all items of certain types in an editor window and lets you jump directly to any of those items.

The Document View window is modeless (unlike the Procedures and Functions list it replaces) and dockable. It displays procedure and function names, class names, method names, and, optionally, constant definitions and preprocessor directives. The context menu lets you determine which items appear. The context menu also provides sorting options—you can see the list in alphabetical order, in the order the items appear in the file, or organized by item type. **Figure 10** shows part of the Document View window for the VFPXTab program that comes with Visual FoxPro. The icon next to each item indicates the type of item: The red "#" symbol marks constants, the yellow "#" symbol marks other preprocessor directives, the blue-green item that looks like a form is for methods and functions, and the multi-colored diagram is for class definitions.

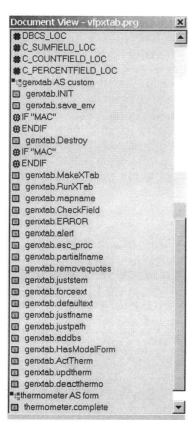

Figure 10. *The Document View window provides direct access to class definitions, methods, procedures, functions, constant definitions, and preprocessor directives. Choosing one of the items in the list moves focus in the code window to the chosen item.*

Document View always shows items from the code window with focus, so you can open several windows and switch among them, keeping Document View in synch.

Document View works with classes and forms as well as with all kinds of code windows. When the Class Designer or Form Designer has focus, Document View shows the methods of the class or form that contain code. Choosing a method name brings the method editor to the front, focused on the chosen method. Document View also works with stored procedure editing windows, though you have to open the window explicitly to get the list into Document View. (That is, MODIFY DATABASE is not sufficient to list all of the database's stored procedures.)

Document View doesn't keep track of what you've typed into the current editing window. However, it updates its list each time a different editing window gets focus. For forms and classes, you need to do something that compiles the new method for Document View to see it.

Two new functions provide Document View support programmatically. AProcInfo() fills an array with the information needed to find the different kinds of items. Depending on the parameters you pass, it can include all of the items available in Document View (procedures, functions, classes, methods, constants, and directives) or various subsets. The array created includes, at least, the name of the item and the line number where it appears. Unlike Document View, however, AProcInfo() works only with PRG files.

The new EditSource() function opens an editor at a specified location. Although it can work with the array created by AProcInfo(), it actually has wider applicability. (In fact, it seems clear that it was added to VFP to allow the Task List application to be created.) EditSource() accepts either a shortcut ID (see Chapter 3, "New and Better Tools," for an explanation of shortcut IDs) or the name of a file, and the location at which to open the file.

There are several ways to specify the location in the file. For PRG files, text files, and stored procedures, you can provide just a line number (which is, no doubt, why AProcInfo() puts line numbers in the array). For forms, you specify the name of a method; if you want, you can also include the line number within the method. For class libraries, you specify the name of the class; you can also specify a method within the class and a line number within the method.

Better access to files

In previous versions of Visual FoxPro, when a file is open for editing, no other program can touch it. It can't be copied or even just read by another program. In VFP 7, files are available as read-only when they're open in the editor. So you can copy or zip a program file even while it's being edited. (Of course, unsaved changes won't be included in the copy.)

Under the hood, what's going on is that the editor in previous versions gave the file an attribute of "Deny Read" when it opened it. In VFP 7, the "Deny Write" attribute is used instead.

Summary

Creating, formatting, and editing files is easier than ever in VFP 7. New tools, settings, and commands provide more ways to work with your code, make it more readable, and find specific sections in order to edit them.

Chapter 3
New and Better Tools

If you thought the first two chapters were chock-full of new and improved features, wait until you read this one! VFP 7 has improvements in almost every tool that comes with it, plus it adds several cool new utilities.

FoxPro has always included "power tools" that improve a developer's productivity. Among the early ones were the Screen and Menu Designers, which allowed you to visually design a screen or menu and generated the reams of code you'd have to write manually without the tool. VFP added lots of new tools, including the Class and Form Designers and the Class Browser. With the exception of VFP 6, which added the Component Gallery, most of the enhancements or additions to the VFP tool suite have been incremental. VFP 7 changes that—new tools include a replacement for the VFP Setup Wizard, an automated testing facility, and a task list for managing editor shortcuts and your "to do" list. Existing tools have many new features as well, including modernization of application menus, productivity improvements in the Class, Form, and Report Designers, new window behaviors, more FoxPro Foundation Classes, and more samples.

Modern menus

Visual FoxPro's menus have been enhanced to keep up with the latest interaction techniques. The DEFINE BAR command has several new clauses. PICTURE and PICTRES let you add pictures to menu items. With PICTURE, you specify a file, including path. With PICTRES, you specify the bar number for an item from the FoxPro system menu and the graphic associated with that item is used. In order to use graphics, the menu popup containing the bar must be defined with the MARGIN clause. Support for the PICTURE and PICTRES clauses has been added to the Menu Designer. **Figure 1** shows the Prompt Options dialog with the graphic from _mtl_wzrds (Tools | Wizards) chosen.

The other two new clauses, INVERT and MRU, are not supported by the Menu Designer. You need to write code for such menus by hand or trick the Menu Designer into including it by adding it to the SKIP FOR clause. (Later in this section we describe an improvement in handling such clauses.)

INVERT allows you to make a bar appear with a lighter background and as though it were depressed. This is the way the lesser-used items in the Office applications appear (when they appear at all).

The final new clause, MRU, is the most complex because you need to write code to make it useful. MRU stands for "most recently used." When you add this clause to a bar, the bar appears as a chevron character pointing downwards and implies that the menu can be expanded. When the user holds the mouse over that item or clicks on it, you can respond by adding menu items (or with any other code you want to run). Presumably the items you add will be inverted; otherwise, they'd have been displayed initially.

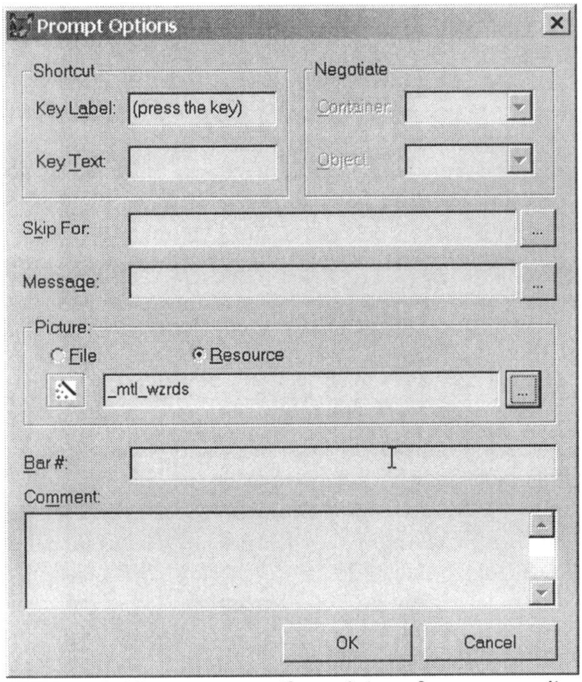

***Figure 1**. You can specify a picture for a menu item in the Menu Designer.*

The program in **Listing 1** creates a new menu pad on the system menu with three items. The first two have pictures associated with them. The third is an MRU item. When the user chooses the MRU item, a separate program is called that changes the menu popup.

***Listing 1**. The new MRU menu option lets you create menus that can be expanded.*

```
* MRUMenu.PRG
* Create a menu with an MRU item.

DEFINE PAD MRUSample OF _MSYSMENU PROMPT "MRU Demo"

DEFINE POPUP MRUpop MARGIN RELATIVE

ON PAD MRUSample OF _MSYSMENU ACTIVATE POPUP MRUPop

DEFINE BAR 1 OF MRUPop PROMPT "End MRU Demo" PICTURE HOME() + "Fox.BMP"
DEFINE BAR 2 OF MRUPop PROMPT "Second" PICTRES _mfi_save
DEFINE BAR 3 OF MRUPop MRU

ON SELECTION BAR 1 OF MRUPop DO ReleaseMRU
ON SELECTION BAR 2 OF MRUPop WAIT WINDOW "Not really saving anything"
ON SELECTION BAR 3 OF MRUPop DO ChgMRUPop
```

Listing 2 shows ChgMRUPop, which is called when the user chooses the MRU item. It modifies the popup, reactivates it, and then, after the user makes a choice, restores the menu to its original state.

Listing 2. *You have to write code to change the menu after the user chooses the MRU item.*

```
* ChgMRUPop.Prg
* Change the contents OF MRUPop menu popup in response to the MRU choice

* Remove the MRU bar
RELEASE BAR 3 OF MRUPop

* Add the new bars
DEFINE BAR 3 OF MRUPop PROMPT "Inserted (bar #3)" INVERT AFTER 1
DEFINE BAR 4 OF MRUPop PROMPT "Fourth" INVERT

ON SELECTION BAR 3 OF MRUPop WAIT WINDOW "Hey! This works."
ON SELECTION BAR 4 OF MRUPop WAIT WINDOW "Even the new one at the bottom works"

* Reactivate the popup
ACTIVATE POPUP MRUPop

* After the user makes a choice, clean up
* Remove the added bars
RELEASE BAR 3 OF MRUPop
RELEASE BAR 4 OF MRUPop

* Need to redefine the MRU bar,
* if the user didn't close this menu
IF POPUP("MRUPop")
    DEFINE BAR 3 OF MRUPop MRU
    ON SELECTION BAR 3 OF MRUPop DO ChgMRUPop
ENDIF
```

Finally, **Listing 3** contains the ReleaseMRU program that cleans up the menu when the user chooses the End MRU Demo choice.

Listing 3. *Like other menus, you have to clean up from expandable menus.*

```
* ReleaseMRU.PRG
* Clean up MRUMenu

RELEASE POPUP MRUpop
RELEASE PAD MRUSample OF _MSysMenu
```

 *All three programs are included in the Developer Downloads available at **www.hentzenwerke.com**.*

Figure 2 shows the menu as it first appears, while **Figure 3** shows the expanded menu.

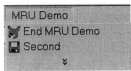

Figure 2. Menu enhancements—this menu popup shows pictures for menu bars and the MRU menu item.

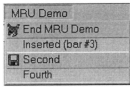

Figure 3. Menu expansion—you can write code to respond to the MRU item to add bars to the menu. The new INVERT clause provides the ability to have bars that are set back and dimmed.

With the new MRU and INVERT clauses, you can even write code to mimic Office's behavior of showing only the most frequently used items in a given menu. In that case, every menu item needs to include code to track its usage, and the code to create and expand the menu needs to check the usage data to see which items should be displayed initially and which should show up only on expansion of the menu.

There's one additional change related to menus. VFP developers have long used the SKIP FOR option for menu items to add clauses not supported in the Menu Designer interface. By specifying False, and then following it with the desired clauses, the menu generator program, GENMENU, is tricked into adding the desired clauses to the menu program. In VFP 7, GENMENU has been modified so that SKIP FOR .F. clauses are automatically eliminated. That way, the additional clauses are added without the baggage of a useless SKIP FOR specification.

You can take advantage of the SKIP FOR clause to add an MRU item to a menu. To do so, put ".F. MRU" in the Skip For item of the Prompt Options dialog (shown in Figure 1). The code generated for that item would look something like this (assuming you give the item a prompt of MRU, as documentation):

```
DEFINE BAR 7 OF MyMenu PROMPT "MRU" MRU
```

Without the change to SKIP FOR, the code would have looked like this:

```
DEFINE BAR 7 OF MyMenu PROMPT "MRU" SKIP FOR .F. MRU
```

More importantly, the SKIP FOR clause would have needed to be evaluated every time the menu was updated.

Class and Form Designers

The Class and Form Designers have several productivity-boosting enhancements: the ability to quickly drill down into containers, easier identification of the properties, events, and methods (PEMs) of ActiveX controls and of inherited methods in the Properties Window, preservation of case in the parameters statement of methods of subclasses or instances, and "real" grid coordinates.

Drilling down into containers

Imagine you have a form with a page frame on it. Page 2 of the page frame has a container class on it. The container class includes an option group with three option buttons. After opening the form in the Form Designer (or the Class Designer if it's a form class), you have to do the following to select the second option button:

1. Right-click on the page frame.

2. Choose Edit from the shortcut menu.

3. Click on Page2.

4. Right-click on the option group.

5. Choose Edit from the shortcut menu.

6. Click on the second option button.

Alternatively, you could navigate through the hierarchy of objects in the Objects combo box in the Properties Window. Either way, it's kind of a pain selecting contained objects.

In VFP 7, you can now hold down the Ctrl key while clicking on a container to drill down into the container one level at a time. That essentially takes the place of right-clicking and choosing Edit. Even better is the ability to directly select a contained object, regardless of how deep it is in the hierarchy, by holding down the Ctrl and Shift keys and clicking on it. That shortens the earlier sequence to:

1. Ctrl-Click on the page frame.

2. Click on Page2.

3. Ctrl-Shift-Click on the second option button.

Identifying ActiveX PEMs

When you drop an ActiveX control on a form, you're really dropping an OLEControl object on the form. The OLEControl object is a container that hosts the ActiveX control. While this distinction seems trivial, it's actually very powerful: It allows VFP developers to "subclass" ActiveX controls. Of course, you aren't really subclassing the ActiveX control; you're subclassing the OLEControl that hosts the ActiveX control. However, that's a technical detail, since the effect is the same.

One problem caused by the containership of an ActiveX control is distinguishing which PEMs belong to the OLEControl and which belong to the ActiveX control, since the Properties Window shows them co-mingled. Why would you care? Because there are cases where the OLEControl and ActiveX control have PEMs of the same name. It's possible the OLEControl and ActiveX control treat the same-named PEM differently. For example, the KeyPress event in VFP objects accepts two parameters (the key code and a value indicating whether the Shift, Alt, or Ctrl keys were pressed), while the TreeView ActiveX control version accepts only one.

The Properties Window in VFP 7 now distinguishes native and ActiveX PEMs using different colors: It shows native PEMs in black and ActiveX PEMs in blue. You can change the color of ActiveX PEMs by right-clicking in the Properties Window, choosing ActiveX Color from the shortcut menu, and selecting the desired color.

Identifying inherited methods

A form isn't working quite right, so you open the code window for the appropriate method in the Form Designer, but there's no code there. So, you open the class the form is based on in the Class Designer, open the code window for the method, and there's no code there either. You then open the parent of that class... Sound familiar?

VFP 7 makes it easy to determine where to find the code for a method. As you can see in **Figure 4**, the Properties Window shows "Inherited <class> <class library>" for inherited methods you haven't overridden rather than "[Default]" as previous versions did.

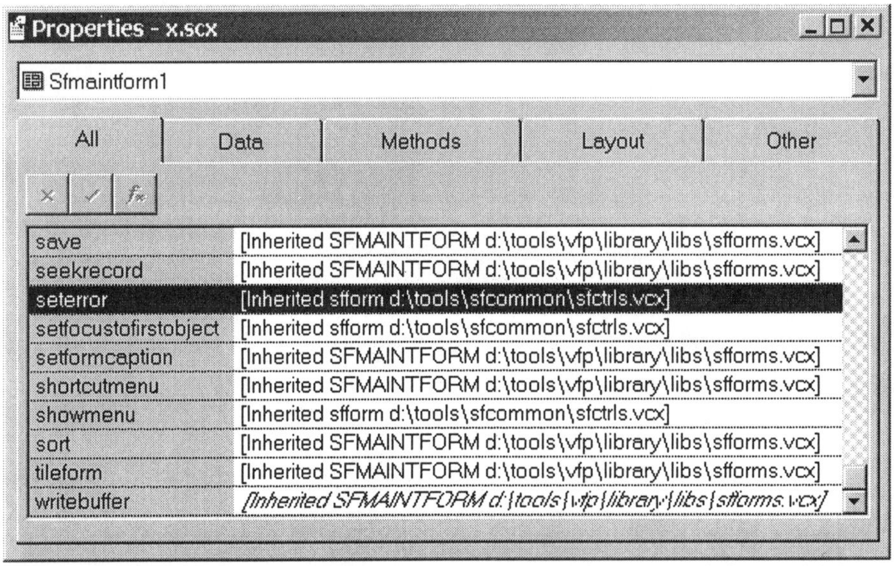

Figure 4. The Properties Window shows which methods inherit from which parent classes.

Preserving case in parameters statements

Some developers are very particular when it comes to coding standards. For example, Doug prefers lowercase for VFP keywords and Hungarian notation with "camel case" for variables (such as lcMyVariable for a local character variable). So, in his code, the parameters statement of a method typically looks like this (putting each parameter on a separate line makes it easier to read and easier to insert new parameters in the proper place):

```
lparameters tcParameter1, ;
  tnParameter2, ;
  tlParameter3
```

Earlier versions of VFP mangled this statement to the following in a subclass or instance:

```
LPARAMETERS tcparameter1, tnparameter2, tlparameter3
```

VFP 7 now preserves the case of parameters statements in subclasses and instances. However, it still doesn't handle multi-line statements properly; it removes the semicolons and Returns, so the statement looks like this:

```
lparameters tcParameter1,     tnParameter2,     tlParameter3
```

Hopefully, this will be fixed in a service pack.

"Real" grid coordinates

The Class and Form Designers now display grid lines ("grid" meaning the lines that appear in the designers, as opposed to the Grid control) in actual grid coordinates rather than in double the grid scale as previous versions did. **Figure 5** shows forms in VFP 6 and VFP 7 with the same grid scale.

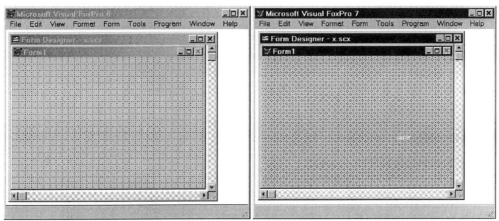

Figure 5. VFP 7 uses actual grid coordinates, while VFP 6 used double grid scale.

Project Manager

There's only one small change in the Project Manager: The Rename File function now has F2 as its shortcut key to make it consistent with other applications such as the Windows Explorer.

Report Designer

Keyboard-only users found the Report Designer quite difficult to work with in previous versions. For example, the only way to display the Properties dialog for a report band was to double-click on the gray bar at the bottom of the band. VFP 7 has the following improvements for those who must or prefer to work exclusively with the keyboard:

- Selecting the new Bands item in the Report menu displays a dialog from which you can select a particular band and edit its properties.

- The new Insert Control item in the Report menu has a submenu with the same controls available in the Report Controls toolbar. Selecting a control from the menu adds it in the upper left corner of the report.

- The new Background Color and Foreground Color items in the Format menu allow you to set the colors for the selected objects in the report.

- The Report Designer has improved keyboard navigation. Press Ctrl-E to edit the text of the selected label. Press Ctrl-Tab to toggle in and out of a new "tab" mode; while in tab mode, press Tab to move to the next object and Shift-Tab to move to the previous object.

There are two other changes related to reports. In previous versions, the Windows Print Spooler dialog displayed "Visual FoxPro" for reports waiting to be printed. This caused concern for those developers who don't want their users to know what language their applications were written in, and also made it difficult to determine which report was which in the queue when several reports were printed. In VFP 7, the Print Spooler shows the name of the FRX or LBX file being printed. Also, the page limit has been increased from 9,999 to 65,534.

VFP developers working in languages that read right-to-left will appreciate the new Reading Order function in the Format menu. Similar to the RightToLeft property of some controls, it allows you to specify the reading order for the selected object.

Distributing applications

The expression "long in the tooth" applied to the VFP Setup Wizard and the installation technology it relied on several years ago. By today's standards, it's positively ancient. The setup executable it creates looks like the 16-bit application it is, has a clunky interface with confusing dialogs (one of the dialogs implies your application was written by Microsoft), and has limited ability to do anything but copy and register files on the user's system (you're responsible for other tasks such as creating shortcuts). As a developer tool, the Setup Wizard also has several shortcomings, including a clunky interface and the inability to customize anything about the installation dialogs other than the caption and copyright notice.

Fortunately, VFP 7 replaces the Setup Wizard with a VFP-specific version of InstallShield Express. This setup tool, from InstallShield Software Corporation (**www.installshield.com**), is a wonderfully easy-to-use yet highly customizable utility. Both the tool and the resulting setup executable have a clean, modern user interface. Although it comes with extensive Help, you'll probably find you can use it without referring to the documentation at all.

InstallShield Express uses Microsoft Installer (MSI) technology. The technology was introduced a couple of years ago and has become the standard way of installing applications on Windows systems. Although you can use the Visual Studio Installer (VSI), available for download from Microsoft's Web site, to create VFP setups, InstallShield Express provides a much friendlier interface and adds capabilities missing from VSI. For information on using MSI to install VFP applications, see the white paper titled "Using Microsoft Visual Studio Installer for Distributing Visual FoxPro 6.0 Applications" at **http://msdn.microsoft.com/ library/techart/usingvsi.htm**. Although this document is for VFP 6, it has some good background information on MSI and how it relates to VFP.

InstallShield is available in several versions. The version that comes with VFP 7 is a stripped-down ("limited edition") version of InstallShield Express; several of the customization capabilities have been disabled. You can upgrade from that version to the full version of InstallShield Express if you want those capabilities. InstallShield Professional is a much more powerful installation tool, providing almost limitless customization, albeit at a high price, both in dollars and learning curve.

Creating an InstallShield Express project

The first step in creating a setup executable for your application is to create a new InstallShield project. Run InstallShield by choosing the "Express – Visual FoxPro Limited Edition" shortcut in the InstallShield folder of Start | Programs. Click on Create a new project in the right pane, select Blank Setup Project, enter the desired path and name for the project (InstallShield projects have an ISM extension), select the desired project language (this option only appears if your system is configured for multiple languages in the Regional Options Control Panel applet), and click on the Create button.

After InstallShield has created your project, it displays a list of the steps necessary to create a setup executable in the left pane and settings for the selected step in the right pane (see **Figure 6**). Although there may appear to be a lot of steps, not all are necessary for every application. As you visit each step, a red check mark appears beside it in the left pane.

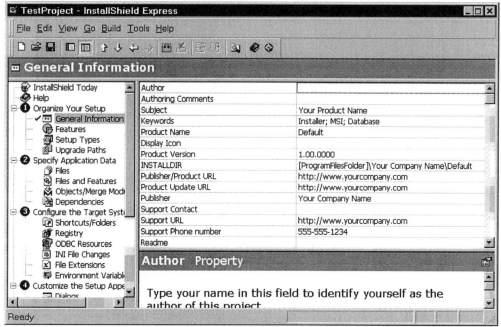

Figure 6. *InstallShield includes a list of the setup steps in the left pane and the settings for the selected step in the right pane.*

Organize your setup

The first set of steps is titled "Organize Your Setup." In these steps, you specify information about your application and what choices the user can make to install it.

General information step

In the General Information step, enter information about your application (see Figure 6), such as the name and version number of the application, the URLs for your company, update, and support sites, and so on. In addition to properties of the application, there are three important settings in this step:

- INSTALLDIR: This represents the default installation location on the user's system. As you can see in Figure 6, the default value contains [ProgramFilesFolder]; this is a placeholder in InstallShield that represents the location of the "Program Files" folder on the user's system. INSTALLDIR appears in uppercase because it's used as a placeholder itself in other places in InstallShield where you want to represent the installation directory the user selected.

- DATABASEDIR: This item (not visible in Figure 6) contains the default location for database files on the user's system. Its default value is a subdirectory of [INSTALLDIR]. As with INSTALLDIR, it can be used as a placeholder in other settings.

- Disable Change Button, Disable Remove Button, and Disable Repair Button: These three settings (not visible in Figure 6) indicate what behavior your setup executable will have in the Add/Remove Programs applet of the Windows Control Panel. For example, if you only want the user to be able to remove the application, set Disable Remove Button to No and the other two to Yes.

Features step
This step allows you to define which optional components ("features") your user may decide to install or not (for example, when you installed VFP, you may have decided to not install the samples and ActiveX controls that came with it).

Setup types step
This step is related to features: It allows you to specify which setup types the user can choose from (Typical, Minimal, and Custom) and which features each type will install. Since most VFP applications don't use optional components, you'll likely skip the Features step and disable the Minimal and Custom types.

Upgrade paths step
The last step in "Organize Your Setup" is Upgrade Paths. In this step, you specify information used when the user is upgrading from a previous version of your application without having to uninstall that version first. Note: This step is only available in the full edition of InstallShield Express.

Specify application data
The next set of steps is called "Specify Application Data." This is where you define all the pieces that make up your application.

Files step
The first step is the application's files. This is a refreshing change from the VFP Setup Wizard, where you have to create a distribution directory containing all the files in your application. InstallShield presents a Windows Explorer-like interface in which you drag and drop files from anywhere on your system to folders on the destination computer. Start by creating one or more folders on the destination system. To do that, right-click on Destination Computer in the lower pane and either choose Add to create a new folder or (more likely) choose one of the predefined folders such as [INSTALLDIR]. Then, drag files from your system in the upper pane to the desired folders in the lower pane (see **Figure 7**).

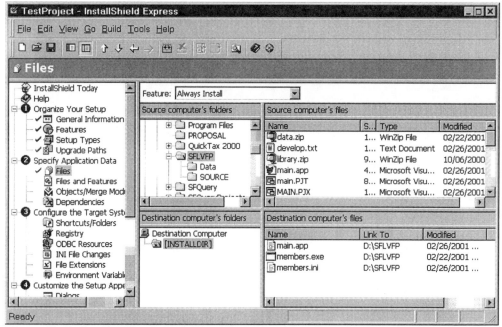

Figure 7. Define the files to install and their target locations by dragging them from your system in the upper pane and dropping them in the appropriate folder on the destination computer in the lower pane.

Files and features step

This step associates each file with the features you defined in the Features step. If you're not using features, you can skip this step.

Objects/merge modules step

You specify which components your application needs in addition to its own files in the Objects/Merge Modules step. A merge module is a prepackaged set of files that always go together, along with information about how to install and register them. For example, the VFP run time files are packaged in one merge module and the ActiveX controls in MSCOMCTL.OCX (such as the TreeView and ImageList controls) are in another. As you may know if you've examined the files installed by the VFP Setup Wizard, a VFP application requires more than just the application's files and the VFP run time libraries. You need to select the following merge modules as a minimum:

- Microsoft Visual C++ 7 Runtime Library (MSVCR70.MSM, MSVCP70.MSM, and MSVCI70.MSM): The Visual C version 7 run time libraries (be sure to select all three of them).

- Microsoft Visual FoxPro 7 Runtime Libraries (VFP7Runtime.MSM): The VFP 7 run time files.

Other merge modules you may need, depending on which features your application uses, include:

- Microsoft Component Category Manager Library (COMCat.MSM): Include this if your application uses any ActiveX controls. You must also include the appropriate merge module for the ActiveX controls; for example, Windows Common Controls ActiveX Control DLL (MSComCtl.MSM) contains the version 6 TreeView, ImageList, and ListView controls.

- Microsoft OLE 2.40 for Windows NT (TM) and Windows 95 (TM) Operating Systems (OLEAut32.MSM): Provides COM support.

- Microsoft Visual FoxPro OLE DB Provider (VFPOLEDB.MSM): Add this to install the VFP OLE DB provider (see Chapter 5, "Data," for information). You should also include one of the Microsoft Data Access Components merge modules; see below.

- Visual FoxPro ODBC Driver Merge Module (VFPODBC.MSM): This merge module installs the VFP ODBC driver. You should also include one of the Microsoft Data Access Components merge modules; see the next point.

- MDAC25 (version 2.5; MDAC25.MSM) or MDAC26ENU (version 2.6 English; MDAC26.MSM): The Microsoft Data Access Components merge modules. These have a dependency on DCOM95, so that merge module (DCOM95.MSM) will be selected automatically when either of the MDAC modules is selected.

- Microsoft Visual FoxPro HTML Help Support Library (VFPHTMLHelp.MSM): Include this if your application uses HTML Help. In addition, you may need to install the HTML Help viewer files. Unfortunately, these aren't available as a merge module; instead, the user has to run HHUPD.EXE. Be sure to include this file (available from MSDN or in the REDIST subdirectory of the directory where HTML Help Workshop is installed on your system if you have that application) with your distribution files and tell the users they need to run this EXE.

- Microsoft Visual FoxPro 7 Runtime Resource Library (VFP7R???.MSM): These merge modules install locale-specific resource files. See VFPDeploy.DOC in the Technical Articles directory of the VFP 7 CD for details on which module to use for a given language.

- SOAP SDK Files (SOAP_Core.MSM) and Visual Basic Virtual Machine (MSVBVM60.MSM): Needed if your application uses Web Services or SOAP (see Chapter 15, "Working with Web Services," for a discussion on Web Services in VFP 7).

- Microsoft Visual FoxPro Active Document Support Library (VFPActiveDoc.MSM): Needed for ActiveDoc support.

Because of dependencies between merge modules, some of these may be selected automatically. For example, selecting the Windows Common Controls ActiveX Control DLL (MSComCtl.MSM) automatically selects both Microsoft Component Category Manager

Library (COMCat.MSM) and Microsoft OLE 2.40 for Windows NT (TM) and Windows 95 (TM) Operating Systems (OLEAut32.MSM).

Dependencies step

If you're not sure what merge modules your application requires, the Dependencies step can help. The Perform Static Scanning option examines your application's files (EXE, DLL, and OCX) and adds any dependencies it finds to the project. Perform Dynamic Scanning watches your system as you run the application, adding any DLLs and OCXs it accesses to the project. Note: This step is only available in the full edition of InstallShield Express.

Configure the target system

The set of steps titled "Configure the Target System" allows you to perform additional setup tasks on the user's computer.

Shortcuts/folders step

In this step, you define where shortcuts should appear, such as in the Programs folder of the Start menu or on the user's desktop. To create a folder under Programs, right-click on Programs Menu, choose New Folder, and enter the folder name. To create a shortcut, right-click on the item where the shortcut should go (such as a folder you created or Desktop), choose New Shortcut, enter the shortcut name, and fill in the properties for the shortcut in the right pane. Selecting the target file and working directory for the shortcut is easy: You simply select them from the combo box that appears when you click on each item. **Figure 8** shows shortcuts called My Application in a folder called Test Folder in the Programs Menu and on the Desktop.

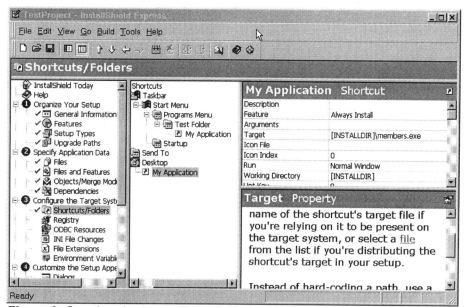

Figure 8. Creating shortcuts to your application is easy in InstallShield.

Registry step

This step allows you to define Registry keys on the target system. You can either create a new key or drag a key from your Registry and drop it on the target system's Registry. Although you can easily create your own keys within the application using the Registry class included in the FoxPro Foundation Classes (FFC), it's a good idea to at least create the top-level key for your application in InstallShield. That way, if the user uninstalls your application, InstallShield will remove the application's Registry keys rather than leaving them as orphans. **Figure 9** shows the results of dragging a key from the source computer to the target computer.

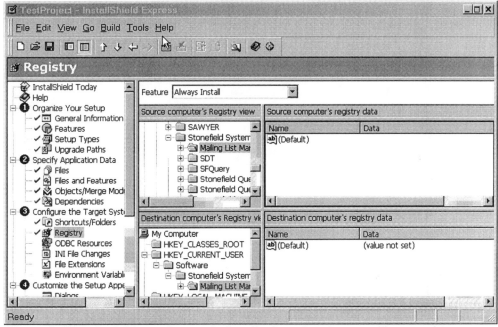

Figure 9*. Registry keys can be created on the target system as either new keys or keys copied from your system.*

Other steps

The remaining steps in "Configure the Target System" are less frequently used for VFP applications. The ODBC Resources step allows you to select which existing ODBC data sources (DSNs) on your system should be created on the user's system. You can edit the properties of a DSN as necessary (for example, to point to a different server on the target system). In the INI File Changes step, you can create new INI files on the user's system or edit existing ones (including Windows files such as Boot.INI and WinInit.INI). The File Extensions step allows you to create file associations on the target computer so when the user opens a file with a certain extension, your application is automatically launched. The last step, Environment Variables, allows you to create, edit, or remove environment variables on the target system; this step is only available in the full edition of InstallShield Express.

Customize the setup appearance

The "Customize the Setup Appearance" set of steps allows you to determine how the setup executable will appear to the user. This is something the VFP Setup Wizard completely lacked, so VFP 7 developers will appreciate it.

Dialogs step

You can't create your own custom dialogs; for that, you have to upgrade to InstallShield Professional. However, the Dialogs step, shown in **Figure 10**, does allow you to select which of a predefined list of dialogs should appear and customize to some extent what information appears in them. For example, you can have a license agreement displayed and specify both the image displayed and the text of the agreement. In the Customer Information dialog, you can indicate that a serial number is required and specify which function in a DLL ensures the serial number is valid.

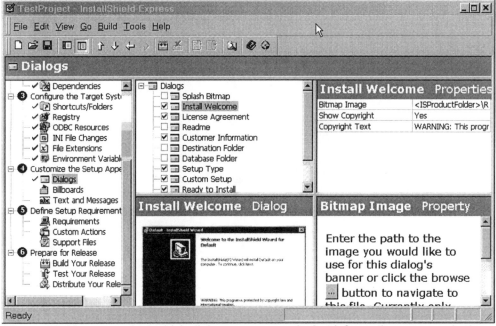

Figure 10. You can select which dialogs appear and what information appears in them in the Dialogs step.

Other steps

The Billboards step allows you to specify images to display during the installation process that describe your application or provide advertising for other products and services you offer. The Text and Messages step allows you to customize every string displayed in every dialog, so, for example, no dialogs display "InstallShield" anywhere. Note: Both of these steps are only available in the full edition of InstallShield Express.

Define setup requirements

The "Define Setup Requirements" set of steps allows you to customize the setup even further.

Requirements step

Using the settings in the Requirements step, you can ensure your application is only installed on certain operating systems (for example, if you require COM+, you only want the application installed on Windows 2000), with minimum settings for processor, RAM, screen resolution, and color depth.

Custom actions step

The Custom Actions step is similar to the ability to define a post-setup executable in the VFP Setup Wizard, except you can use either a DLL or EXE, call it from any step in the installation process rather than just at the end, and indicate whether it's called during installation or uninstallation (calling a custom action during uninstallation allows you to clean up things your application does that InstallShield doesn't know about, such as files or Registry entries it creates). Note: This step is only available in the full edition of InstallShield Express.

Support files step

You can use the Support Files step to define files required only during the installation process, such as the DLLs or EXEs called for custom actions. InstallShield places these files in a temporary directory during installation and removes them after installation is complete. Note: This step is only available in the full edition of InstallShield Express.

Prepare for release

The final set of steps, "Prepare for Release," is where you build, test, and distribute your setup executable.

Build your release step

In the Build Your Release step, you select the type of media the setup is targeted for: CD, DVD, single image (such as for Web sites), and custom. The type of media determines how the setup files are split up; for example, in the custom type, you can specify a media size of 1.44MB if your setup will go on floppy disks (does anyone still do that?) and InstallShield will create components no bigger than that size. In addition to the media size, you can specify whether InstallShield should use compression (you can turn this off if, for example, you're using CDs for distribution and your setup doesn't take 600MB), include the Windows Installer engine for different platforms (if you don't allow the application to be installed on Windows 95, you can turn that setting off), and generate an AutoRun.INF file for automating CD and DVD installation.

Test your release step

The Test Your Release step allows you to run the setup process exactly as a user would or test the setup process without actually copying any files. This step is important to ensure it works correctly and you're happy with the dialog choices.

Distribute your release step
The final step, Distribute Your Release, copies the setup files to a specified location, such as to a CD or FTP site.

Other InstallShield Express information
In addition to certain steps mentioned earlier, the full version of InstallShield Express has a couple of other features missing in the VFP Limited Edition. One is the ability to globalize the setup by exporting, translating, and reimporting the strings used in the InstallShield project. Another is dynamic file linking, in which you add the contents of an entire directory to the project. InstallShield reads the contents of the directory every time you create a build, so new or removed files are handled automatically.

The first time you use InstallShield Express, you'll forget you ever saw the VFP Setup Wizard. While there are more steps involved in creating a distribution executable using InstallShield, the additional features and modern interface of this tool are more than worth it. This is a very welcome addition to VFP 7!

Window behavior
The behavior of "system" windows is significantly improved in VFP 7.

Dockable windows
The biggest change in window behavior in VFP 7 is dockable windows. Like dockable toolbars, the following VFP system windows have the ability to dock at any edge of the VFP screen:

- Call Stack
- Command
- Data Session
- Debug Output
- Document View
- Locals
- Property
- Trace
- Watch

To enable or disable window docking for these windows, right-click in the title bar and choose Dockable; a check mark in front of this item indicates that the window is currently dockable. You can also choose this item in the Window menu when the window is active. There are more differences between dockable and non-dockable windows than just docking ability; **Table 1** shows the differences in characteristics and behavior between them.

***Table 1**. Dockable and non-dockable windows display different characteristics and behavior.*

Non-dockable	Dockable
Title bar has icon, close box, and minimize and maximize buttons	Title bar has no icon or minimize or maximize buttons (no support for minimize and maximize behavior)
Can be moved under other windows	Always on top
Cannot be moved outside the VFP desktop	Can be moved outside the VFP desktop
No docking behavior	Supports normal, linked, and tabbed docking
Trace and Debug Output windows (when the Debugger is in FoxFrame mode) no longer have lower-right corner resize control	Resize control appears in Trace and Debug Output windows
Window name added to bottom of Window menu	Window name not added to bottom of Window menu (Command, Data Session, and Properties always there)

VFP supports three types of docking: normal, linked, and tabbed. Normal docking means docking the window like a toolbar at an edge of the VFP screen. To dock a window, drag its title bar until the mouse pointer is within 25 pixels of an edge of the VFP screen; the dragged window image changes width or height to indicate it will be docked when you release the mouse button. To undock a window, drag its title bar away from the edge of the screen. Double-clicking the title bar reverses its docked status. That is, double-clicking an undocked window docks it, while double-clicking a docked window undocks it. To avoid docking a window, hold down the Ctrl key while dragging it. **Figure 11** shows an example of the VFP screen with the Command Window docked at the left and the Data Session Window moved outside the boundaries of the VFP screen.

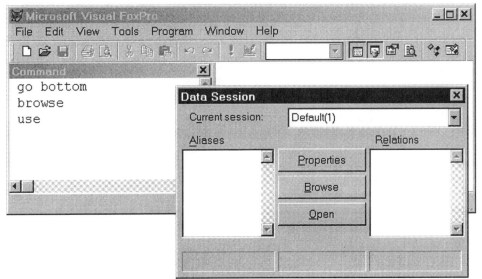

***Figure 11**. The Command Window is docked and Data Session Window is outside the VFP screen.*

Link docking is cool—it allows you to combine dockable windows together, similar to the Debugger window when you use the "Debug Frame" option. To link dock two windows, drag the title bar of one to any inner edge of the "client area" of the other. VFP creates a new container window to hold the two windows. You can add other windows to the container by dragging them into it. To remove a window from the container, drag it out; when only one window remains, the container window disappears. You can resize the container window, adjust the split in size between the windows inside the container, dock the container window at any edge of the VFP screen, or move it outside the VFP screen boundaries. **Figure 12** shows the Command and Data Session windows link docked together.

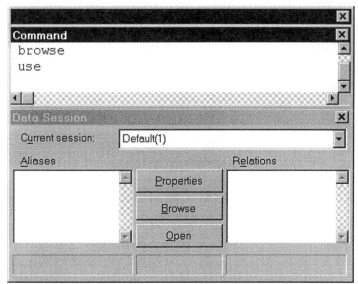

Figure 12. The Command and Data Session windows link docked.

Tab docking is even cooler! Like link docking, tab docking allows you to combine two or more windows into a container window. However, with tab docking, each window takes up the full size of the container; tabs at the bottom of the container allow you to select which window to display. To tab dock two windows, drag the title bar of one onto the title bar of the other. To remove a window, drag its tab out of the container. As with link docking, you can resize the container window, dock it at any edge of the VFP screen, or move it outside the VFP screen boundaries. **Figure 13** shows the Command and Data Session windows tab docked together.

Note that while other types of docking are preserved between VFP sessions, tab docking is not.

A new function, WDockable(), returns the current dockable state of a window and can change it. For example, the following code saves the current state of the Command Window, makes it dockable, and then restores the former state:

```
llState = wdockable('Command')
wdockable('Command', .T.)
wdockable('Command', llState)
```

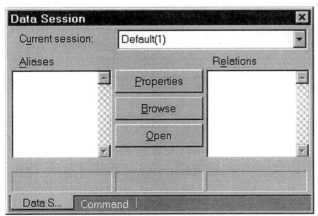

Figure 13. *The Command and Data Session windows tab docked, with Data Session currently selected.*

Properties Window enhancements

In addition to the two enhancements mentioned earlier in this chapter (identifying ActiveX PEMs and inherited methods), the Properties Window has a couple of new behaviors. First, selecting the new Properties Window item in the Window menu displays the Properties Window showing the properties of the VFP desktop. This makes it easier to change things like the color, font, and caption of the VFP window than doing it programmatically by setting properties of the _Screen object.

Second, the Properties Window can be made dockable. In addition to the behavior described for other dockable windows, when the Properties Window is dockable, it stays open when the Form and Class Designers are closed, displaying the properties of _Screen. If you find this annoying, turn off the dockable status for the Properties Window.

Other window enhancements

VFP has three other enhancements to windows:

- The Data Session Window is now resizable.

- Like IntelliSense's Auto Field Names list (discussed in Chapter 1, "IntelliSense"), the Database Designer, View Designer, and DataEnvironment of a form or report now show value tips displaying the data type and size for the selected field, followed by the caption (in parentheses) and comment for the field if they were specified. **Figure 14** shows an example.

- VFP "system" windows (those used for things like error messages, Wait Window, tool tips, list tips, value tips, and so forth) now respect your Windows font settings. Also, pressing Ctrl-C copies the contents of an error window to the Clipboard.

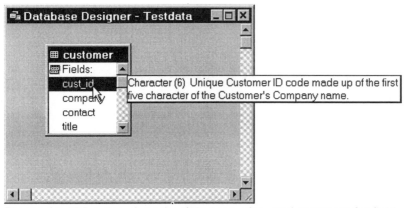

Figure 14. Value tips show the data type, size, and comment for fields.

Task List

As discussed in Chapter 2, "Editor Enhancements," the VFP 7 code editor provides bookmarks and shortcuts, features that allow you to quickly return to a line of code. The difference is that, unlike bookmarks, shortcuts persist when you close an edit window. That obviously means they must be saved somewhere, and that somewhere is the FoxTask table. The name and location of that table can be specified in the File Locations page of the Options dialog or in the new _FoxTask system variable. The default location is the VFP application data directory (C:\Documents and Settings\<user name>\Application Data\Microsoft\Visual FoxPro\FoxTask.DBF).

VFP 7 comes with an application called the Task List Manager that provides a front end for the FoxTask table. The name and location of this application can be specified in the File Locations page of the Options dialog or in the new _TaskList system variable; the default is TaskList.APP in the VFP home directory. This application, which can be executed from the Task List item in the Tools menu, provides more than just a list of the shortcuts you've defined; you can also use it to manage a "to do" list. **Figure 15** shows the Task List Manager.

!			Contents	File Name	Due Date
			Click here to add a new task		
↓	☐	🔖	PROCEDURE SolutionErrHandle	D:\Program Files\Microsoft Visual FoxPro 7.0\S;	/ /
↓	☐	🔖	loMatches = loRegEx.execute(tcStr	D:\Program Files\Microsoft Visual FoxPro 7.0\Ff	/ /
!	☑	🔖	Finish final testing before release		04/09/01

Figure 15. The Task List Manager can manage "to do" lists as well as editor shortcuts.

The first column in the task list indicates a task's priority; the choices are low (the default), normal, or high and are indicated with an icon in the list. You can change the priority by clicking in that column and selecting the desired value from the combo box that appears. To indicate that a task has been completed, place a check mark in the second column; the columns in a row marked "completed" appear with stricken out text (see the bottom row in Figure 15). The third column contains an icon specifying the task type: an editor shortcut (the first two tasks in Figure 15) or a user-defined task (the bottom row in Figure 15). The remaining columns show the description of the task (in the case of a user-defined task) or line of code (in the case of a shortcut), the name and path of the associated file, and the due date of the task. To sort the task list on a particular column, click on the column header, which then appears in blue. Click again to sort in descending order.

To add a user-defined task, click in the Contents column of the first row (where "Click here to add a new task" is displayed) and type the description of the task; after you tab out of this column, the new task appears at the bottom of the task list. You can also fill in a file name (if the task is associated with a file) and the due date for the task. Tasks for which the due date has passed appear in red, while those due today appear in blue.

The FoxTask table has more fields than those shown in the task list. To edit other properties for a task, right-click on the task and choose Open Task from the shortcut menu to display the Task Properties dialog (shown in **Figure 16**). The Class, Method, and Line properties are used (along with File Name) by shortcut tasks to reference the exact location of the shortcut. If you check the Read check box, the task appears normal rather than bold in the task list. The Fields tab displays user-defined fields, discussed later.

Figure 16. You can specify additional information about a task in the Task Properties dialog.

In addition to opening a task, the shortcut menu for the Task List Manager has the following functions:

- Open File: opens the file associated with the task (in the case of a shortcut, you can also double-click anywhere on the task to open the file).

- Mark as Complete, Mark as Incomplete, Mark as Read, and Mark as Unread: marks the task appropriately.

- Delete Task: removes the task.

- Remove This Column: removes the selected column from the grid.

- Column Chooser: displays the Column Chooser, from which you can add an undisplayed FoxTask field to the grid.

- Show Tasks: allows you to filter which types of tasks are displayed.

- Options: displays a dialog in which you can define new properties for tasks.

The "_FOXTASK System Variable" topic in the VFP Help file explains the structure of the FoxTask table. You can use the Task List Manager Options dialog to define new properties for tasks. These additional properties are stored in a separate table; you specify the name and location of that table in the Options dialog (the default is "UDFTable.DBF"), and then add the fields you desire to the table. These fields appear in the Fields page of the Task Properties dialog; you can also add them to the task list by right-clicking in the task list, selecting Column Chooser from the shortcut menu, and dragging the field name from the Column Chooser dialog to the grid.

Complete source code for the Task List Manager is provided in the Tools\XSource\ TaskList subdirectory of the VFP home directory, including documentation in Microsoft Word format.

Improved debugging

There are several changes in VFP 7 that give you more control over the debugging process. The one you're likely to notice first is that the list of events created when you turn Event Tracking on now includes a timestamp in seconds (like the one used in Coverage logs). Here's an example:

```
53366.089, screen.MouseUp(1, 0, 391, -70)
53369.634, frmcolors.Load()
53369.664, frmcolors.dataenvironment.Init()
53369.664, frmcolors.shpbox.Init()
53369.664, frmcolors.imgfox.Init()
53369.664, frmcolors.lblsurprise.Init()
```

A new SYS() function provides a welcome enhancement to Event Tracking. SYS(2801) lets you decide whether you want to track only VFP's events, only Windows mouse and keyboard events, or both. There are times when the information VFP offers from its events isn't sufficient to figure out what's going on under the hood. The ability to track Windows events as well can help unravel some tricky situations. Be forewarned—if you thought event logs were huge already, you're in for a shock. They'll be much larger when you track Windows events. The Windows-level MouseMove event fires frequently, and removing VFP's MouseMove from the list of tracked events doesn't affect this one.

Another new SYS() function is for those situations where you're trying to debug something that involves one of the VFP tools that's also written in VFP, like the Class Browser or Coverage Profiler. In VFP 6 and earlier versions, breakpoints and other debugging features see these tools and are affected by them. But most of the time, that's not what you want. You don't want to debug the code provided with VFP; you want to debug your code that's using the tool.

So, in VFP 7, the default behavior has changed. Most of the Debugger's features ignore these built-in tools. However, you can replace these tools with your own homegrown versions. In that case, you need to be able to debug the code. So, SYS(2030) lets you control whether or not these VFP-coded tools respond to breakpoints, appear in coverage logs, and so forth. Pass the default 0 to leave VFP tools out of debugging; pass 1 to turn on debugging features for these tools.

There's one other, minor, change that makes debugging easier. The Breakpoints dialog is now available on the Tools menu with a shortcut of Ctrl-B. So you don't have to open the Debugger to set complex breakpoints.

Active Accessibility and the Accessibility Browser

Creating applications that can be used by everyone, regardless of disabilities, is increasingly important. Not only do many countries now have laws requiring employers to provide facilities for employees with disabilities, but as the population ages, the number of people who are limited in one way or another is increasing.

Microsoft has been improving Windows' ability to accommodate users with disabilities; with version 7, VFP joins the bandwagon. Active Accessibility provides a standard interface for accessibility aids (such as screen reader and magnification utilities). Earlier versions of VFP didn't support the IAccessible interface that underlies Active Accessibility. VFP 7 remedies that problem. This means that tools like Windows 2000's Narrator and Magnifier can work with VFP applications.

SYS(2800) controls the availability and behavior of VFP's native controls through Active Accessibility. By default, VFP controls are available. Using this function, they can be made invisible to accessibility aids. The function also lets you change their response to accessibility aids—for example, one setting indicates that controls should provide their name rather than their caption to such aids.

To help you build accessible applications, the VFP team has provided a new tool, the Accessibility Browser. It's installed in the Tools\MSAA subdirectory of the VFP installation and run by issuing DO AccBrow from that directory.

The Accessibility Browser lets you see how your forms appear through the IAccessible interface. **Figure 17** shows the Accessibility Browser displaying information for the form shown in **Figure 18**.

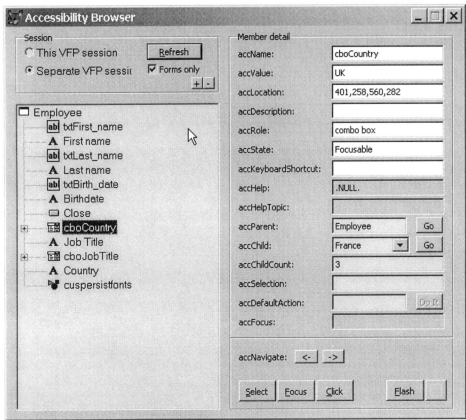

Figure 17. *The Accessibility Browser shows how forms look to accessibility aids.*

Figure 18. *The form whose internals are shown in Figure 17.*

The Accessibility Browser can examine forms in the same VFP session in which it's running or in a special session that it opens. Regardless of which mode it's in, the Refresh button tells the Browser to see what forms are active and add them to the treeview in the left panel. The Forms only check box determines whether the Browser sees other objects, such as the system menu, as well.

The right-hand side of the form shows data for the object currently highlighted in the treeview. The two Go buttons change the position of the highlight in the treeview. You can navigate to the parent or any child of the currently highlighted item.

The Do It, Select, Focus, and Click buttons take actions in the form containing the currently highlighted item. Do It performs the default action for that item. For example, if the Close button of the Employee form is highlighted in the treeview, clicking Do It clicks the Close button (and, in fact, closes the form). Select, Focus, and Click control the keyboard and mouse focus. Click places the mouse focus on the specified control, Focus puts the keyboard focus on the control, and Select selects the object. You can use the Ctrl and Shift keys with the buttons for extending selections.

The Flash button briefly puts a yellow highlight around the object with focus. The button next to it (with the yellow square) is really a check box. When it's checked, a yellow focus highlight is visible and follows the focus.

Once you've worked a little with the Accessibility Browser, the question you're likely to ask is what you need it for. In building VFP applications, the answer is not much. It's useful for getting a feel for how Active Accessibility works, but the best use for the Accessibility Browser is to open it up in VFP and check out the code. It provides a good look at the API functions that support Active Accessibility and the PEMs involved.

Automated testing

Active Accessibility isn't just for helping users with disabilities. The information that's exposed by the IAccessible interface is exactly that needed for automated testing, a task that's always been difficult with Visual FoxPro.

To demonstrate this new ability, VFP 7 includes the Active Accessibility Test Harness. Located in the Tools\Test directory of the VFP installation, the Test Harness is a VFP application that allows you to record and play back test scripts. As with the Accessibility Browser, source code is provided, so not only can you use the tool, you can also learn from its techniques.

The Test Harness (its main form is shown in **Figure 19** and its toolbar is in **Figure 20**) works with applications running in a separate VFP session. When you begin to record a script, you're prompted to choose the VFP session in which to record. You can record activity only in an interactive VFP session, but the selection dialog allows you to start a new VFP session.

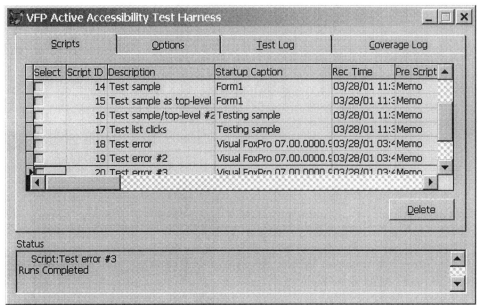

Figure 19. *The main form of the Active Accessibility Test Harness tracks recorded scripts.*

Figure 20. *The Active Accessibility Test Harness's toolbar lets you record and play back scripts, as well as examine and edit existing scripts.*

The script records keystrokes and mouse presses (that is, mouse up and mouse down). Be careful with actions like down arrow to choose from a list—if the list changes, so will the selection. Also, be aware that you can't successfully run a script recorded with small fonts in a large fonts environment and vice versa. The mouse clicks won't hit at the right places.

You can play back multiple scripts in series by checking them in the first column of the grid.

Script data is stored in a table (AAScripts), and each record contains both the script itself and the corresponding event log. The event log takes advantage of VFP's new ability to record system events (key presses and mouse actions—see "Improved debugging" earlier in this chapter).

When you play back a script, a log of that test is created. The Test Log page of the Test Harness (which corresponds to the AATestLog table) lists the logs. That table also tracks the memory used by the test and how long the test took.

There are a number of options that can be set for the Test Harness (see **Figure 21**). As you'd expect, **Overwrite existing script** is essentially SET SAFETY OFF for script names. If you'll generally want to do your recording in a new VFP session, you can save a couple of steps by checking Always launch new VFP window.

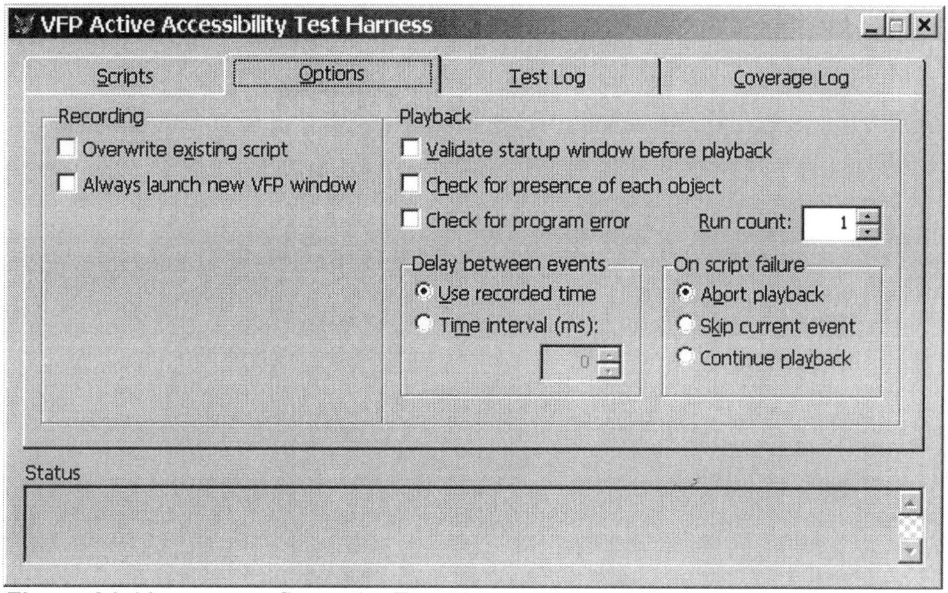

Figure 21. You can configure the Test Harness to work the way you want it to.

The Validate startup window before playback check box tells the Test Harness to ensure that you're playing back a script in the window in which it was recorded. If that item is unchecked, a message about the problem is added to the test log, but playback continues.

The Check for presence of each object check box determines whether script playback requires the original object to exist with the original name. When this option is on, playback fails if an object has been renamed or removed.

Check for program error controls what happens if a VFP error is triggered during playback. When it's checked, the test log is supposed to contain a record of the error message. Unfortunately, in our testing, this feature didn't work.

Run count specifies how many times each selected script is played back. Each run is treated separately and gets its own entry in the test log. When multiple scripts are selected for multiple runs, the whole sequence of scripts is run in order and that sequence repeated as many times as specified.

By default, scripts are played back at the same speed at which you recorded them. The Delay between events option group lets you slow things down by waiting between each event.

You have three options when an event in the script can't be executed. You can stop the playback—in that case, the test is marked as failing. The second choice is to skip over that event as if it weren't in the script. The third choice is to record the failure in the test log, but continue with the script. Both the second and third choices result in a "Pass" indication for the script, even if many individual events fail.

You can integrate coverage logging with playback of scripts. The Coverage Log page of the Test Harness lets you turn on coverage logging, as well as providing direct access to the coverage log created and to the Coverage Profiler.

Modify Procedure and View

The Modify Procedure and Modify View commands now support a Nowait clause. This clause tells VFP to continue program execution after the stored procedures code window or View Designer open. With the exception of Modify Structure, all the Modify commands now support this clause.

New FFC classes

The FoxPro Foundation Classes (FFC) is an underutilized resource. Although there are a few classes that could charitably be described as "demoware," the majority of these classes are a valuable addition to any developer's toolbox. VFP 7 includes several additions to the FFC. Samples are available for all of the new classes; the easiest way to get at the sample is to open the VFP Component Gallery (available in the Tools menu), right-click on the desired class in the appropriate folder of the Foundation Classes node of the Visual FoxPro catalog, and choose Open or Run from the View Sample shortcut submenu.

The following are the new classes (all specified files are located in the FFC subdirectory of the VFP home directory, and all classes are shown in the Utilities subfolder of the Foundation Classes folder in the Component Gallery unless otherwise specified):

- _Agent: Love 'em or hate 'em, Microsoft has made the technology used to display "assistants" (such as the paper clip) in Microsoft Office available for developers to add to their applications. _Agent (in _Agent.VCX and appearing as the "Microsoft Agent Utility" node in the Component Gallery) is a wrapper for the Microsoft Agent ActiveX controls. It provides simple methods to instantiate an agent and have it perform the desired actions without having to worry about coordinate systems or whether the user closed the agent. See the "Microsoft Agent Utility Foundation Class" topic in the VFP Help file for information about this class.

- _SetAllX: The SetAll() method of container classes such as Form sets the specified property of all contained objects to the specified value. _SetAllX (in _SetAllX.VCX and appearing as the "SetAllX Extension" node in the Component Gallery) is like SetAll() on steroids. You can pass it expressions to evaluate for both the property and the value, specify a list of base classes (all other types of contained objects are ignored), and tell it to not drill down into containers such as page frames. The "SetAllX Extension Foundation Class" topic in the VFP Help file has details on this class.

- _RegExp: Sometimes finding and replacing text is more difficult than just searching for one string and replacing it with another. For example, you may only be interested in finding a word when it's near another, or maybe you want all occurrences of a word and any variations. A notation called *regular expressions* was developed for this type of searching. Details of regular expressions are available in MSDN and in two HTML files in the Samples\Solution\FFC directory of the VFP home directory: RegExp1.HTM and RegExp2.HTM.

The _RegExp class, defined in _RegExp.VCX and displayed as "Regular Expressions" in the Component Gallery, is a wrapper for the RegExp class in the Microsoft Visual Basic Scripting Edition (for documentation on VBScript, see **http://msdn.microsoft.com/scripting/**). Set the Pattern property to the regular expression to search for and then call the Execute() method with two parameters: the text to search and a logical value to indicate whether a case-sensitive search is required (True for case-sensitive). The Matches array property contains the results of the search. For more information on this class, see the "Regular Expressions Foundation Class" topic in the VFP Help file.

- _System: This class is a wrapper for the SHGetFolderPath Windows API function, which returns the path for common system directories such as Windows, System, My Documents, and Application Data. Call the class's GetFolder() method, passing the ID of the desired directory (see the "Common System Folders Foundation Class" topic in the VFP Help file for details) and True if the directory should be created if it doesn't exist. This class is defined in _System.VCX and appears as "Common System Folders" in the Component Gallery.

- _SysMetrics: The GetSystemMetrics Windows API function returns information about the system, such as how many monitors are installed and how many buttons are on the mouse. This class is a wrapper for GetSystemMetrics. It has several properties, such as nMonitors and lMouseWheelPresent, that have access methods calling the protected CallSysMetrics() method, which in turn calls GetSystemMetrics() to obtain the desired information. You can subclass _SysMetrics to provide additional information if required. This class is contained in _System.VCX, appears as "System Metrics" in the Component Gallery, and is documented in the VFP Help file in the "System Metrics Foundation Class" topic. The sample form for this class is the same as the _System class.

- _UserPriv: The GetUserPriv() method of this class, which is also contained in _System.VCX, returns the privilege level of the specified user: 0 means guest, 1 means power user, and 2 means administrator. _UserPriv appears in the Component Gallery as "User Privileges" and is discussed in the "User Privileges Foundation Class" topic of the VFP Help file. The sample form for this class is the same as the _System class.

- _CryptAPI: Unbeknownst to most, Windows contains several API functions for encrypting and decrypting information. _Crypt.VCX contains the _CryptAPI class, which is a wrapper for some of these functions. You can use it to encrypt strings, entire files, and fields in a table using a variety of mechanisms; it also provides file signing features. This is one of the most complex classes in the FFC, and unfortunately its topic in the Help file, "Crypto API Foundation Class," has very little documentation. Fortunately, it comes with a pretty good sample file (easily accessed from the "Crypto API" item in the Component Gallery) that shows how to use it for different types of tasks.

- _ComDlg: Like several other classes, this class is defined in _System.VCX; it appears as "Common Dialog" in the Dialogs folder in the Component Gallery. _ComDlg provides a wrapper for the Windows API functions that display File Save and Open dialogs. Using this class may be more convenient than using the CommonDialogs ActiveX control that comes with VFP because you don't have to worry about whether the ActiveX control is properly installed and registered on the user's system. See the "Common Dialog Foundation Class" topic in the VFP Help file for details.

In addition to these, another class library, _WebServices.VCX, exists in the FFC subdirectory. This VCX contains classes that implement Web Services in VFP 7; Web Services are discussed in detail in Chapter 15, "Working with Web Services."

New samples

VFP 7 comes with several new samples to help you get started in a particular area. The Solution application (Solution.APP in the Samples\Solution subdirectory of the VFP home directory) has a "New Features for VFP 7.0" heading, with samples showing new features such as DBC events (covered in this book in Chapter 5, "Data"), hot tracking and MouseEnter/MouseLeave events (discussed in Chapter 6, "OOP Enhancements"), and using new features of the Menu Designer (see "Modern menus" earlier in this chapter).

The Samples\COM+ subdirectory includes samples showing how to use COM+ features in VFP applications, including COM+ Transactions, COM+ Events, Queued Components, and compensating resource managers. See Readme.HTM in the same directory for details on what these samples show and how to run them (also see Chapter 14, "Playing in the COM+ Sandbox").

Summary

VFP 7 has more than a few minor improvements in its tool suite. It has a long-needed replacement for the Setup Wizard, a new Task List Manager that can help you avoid those little sticky notes that litter your office, the ability to create menus that look like those in today's applications, a tool that automates regression testing of your applications, and many more new and improved features.

Chapter 4
More IDE Changes

Not all the changes in VFP 7 fit neatly into cubbyholes. This chapter covers IDE changes that aren't related to IntelliSense, editing, or tools.

There are a variety of changes in the VFP 7 IDE that can't be easily categorized. Quite a few of these are actually items for which support has been discontinued, others relate to Windows 2000 logo requirements, some have to do with VFP's interaction with Windows, and a few are just little tweaks, perhaps in response to developer requests.

Things that aren't there anymore

Several items that were included with earlier versions of VFP have been eliminated in VFP 7. The first two, the Setup Wizard and the runtime for Microsoft Graph, are gone because VFP 7 includes a new approach to distributing applications. See Chapter 3, "New and Better Tools," for a discussion of InstallShield Express Visual FoxPro edition.

Visual FoxPro and its predecessors have included a spelling checker for quite a few versions. In VFP 7, it's gone. Since that tool couldn't be distributed with applications, it doesn't seem much of a loss.

A number of commands that execute old development tools have been dropped in VFP 7. The list is FOXGRAPH, FOXVIEW, FOXGEN, FOXCODE, and CENTRAL. Interestingly, the _FOXGRAPH system variable has not been removed.

Several ActiveX controls that used to be installed with VFP are no longer included. They are the Calendar, Outline, and FoxHWnd controls.

Windows 2000 logo requirements

A few things have been changed in order to allow VFP 7 to meet the Windows 2000 logo requirements. The default location of the resource file (FoxUser.DBF, by default) has been changed. In VFP 7, it's put in the VFP "user" folder (in Windows 2000, C:\Documents and Settings\<user name>\Application Data\Microsoft\Visual FoxPro). You can change the location for the resource file using the SET RESOURCE TO command, by specifying the location on the File Locations page of the Options dialog, or by specifying the Resource setting in the Config.FPW file.

Similarly, the default startup location has been changed to the "desktop folder" (in Windows 2000, C:\Documents and Settings\<user name>\Desktop). You're unlikely to want to store files in that folder. You can change it in a couple of ways. First, if you set up a shortcut for VFP 7 on your desktop, fill in the Start in text box with the folder where you really want to start. You can also set the Default Directory on the File Locations page of the Options dialog (Tools | Options from the menu).

Interaction with Windows

Several changes impact the way VFP interacts with the Windows environment. First, when you Open a file associated with VFP from the Windows shell (for example, from Explorer), a new instance of VFP is started. In earlier versions, if VFP is already running, the file is opened in that instance of VFP.

In earlier versions of VFP, double-clicking on a VFP program file in Explorer runs the program. In VFP 7, the default for program (PRG) and query (QPR) files is to open them in the appropriate editor, rather than run them. No more accidentally running a program from Explorer.

Although VFP 7 seems quite stable, inevitably, it will crash. However, Microsoft has made it easier for the VFP team to figure out what's causing such problems. When VFP 7 crashes, it creates a log file containing the error message and the call stack at the time of the crash. You can use this information to determine where your code crashed. More importantly, you can send it to Microsoft to help them track down any remaining fatal bugs.

What's left?

VFP 7 has an assortment of other changes that affect interactive use. Many of these are items that make the product much easier to use.

Shareable resource file

Probably the most important change in this group is that the resource file is now shareable. That means that you can open multiple instances of VFP and all of them can use your stored settings. In addition, multiple users can access the same resource file.

Persistent Command Window

Another useful new behavior is persistence of the Command Window contents. When you close VFP normally, everything in the Command Window is saved to a file named _Command.PRG. As with other such files, it's stored in the "user" folder. When you start VFP, the contents of the file are copied into the Command Window, so that you can reuse commands across sessions the same way you use them within sessions.

When you have multiple VFP sessions open, the commands from the last session to close "win." That is, only commands from that session are stored for future sessions.

There's no way to turn Command Window persistence off, but you can clear out the file's contents between sessions, if you prefer to start with a clean slate. You can also use the Clear option on the context menu to empty the Command Window. Then, only commands issued after that in the current session are stored for the next session.

Menu changes

VFP 7 follows current user interface trends by including icons in the menu. Many items on the VFP menu have an icon to the left. In general, when the item has a corresponding toolbar button, the two use the same icon.

VFP 7 also supports icons in menus you create. See Chapter 3, "New and Better Tools," for details.

There are also some changes in menu contents. Most of them are discussed in other chapters. However, there are a few leftover changes.

The Run Active Document item is gone from the Tools menu. However, the Active Document launcher program (RunActD.PRG) is still available in the main VFP directory.

The Tools menu has been reorganized, with more logical groupings of its items.

The Window menu now includes a Cascade item that overlaps all open windows starting from the upper left corner.

The Help menu no longer has separate items to get to the Contents, Index, and Search pages of the Help file. Instead, you can simply open the Help file with the Microsoft Visual FoxPro Help item. In addition, there are some new items. MSDN Search opens an installed version of MSDN to the Search page. The Microsoft on the Web item, which opened a submenu in VFP 6, has been replaced with a single Visual FoxPro on the Web item that navigates Microsoft's VFP site.

Options dialog changes

There are quite a few changes to the Options dialog accessed from the Tools menu. Many of them are discussed along with the items they affect in other chapters. For example, the new IDE page of Options is covered in Chapter 2, "Editor Enhancements." But there are a couple of differences that are unrelated to other changes in the product.

The File Locations page includes several new items. In addition to those discussed elsewhere (like FoxCode Table and Object Browser), CrossTab Generator (corresponding to the _GenXTab system variable) has been added. In addition, the prompt for the _Beautify item has been changed to Beautify. In older versions, it was labeled Documenting Wizard.

Starting VFP

VFP has a whole collection of switches you can add to the command line that runs the program. VFP 7 adds a new switch that you're not likely to use in any desktop shortcuts or batch files, but which should come in handy nonetheless. The new switch is "/?" and it brings up a dialog showing all the command line switches for VFP (see **Figure 1**). Just the ticket when you're trying to build a command line and can't remember which switch you need.

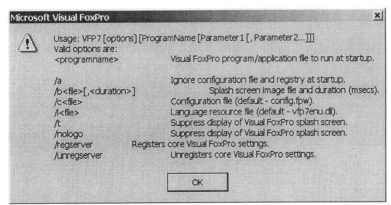

Figure 1. Using the new "/?" switch on the VFP command line displays a dialog showing all the available switches.

Final IDE thoughts

The developer interface includes many changes in VFP 7, from major ones that will change the way you work (like IntelliSense and the Object Browser) to others, not as significant, that just make things easier (such as the "/?" command line switch).

Some of the changes (like the new locations for some files) are neutral, as long as you know they're there. Overall, VFP 7 makes it easier to be productive than any previous version of the product.

Section 2
Developing Desktop
Applications

Chapter 5
Data

The defining characteristic of VFP is its built-in database engine. It's been a while since Microsoft made improvements in the engine, but VFP 7 has several.

VFP developers like to brag that VFP is the fastest desktop database engine on the planet. While VFP 7 doesn't improve database performance (there probably isn't much more speed that can be wrung out of the engine), it does include several improvements in other areas of the engine. This chapter looks at these improvements in three sections: new and enhanced language elements, database (DBC) events, and the VFP OLE DB provider.

New and enhanced language elements

Like most other areas of VFP, the database engine has some new and improved language elements. Some of them, such as the improvements to Browse and SYS(3054) and the new ATagInfo() function, are targeted at developers, while others, such as the new capability of SQL Select, can make your run-time code leaner or cleaner.

ASessions()

This new function fills an array with the DataSessionID values of all existing data sessions. The following code shows how it works by creating two Session objects, using ASessions() to fill an array, and then displaying the contents of the array.

```
loSession1 = createobject('Session')
loSession2 = createobject('Session')
asessions(laSessions)
clear
display memory like laSessions
```

In VFP 6 and earlier, a common technique used when an application is being shut down due to an error is to revert any data changes in all data sessions. One way to do this is to spin through all open forms, Set DataSession to their DataSessionID, and use TableRevert() on all open tables:

```
local lnI

* Rollback all transactions.

do while txnlevel() > 0
  rollback
enddo while txnlevel() > 0

* Go through all forms and revert all tables in their data sessions.

for lnI = 1 to _screen.FormCount
  if _screen.Forms[lnI].DataSessionID <> 1
```

```
      set datasession to _screen.Forms[lnI].DataSessionID
      RevertTables()
   endif _screen.Forms[lnI].DataSessionID <> 1
next lnI

* Revert all cursors in the default data session.

set datasession to 1
RevertTables()

function RevertTables
local laCursors[1], ;
  lnCursors, ;
  lnI, ;
  lcAlias

* Revert all changes in all buffered tables.

lnCursors = aused(laCursors)
for lnI = 1 to lnCursors
  lcAlias = laCursors[lnI, 1]
  if cursorgetprop('Buffering', lcAlias) > 1
    tablerevert(.T., lcAlias)
  endif cursorgetprop('Buffering', lcAlias) > 1
next lnI
return
```

One problem with this code: It won't handle any private data sessions created by Session objects. So, here's the VFP 7 version of this routine:

```
local laSessions[1], ;
  lnI, ;
  laCursors[1], ;
  lnJ, ;
  lcAlias

* Rollback all transactions.

do while txnlevel() > 0
  rollback
enddo while txnlevel() > 0

* Go through all data sessions and revert all tables in them.

for lnI = 1 to asessions(laSessions)
  set datasession to laSessions[lnI]
  for lnJ = 1 to aused(laCursors)
    lcAlias = laCursors[lnJ, 1]
    if cursorgetprop('Buffering', lcAlias) > 1
      tablerevert(.T., lcAlias)
    endif cursorgetprop('Buffering', lcAlias) > 1
  next lnJ
next lnI
```

*The Developer Download files at **www.hentzenwerke.com** include this code in RevertAllTables.PRG.*

ATagInfo()

ATagInfo() does in a single function what in earlier versions of VFP you had to use nine functions and about 40 lines of code to do: get all of the information about the tags of a table. It even works with non-structural indexes as long as they're open. This function fills the specified array with the name, type, expression, filter, order, and collate sequence for each tag and returns the number of tags. This information is essential for creating metadata that can later be used to re-create the indexes if they become corrupted. The following code shows how ATagInfo() works:

```
open database (addbs(_samples) + 'Data\Testdata')
use Customer exclusive
index on upper(Address) tag Address of Temp.CDX
ataginfo(laTags)
display memory like laTags
close databases all
erase Temp.CDX
```

 *The Developer Download files at **www.hentzenwerke.com** include this code in TestATagInfo.PRG.*

Browse

At long last, this command has a NoCaption option to display the actual field names rather than the captions defined for the fields in the database container.

GetNextModified()

GetNextModified() returns the record number of the first or next modified record (depending on what parameters are passed) in a table-buffered cursor. This can be used, for example, to determine whether Save and Revert buttons in a toolbar should be enabled.

 *The Developer Download files at **www.hentzenwerke.com** include the three programs described in this section: DataChanged6.PRG, DataChanged7.PRG, and TestGetNextModified.PRG.*

The following routine, DataChanged6.PRG, is an example of how GetNextModified() can be used. It returns True if any record in any open cursor has been changed.

```
local llChanged, ;
  laTables[1], ;
  lnTables, ;
  lnI, ;
  lcAlias, ;
```

```
   lcState

* Check each open table to see if something changed.

llChanged = .F.
lnTables  = aused(laTables)
for lnI = 1 to lnTables
  lcAlias = laTables[lnI, 1]
  do case

* This cursor isn't buffered, so we can ignore it.

    case cursorgetprop('Buffering', lcAlias) = 1

* This is a row-buffered cursor, so check the current record.

    case cursorgetprop('Buffering', lcAlias) < 4
      lcState   = getfldstate(-1, lcAlias)
      llChanged = not isnull(lcState) and ;
        lcState <> replicate('1', fcount(lcAlias) + 1)

* This is a table-buffered cursor, so look for any modified record.

    otherwise
      llChanged = getnextmodified(0, lcAlias) <> 0
  endcase
  if llChanged
    exit
  endif llChanged
next lnI
return llChanged
```

There's one major problem with this routine: GetNextModified() fires the rules (field, table, and index uniqueness) for the current record before figuring out what the next modified record is. This prevents the routine from working if there's anything wrong with the current record.

In VFP 7, GetNextModified() can now accept True as a third parameter to prevent rules from firing. DataChanged7.PRG has the same code as DataChanged6.PRG except it has True as the third parameter to GetNextModified(). To see the difference in behavior, run the following program (TestGetNextModified.PRG):

```
* Set up an error handler.

on error llError = .T.
llError = .F.

* Open the Customer table and table buffer it.

open database (addbs(_samples) + 'Data\Testdata')
use Customer
set multilocks on
cursorsetprop('Buffering', 5)

* Do some data updates; the second one duplicates the primary key of the first
* record.
```

```
replace Company with 'Howdy'
skip
replace Cust_ID with 'ALFKI'

* Try using GetNextModified; an error will occur.

llChanged = DataChanged6()
if llError
  aerror(laError)
  wait window laError[2]
  llError = .F.
else
  wait window 'Data ' + iif(llChanged, 'was', 'was not') + ' changed'
endif llError

* Try again with the lNoFire parameter; no error should occur.

llChanged = DataChanged7()
if llError
  aerror(laError)
  wait window laError[2]
  llError = .F.
else
  wait window 'Data ' + iif(llChanged, 'was', 'was not') + ' changed'
endif llError

* Clean up and exit.

tablerevert(.T.)
on error
```

In clause

This isn't really a command or function itself, but the In clause was added to several existing commands: Blank, Calculate, Pack, Recall, and Set Filter. This eliminates the need to save the current work area, perform the action, and then restore the work area as you do in previous versions of VFP. For example, here's how you used to set a filter on a table in a different work area:

```
lnSelect = select()
select Customer
set filter to City = 'New York'
select (lnSelect)
```

In VFP 7, you can simply use:

```
set filter to City = 'New York' in Customer
```

IsReadOnly()

Previously, IsReadOnly(), which returns True if the specified item was opened with the NoUpdate clause or is read-only, only worked with tables. Now, you can determine whether the current database is read-only by passing 0 as the parameter.

SQL Select

As you probably know, a cursor created with a SQL Select statement is read-only. While this isn't often an issue, because cursors are typically used for reports or other read-only processing, it can be if you have to perform further processing on the cursor before it's used, such as adding summary records. Before VFP 7, you made a cursor read-write by opening it in another work area, using code similar to the following:

```
select ... into cursor Temp1
select 0
use dbf('Temp1') again alias Temp2
use in Temp1
* Temp2 is a read-write copy of the cursor
```

In VFP 7, you can cut this down to a single command by adding the new ReadWrite clause to the Select statement:

```
select ... into cursor Temp1 readwrite
```

Set Reprocess

The new System clause for this command allows you to control record locking in the "system" data session, which is used for internal access to tables such as databases, the FoxUser resource file, SCX and VCX files, and so forth. To see an example of this, fire up two instances of VFP 7 and type the following in the Command Window of each one:

```
set reprocess to automatic system
```

Modify a class in a VCX in one instance and try to modify the same class in the same VCX in the second. VFP will wait to get a lock on the class's records in the VCX until you either close the class in the other instance or press Esc. Press Esc to cancel the attempt. Now type the following:

```
set reprocess to 2 seconds system
```

Try to modify the class again. This time, VFP tries for two seconds to lock the records, and gives up when it can't.

To determine the value of this setting, use Set('Reprocess', 'System').

SYS(3054)

This indispensable function, which tells you the Rushmore optimization levels for SQL Select commands (including those executed when a view is opened), works even better in VFP 7. Passing 2 or 12 for the first parameter (following the 3054) tells VFP to include the SQL statement in the output, making it easier to figure out which of several SQL statements the output applies to. A new second parameter sends the results to a variable rather than _Screen, which allows you to control the output (for example, you could log it to a file) or to automate analysis (such as warning the developer if "none" or "partial" appears in the results but not if "full" does). You must specify the variable name as a string rather than a name (that is, as "VariableName" instead of VariableName).

The following code shows the use of these new features:

```
close tables all
open database (addbs(_samples) + 'Data\Testdata')
use Customer
use Orders in 0
sys(3054, 12, 'lcRushmore')
select Customer.Company, ;
   max(Orders.Order_Date) ;
  from Customer ;
    join Orders ;
      on Customer.Cust_ID = Orders.Cust_ID ;
  group by Customer.Cust_ID ;
  into cursor Test
clear
? lcRushmore
sys(3054, 0)
```

Use

Whether you use remote views in production applications or not (discussions in threads on the Universal Thread, **www.universalthread.com**, and in documents on the FoxWiki, **http://fox.wikis.com**, have been just a tad heated!), they are still useful tools. For example, even if you normally use SQL Passthrough or ADO when accessing non-VFP data in production, you may sometimes find it handy to create a DBC and some remote views in a development environment so you can quickly browse the data. One downside of remote views compared to SQL Passthrough, though, is that the connection information is hard-coded, either in a connection stored in the database or in an ODBC datasource (DSN). This means this information can't be changed, so you can't use the same remote view to access data on a different server, for example. Also, user names and passwords stored in the DBC aren't encrypted, so that's a potential security risk.

VFP 7 adds the ability to specify a connection string on the fly, by simply adding it to the Use command for a remote view. If one is specified, it overrides the defined connection information for the view. If an empty string is specified, VFP displays the Select Data Source dialog.

 *The Developer Download files at **www.hentzenwerke.com** include the Test database used by the examples described next.*

To see an example of this new capability, do the following steps. First, create an ODBC DSN called "Northwind" for the Northwind database that comes with Access using the Access ODBC driver (if you don't have Access installed, use the SQL Server Northwind database and the SQL Server driver instead). Next, type the following in the Command Window:

```
open database Test
use RV_Customers connstring 'dsn=Northwind'
```

What's so remarkable about this? Well, the RV_Customers view is defined as:

```
create sql view "RV_Customers" ;
  remote connect "NorthwindConnection" ;
  as select * from Customers Customers
```

The NorthwindConnection connection specified in this view uses the SQL Server driver to access the Northwind database on the server named DHENNIGW2K:

```
create connection NorthwindConnection ;
  connstring 'DRIVER=SQL Server;SERVER=DHENNIGW2K;UID=sa;PWD=;' + ;
    'DATABASE=Northwind'
```

Specifying a connection string in the Use command allows you to create a cursor from the Customers table in the Access database on your system instead.

The benefit of this enhancement is that you can store the server, user name, and password in a table, build a connection string, and then use it in the Use command for your remote views. This gives you both flexibility (you can easily change the server, user name, and password in the table) and security (the password can be encrypted in the table and decrypted when the connection string is built).

Validate Database Recover
Formerly, this command could only be used in "interactive mode" (that is, from the VFP Command Window). In VFP 7, this command can now be used in code, so you can use it in a run-time environment. Of course, since this is a potentially dangerous command (it can remove tables from a DBC, for example) that displays dialogs that are confusing to the typical end-user ("What *is* a backlink and why would I want to update or remove it?"), you'll want to use it only in "administrator" functions in your applications.

Database events
Database events are an exciting new addition in VFP 7. Like a trigger, which automatically executes procedural code when a record is inserted, updated, or deleted in a table, a DBC event automatically executes a specific routine when something is done with a member of the DBC (such as a table or view) or the DBC itself. Events are available for almost any action you can take on anything in a DBC, such as opening or closing a table or view, creating a connection, dropping a relation, validating the DBC, and so forth.

It doesn't matter whether you do something visually (for example, selecting a view in the Database Designer and pressing the Delete key) or programmatically (executing the Drop View command), in a run-time or development environment, through VFP code or through ADO; the appropriate DBC event will fire.

By default, DBC events are turned off. There are two ways you can turn on DBC events for a given DBC. One is programmatically using something like:

```
dbsetprop(juststem(dbc()), 'Database', 'DBCEvents', .T.)
```

The other is using the Set Events On check box in the new Database Properties dialog (choose Properties from the Database menu or right-click in the Database Designer and choose Properties from the shortcut menu to display this dialog).

A DBC with events turned on is not backward-compatible with previous versions of VFP, nor can it be accessed through the VFP ODBC driver. Of course, you can always turn events back off again, but only from within VFP 7. If you want to maintain compatibility with older applications but make use of DBC events in your new versions, have your new applications explicitly turn DBC events on when they start.

The Version property of a DBC returned by DBGetProp(), normally 10, is 11 if DBC events are turned on.

Turning DBC events on doesn't mean anything will happen; you have to specify what events you want to handle by creating routines with the names VFP expects for DBC events. The procedure names all begin with "DBC_", followed by the name of the event (for example, DBC_BeforeOpenTable is the name of the procedure VFP executes when a table is opened).

As described in Chapter 1, "IntelliSense," the new ALanguage() function fills an array with VFP language elements. The first parameter is the array to fill and the second is the type of language elements desired. Passing 4 for the second parameter fills the array with the names of database events, although these names don't include the "DBC_" prefix.

DBC event code can be placed in the stored procedures of a DBC or in a separate PRG file. There are two ways you can specify a separate PRG file. One is programmatically using something like the following (where lcPRGName contains the name of an existing PRG):

```
dbsetprop(juststem(dbc()), 'Database', 'DBCEventFileName', lcPRGName)
```

The other way is using the Events File check box and associated Open File button in the Database Properties dialog. Doing this visually doesn't automatically create the PRG; you must select an existing file, even if it's empty.

Although you could type the DBC event names and parameter lists yourself, VFP can generate "template" code for you. Bring up the Database Properties dialog, check the Set Events On check box, and then select the events you wish to handle in the Events list box (any events that already have code will appear in bold) and click on the Edit Code button. (Neglecting the last step and clicking on OK instead simply closes the dialog without generating any template code.) An edit window for either the stored procedures of the DBC or the separate PRG file, depending on which you're using, appears with template code for each of the events you selected. All you have to do is fill in the code to execute for each event. If you want to work on existing code for a single event or generate the template for it, double-clicking on the event will do the trick. Hold down the Ctrl and Shift keys while clicking on the Edit Code button to generate template code with a ? statement showing the event name and parameters passed.

Most actions have both "before" and "after" events. While the after events just receive notification that an action took place, the before events can actually prevent the action from occurring by returning False. For example, if DBC_BeforeOpenTable returns False unconditionally, you won't be able to open any tables or views. Obviously, you want to be careful how you handle these events or you can make your database unusable!

How much overhead do DBC events add? Testing the difference in time to open a table with and without DBC_BeforeOpenTable and DBC_BeforeCloseTable events (but nothing in those events) showed a difference of only 2–3 percent, which isn't a significant amount. Obviously, putting extensive code into events will have an impact on performance.

DBC event descriptions

DBC events are available for the DBC itself as well as for tables, views, relations, and connections.

 The Developer Download files for this chapter, available at **www.hentzenwerke.com**, *include the PRG files that demonstrate how DBC events work.*

DBC events for databases

Almost everything you can do with a database has a DBC event associated with it; the only one missing is a DBC_CompileDatabase event. To see these events in action, run DatabaseEvents.PRG. Every Wait Window has a two-second timeout, so you can just sit back and watch the action.

DBC_OpenData(cDatabaseName, lExclusive, lNoUpdate, lValidate)

This event is called after a DBC is opened. After it fires, if another DBC is current, DBC_Deactivate fires for that database (since it won't be the current database anymore). DBC_Activate for the newly opened database then fires (since that database becomes the current one). Only after DBC_Activate does DBC() return the name of the database.

If DBC_OpenData returns False, the error "file access is denied" is triggered and the database can't be opened. Of course, be sure that you do this only under certain circumstances (for example, if the current user isn't authorized to access the database; see the "Using DBC events" section later in this chapter for further discussion), or you'll be somewhat hosed because you won't be able to reopen the database even to turn that feature off! (You're only "somewhat" hosed because you can always USE the DBC to open it as a table, modify the code directly in the Code memo of the StoredProceduresSource record, close it, and then use Compile Database to compile the changes.)

DBC_CloseData(cDatabaseName, lAll)

Called before a DBC is closed; return False to prevent the DBC from being closed. DBC_Deactivate also fires (after DBC_CloseData), since the database is no longer the current database.

DBC_Activate(cDatabaseName)

Called when the DBC is made current via such means as Set Database, after Open Database completes, clicking on an open Database Designer window, and so on. If another DBC is current, DBC_Deactivate fires for that database first (if that database has events enabled).

DBC_Deactivate(cDatabaseName)
Called when the DBC is made non-current; return False to prevent this from happening (this also prevents the DBC from being closed).

DBC_BeforeAppendProc(cFileName, nCodePage, lOverwrite)
Called before the Append Procedures command starts; return False to prevent the procedures from being updated.

DBC_AfterAppendProc(cFileName, nCodePage, lOverwrite)
Called after the Append Procedures command has completed.

DBC_BeforeCopyProc(cFileName, nCodePage, lAdditive)
Called before the Copy Procedures operation starts; return False to prevent procedures from being copied.

DBC_AfterCopyProc(cFileName, nCodePage, lAdditive)
Called after the Copy Procedures operation has completed.

DBC_BeforeModifyProc()
Called before stored procedures are modified; return False to prevent the editor window from appearing.

DBC_AfterModifyProc(lChanged)
Called when the window for the stored procedures is closed.

DBC_BeforeDBGetProp(cName, cType, cProperty)
Called before DBGetProp() executes. Returning False prevents the property's value from being read, in which case DBGetProp() returns null.

DBC_AfterDBGetProp(cName, cType, cProperty)
Called after DBGetProp() completes but before the value is actually returned.

DBC_BeforeDBSetProp(cName, cType, cProperty, ePropertyValue)
Called before DBSetProp() executes; return False to prevent the property value from being changed.

DBC_AfterDBSetProp(cName, cType, cProperty, ePropertyValue)
Called after DBSetProp() completes.

DBC_BeforeValidateData(lRecover, lNoConsole, lPrint, lFile, cFileName)
Called before Validate Database executes; return False to prevent the DBC from being validated. Note that the cFileName parameter isn't passed if lFile is False.

DBC_AfterValidateData(lRecover, lNoConsole, lPrint, lFile, cFileName)
Called after Validate Database has completed.

DBC_ModifyData(cDatabaseName, lNoWait, lNoEdit)
Called after Modify Database is issued; return False to prevent database modifications.

DBC_PackData()
Called before Pack Database executes; returning False from this event prevents the database from being packed, but also triggers a "file access denied" error, so be prepared to trap for this.

DBC events for tables
There's a DBC event associated with everything you can do structurally with a table. One thing is a little goofy: The Remove Table and Drop Table commands, which do the same thing, have a different set of events. If you want to trap the removal of a table, you have to be sure to handle both sets of events. Another issue is that if you open a table with a different alias, that alias is passed for the cTableName parameter in all table events rather than the name of the table. The workaround is to use CursorGetProp('SourceName') to determine the real name of the table.

To see these events in action, run TableEvents.PRG.

DBC_BeforeAddTable(cTableName, cLongTableName)
Called before a free table is added to the DBC; return False to prevent the table from being added.

DBC_AfterAddTable(cTableName, cLongTableName)
Called after a free table is added to the DBC.

DBC_BeforeCreateTable(cTableName, cLongTableName)
Called before a table is created; return False to prevent table creation.

DBC_AfterCreateTable(cTableName, cLongTableName)
Called after a table is created.

DBC_BeforeDropTable(cTableName, lRecycle)
Called before a table is removed from the DBC using Drop Table; return False to prevent the table from being removed.

DBC_AfterDropTable(cTableName, lRecycle)
Called after a table has been removed.

DBC_BeforeRemoveTable(cTableName, lDelete, lRecycle)
Called before a table is removed from the DBC using the Remove Table command or visually in the Database Designer; return False to prevent the table from being removed.

DBC_AfterRemoveTable(cTableName, lDelete, lRecycle)
Called after a table has been removed.

DBC_BeforeModifyTable(cTableName)
Called before a table structure is modified; return False to prevent modification.

DBC_AfterModifyTable(cTableName, lChanged)
Called after a table structure has been modified. You can't tell what changes are made unless you save the structural information somewhere in DBC_BeforeModifyTable (or use metadata) and then compare the current structure with the saved information in DBC_AfterModifyTable.

DBC_BeforeRenameTable(cPreviousName, cNewName)
Called before a table is renamed; return False to prevent the table from being renamed.

DBC_AfterRenameTable(cPreviousName, cNewName)
Called after a table has been renamed.

DBC_BeforeOpenTable(cTableName)
Called before a table is opened; returning False prevents the table from being opened and triggers a "file access denied" error, which you should be prepared to trap.

DBC_AfterOpenTable(cTableName)
Called after a table is opened.

DBC_BeforeCloseTable(cTableName)
Called before a table is closed; return False to prevent the table from being closed (no error is triggered).

DBC_AfterCloseTable(cTableName)
Called after a table is closed.

DBC events for views
As with tables, anything you can do with a view has a DBC event associated with it. As you may expect, some actions with views, such as creating or opening, cause the source tables to be opened, so the DBC_BeforeOpenTable and DBC_AfterOpenTable events fire for these tables. Interestingly, these events fire even if the tables are already open, giving us a glimpse of some internal processes involved in opening the view (such as opening a second copy of the tables).

As with tables, if a view is opened with a different alias, that alias is passed for the cTableName parameter in the Open and Close events rather than the name of the view.

To see these events in action, run ViewEvents.PRG.

DBC_BeforeCreateView(cViewName)
Called before a view is created; return False to prevent view creation.

DBC_AfterCreateView(cViewName, lRemote)
Called after a view is created.

DBC_BeforeDropView(cViewName)
Called before a view is dropped; return False to prevent the view from being dropped.

DBC_AfterDropView(cViewName)
Called after a view is dropped.

DBC_BeforeModifyView(cViewName)
Called before a view is modified; return False to prevent modification.

DBC_AfterModifyView(cViewName, lChanged)
Called after a view has been modified.

DBC_BeforeRenameView(cPreviousName, cNewName)
Called before a view is renamed; return False to prevent the view from being renamed.

DBC_AfterRenameView(cPreviousName, cNewName)
Called after a view has been renamed.

DBC_BeforeCreateOffline(cViewName, cPath)
Called before a view is taken offline; return False to prevent this from happening.

DBC_AfterCreateOffline(cViewName, cPath)
Called after a view is taken offline.

DBC_BeforeDropOffline(cViewName)
Called before a view is taken back online; return False to leave the view offline.

DBC_AfterDropOffline(cViewName)
Called after a view is taken back online.

DBC_BeforeOpenTable(cTableName)
Called before a view is opened; returning False prevents the view from being opened and triggers a "file access denied" error, which you should be prepared to trap.

DBC_AfterOpenTable(cTableName)
Called after a view is opened.

DBC_BeforeCloseTable(cTableName)
Called before a view is closed; return False to prevent the view from being closed (no error is triggered).

DBC_AfterCloseTable(cTableName)
Called after a view is closed.

DBC events for relations

There are only two types of events for relations: adding and removing. When a relation is modified, it's first removed and then re-added, so both the remove and add events fire.

All of these events receive five main parameters. cRelationID is the name of the relation (which is often something like "Relation 1"), cTableName is the name of the child table, cRelatedChild is the tag for the child table, cRelatedTable is the name of the parent table, and cRelatedTag is the tag for the parent table.

To see these events in action, run RelationEvents.PRG; it modifies an existing relation and shows each of these events firing.

DBC_BeforeAddRelation(cRelationID, cTableName, cRelatedChild, cRelatedTable, cRelatedTag)

Called before a relation is added; return False to prevent the relation from being added.

DBC_AfterAddRelation(cRelationID, cTableName, cRelatedChild, cRelatedTable, cRelatedTag)

Called after a relation is added.

DBC_BeforeDropRelation(cRelationID, cTableName, cRelatedChild, cRelatedTable, cRelatedTag)

Called before a relation is dropped; return False to prevent the relation from being dropped.

DBC_AfterDropRelation(cRelationID, cTableName, cRelatedChild, cRelatedTable, cRelatedTag)

Called after a relation is dropped.

DBC events for connections

There are four types of events for connections: adding, removing, renaming, and modifying. To see these events in action, first create an ODBC datasource called Tastrade that points to the VFP sample Tastrade database, and then run ConnectionEvents.PRG.

DBC_BeforeCreateConnection()

Called before a connection is created; return False to prevent the connection from being created. Note that no name is passed, even if the Create Connection command is used with a connection name.

DBC_AfterCreateConnection(cConnectionName, cDataSourceName, cUserID, cPassword, cConnectionString)

Called after a connection is created.

DBC_BeforeDeleteConnection(cConnectionName)

Called before a connection is deleted; return False to prevent the connection from being deleted.

DBC_AfterDeleteConnection(cConnectionName)

Called after a connection is deleted.

DBC_BeforeModifyConnection(cConnectionName)

Called before a connection is modified; return False to prevent modification.

DBC_AfterModifyConnection(cConnectionName, lChanged)

Called after a connection has been modified.

DBC_BeforeRenameConnection(cPreviousName, cNewName)

Called before a connection is renamed; return False to prevent the connection from being renamed.

DBC_AfterRenameConnection(cPreviousName, cNewName)

Called after a connection has been renamed.

Using DBC events

Okay, enough theory; what can you actually use DBC events for? There are two different kinds of things you can use them for: development tools and run-time behavior.

Development tools

DBC events can be used in a number of tools that can make development easier and more productive. Here are some examples.

Enforcing standards

Your organization might have standards for naming tables, views, fields, and so forth (for example, perhaps all tables in the Accounts Receivable database should start with "AR", the first character of all field names must represent the data type or be a four-letter abbreviation for the table, and so on). You may also require that the Comment property of every table, view, and field be filled in. Maybe every table should have a tag on Deleted() and a primary key on a field called ID with NewID() as its DefaultValue property.

Rather than writing an auditing tool to check for these things after the fact, you could create DBC events that either warn if the standard isn't followed or, in the case of the standard tags, automatically add them (of course, this can only be used for an existing DBC). DBC_AfterAddTable, DBC_AfterCreateTable, DBC_AfterModifyTable, DBC_BeforeRenameTable, DBC_AfterCreateView, DBC_AfterModifyView, DBC_BeforeRenameView, DBC_AfterCreateConnection, DBC_AfterModifyConnection, and DBC_BeforeRenameConnection are all candidates for this.

Handling renamed objects

While changing the name of a table is easy (Rename Table does it with a single command), tracking down every place the former name is used isn't. Stored procedures, forms, reports, and PRG files can all reference the former table name. You can put code in DBC_AfterRenameTable (as well as DBC_AfterRenameView and DBC_AfterRenameConnection) to open a project, go through all files in the project, look for the former name (the cPreviousName parameter contains this), and either replace it with the new name (contained in cNewName) or at least print the location so a developer can make the changes manually. Because a database might be used by more than one project, you might have to provide a way to track which projects to process.

Handling renamed fields and indexes is trickier; because DBC_AfterModifyTable and DBC_AfterModifyView don't tell you what changes were made, you have to store the previous structure somewhere (such as in a cursor in DBC_BeforeModify events or in metadata), and then in the DBC_AfterModify events try to figure out what happened. It's not easy; a renamed field looks no different than if you delete one field and add another.

Handling new or removed fields
When a field is added or removed from a table, you often have to add or remove controls bound to that field in forms and reports. Similar to the previous point, DBC_AfterModifyTable and DBC_AfterModifyView could print a list of all forms and reports using that table or view so you can then modify them as required.

Team development
When anything in the database changes (such as tables or views being added, removed, or altered), DBC event code could automatically send an e-mail to every member of the development team informing them of the changes. You could also log who changed something and when, and even prompt the user to enter a short comment about the change.

Automate FoxAudit
TakeNote Technologies (**www.takenote.com**) sells a great tool called FoxAudit that automatically logs all changes made to records in tables. It works by hooking into the insert, update, and delete triggers for those tables you want to audit, and recording the changes made in a log table. Although FoxAudit comes with a wizard to hook into the triggers and generate the stored procedures code to perform auditing, you have to remember to run the wizard after you create or add a table. DBC_AfterAddTable and DBC_AfterCreateTable could do this for you automatically.

Automatically update metadata
DBCX is a public domain set of classes that maintain a data dictionary, or metadata, for VFP data (a copy of DBCX, including documentation, is available from the Technical Papers page of Stonefield's Web site, **www.stonefield.com**). Several commercial tools, including Visual FoxExpress and Stonefield Database Toolkit, use DBCX as their data dictionary manager. The main DBCX class, DBCXMgr, has a Validate() method that creates or updates the metadata for the specified data object. When you add, modify, or delete a data object, you must either call this method or use the visual interface that came with your commercial tool to do this for you. Failing to update the metadata means DBCX (and therefore the commercial tool) can't perform its job correctly.

 *The Developer Downloads available at **www.hentzenwerke.com** include UpdateMeta.PRG.*

UpdateMeta.PRG shows how you can automate the process of updating DBCX metadata. Every action with an impact on metadata has DBC event code that calls the appropriate DBCX method to ensure the metadata is kept in synch with the data objects.

Some commercial tools, such as Visual ProMatrix and FoxFire, have their own data dictionaries. You could use a similar mechanism to keep those data dictionaries up-to-date as well.

Practical jokes

All work and no play makes Doug a dull programmer! Imagine the fun you can have with your fellow developers when you create DBC_Before events that return False in their DBCs while they're on their lunch breaks. Sit back and watch them try to alter the structure of a table, remove a table, and so on. For even more fun, make the DBC events time-specific, like, say, only between 3 and 4 p.m. on Thursdays. April 1 is a particularly good day to wreak havoc!

Run-time behavior

DBC events can also be used in a run-time environment to provide functionality VFP developers have requested for years.

Table and database security

Returning False from DBC_BeforeOpenTable prevents a table or view from being opened. Obviously, you don't want to do this for every table and view under all conditions (otherwise, the database would be rendered useless), but having table opening based on user security may make sense for some applications. The following stored procedure code (taken from TestSecurity.PRG) demonstrates how this might work. You can't display a login dialog to the user when the DBC is being accessed from ADO or a COM object, so you'll have to use a more complex design in that case.

```
procedure DBC_BeforeOpenTable(tcTableName)
GetUserName()
return gcUserName == 'ADMIN'

procedure GetUserName
if type('gcUserName') <> 'C' or empty(gcUserName)
  release gcUserName
  public gcUserName
  gcUserName = upper(inputbox('User name', 'Database Login'))
endif type('gcUserName') <> 'C' …
```

The Developer Downloads available at www.hentzenwerke.com include TestSecurity.PRG.

As with table security, an entire database can be secured by returning False from DBC_OpenData.

Hacker prevention

Although it's not common, some developers have expressed the desire to prevent someone from altering the structure of a table or view. It's probably not a malicious hack they're worried about, but likely a user who typifies the expression "a little knowledge is a dangerous thing." This user could be using a development copy of VFP or ADO. To prevent this, return False in DBC_BeforeModifyTable and DBC_BeforeModifyView.

To prevent someone from changing or disabling the events for the DBC (which would allow them to get around everything DBC events are providing for you), return False in DBC_BeforeModifyProc, DBC_BeforeAppendProc, and DBC_BeforeDBSetProp if cType is "database" and cProperty is "DBCEvents" or "DBCEventFileName". This has only limited usefulness, since someone with a development copy of VFP can Use the DBC (that is, open it as a table, which is what it really is), modify the code in the Code memo of the StoredProceduresSource record, and then close and Compile Database. To prevent this, use a separate PRG file for the DBC event code, and build that PRG into the EXE so it can't be viewed or altered. The downside is that now the DBC can only be opened when the EXE is running, preventing its access from ADO.

To prevent someone from seeing the stored procedures code, return False in DBC_BeforeModifyProc and DBC_BeforeCopyProc.

The one thing missing in this scheme is that the user can still Use the DBC as a table and then bypass or eliminate DBC event code. An enhancement request was sent to Microsoft asking that they fire the DBC_BeforeOpenTable event when a DBC is opened as a table so this can be prevented.

Automatically index views
Some developers like to index views so they can use Seek to locate records. The problem is that you have to create the index every time the view is opened, be sure to set the buffer mode correctly (indexes can only be created when row buffering is used), change the index creation code if the view structure changes, and so forth. Wouldn't it be nice if VFP could automatically create an index for a view whenever you opened it? DBC_AfterOpenTable can do that for you using code similar to the following:

```
procedure DBC_AfterOpenTable(cTableName)
local lcViewName, ;
  lnBuffer
lcViewName = upper(cTableName)
do case
  case not indbc(cTableName, 'view')

* Index the CustView view, ensuring that buffering is set properly when we do
* so.

  case lcViewName == 'CUSTVIEW'
    lnBuffer = cursorgetprop('Buffering')
    if lnBuffer > 3
      cursorsetprop('Buffering', 3)
    endif lnBuffer > 3
    index on upper(COMPANY) tag COMPANY
    if lnBuffer > 3
      cursorsetprop('Buffering', lnBuffer)
    endif lnBuffer > 3
endcase
```

Of course, this sample code uses hard-coded names and expressions; you likely will want to use metadata (such as DBCX, which supports indexes for views) to store the index definitions.

VFP OLE DB provider

Data access has been evolving for some time. Originally, every database management system (DBMS) had its own mechanism for access. This made it difficult for developers, who had to come up with a different set of code for each DBMS their applications used. The solution to this problem was Open Database Connectivity (ODBC), which provides a common mechanism for accessing data, regardless of the underlying DBMS. Each vendor created an ODBC driver for its system that exposed a common, SQL-based interface to the data.

As the development world moved to object-oriented programming (OOP), the procedural nature of ODBC became cumbersome. In response to the need to objectify data access, Microsoft created the Microsoft Data Access Components (MDAC) set of services, including OLE DB and ActiveX Data Objects (ADO). Like ODBC, OLE DB provides a common mechanism for accessing data, but through ADO, the mechanism and even the data itself is exposed as a set of COM objects. Some DBMSs, such as SQL Server, can be accessed through specific OLE DB providers, while others, such as VFP, are available through the OLE DB provider for ODBC. The benefits of a specific OLE DB provider are better performance (since it can access the DBMS directly rather than going through ODBC) and support for features specific to the DBMS that may not be exposed through ODBC.

New to VFP 7 is an OLE DB provider for VFP (in VFPOLEDB.DLL, installed by default in C:\Program Files\Common Files\System\OLE DB). It has several benefits over the VFP ODBC driver:

- It has a future. Microsoft has announced that the VFP ODBC driver is in "support" mode, meaning no future enhancements will be made to it. That means no support for new features in VFP 7, so you can't access tables in a DBC with DBC events turned on through the ODBC driver.

- In addition to better performance, it uses an improved threading model over the VFP ODBC driver for better scalability.

- It provides support for VFP-specific features such as creating rules, triggers, default values, or stored procedures using ADOX.

This section isn't intended to be a primer on using ADO; for that, see John Petersen's ADO white paper in MSDN (**http://msdn.microsoft.com/library/default.asp?URL= /library/techart/ADOJump.htm**).

Using the OLE DB provider

The OLE DB provider for VFP is very similar to the providers for other DBMSs. Typically, you instantiate an ADO Connection object, set its ConnectionString property to specify the VFP OLE DB provider and which database you want to access, and call its Open() method to establish a connection with the data. Here's an example:

```
local loConn as ADODB.Connection
loConn = createobject('ADODB.Connection')
loConn.ConnectionString = 'Provider=vfpoledb;Data Source=' + ;
  addbs(_samples) + 'Data\Testdata.DBC'
loConn.Open()
```

The connection string accepts the following keywords:

- Provider: This should be "VFPOLEDB" (case is unimportant).

- Data Source: Use this to specify the path to the DBC or the directory containing free tables.

- Mode: This optional keyword specifies how the DBC and tables are opened. The default mode is Share Deny None, meaning the DBC and tables are opened for sharing. Other acceptable values are Read, ReadWrite, Share Deny Read, Share Deny Write, and Share Exclusive (which is really an oxymoron, since it means exclusive access).

- Collating Sequence: Specify the collating sequence to use for character fields in this optional keyword. The default is Machine.

Once you have a connection, you can set the ActiveConnection and other properties of an ADO RecordSet object, and then pass a SQL Select statement to its Open() method to fill it with some data:

```
local loRS as ADODB.RecordSet
loRS = createobject('ADODB.RecordSet')
loRS.ActiveConnection = loConn
loRS.CursorLocation  = 3   && adUseClient
loRS.CursorType      = 3   && adOpenStatic
loRS.LockType        = 3   && adLockOptimistic
loRS.Open('select * from Orders')
wait window transform(loRS.RecordCount) + ' records were returned'
```

You can also instantiate an ADO Command object if you want to execute other types of SQL commands:

```
local loCommand as ADODB.Command
loCommand = createobject('ADODB.Command')
loCommand.ActiveConnection = loConn
loCommand.CommandText = "delete from Orders where Cust_ID = 'LILAS'"
loCommand.Execute()
```

You can use VFP SQL syntax with the VFP OLE DB provider. That means code like the following, which won't work with other providers because they don't support the $ operator, works just fine with VFP's:

```
loRS.Open("select * from Customer where 'FUTT' $ upper(Company)")
```

You can specify the behavior of the OLE DB provider by setting provider-specific properties of the Connection object. These properties are accessed through the Properties collection. The following properties are available:

- SET ANSI

- SET BLOCKSIZE

- SET DELETED

- SET EXACT

- SET NULL

- SET PATH

- SET REPROCESS

- SET UNIQUE

The following code prevents deleted records from being processed:

```
loConn.Properties('SET DELETED').Value = .T.
```

Here's an example that displays all properties in the Properties collection:

```
local loConn as ADODB.Connection, ;
  loProperty as ADODB.Property
loConn = createobject('ADODB.Connection')
loConn.ConnectionString = 'Provider=vfpoledb;Data Source=' + ;
  addbs(_samples) + 'Data\Testdata.DBC'
loConn.Open()
for each loProperty in loConn.Properties
  ? loProperty.Name, loProperty.Value
next loProperty
loConn.Close()
```

See the "Standard and Custom OLE DB Properties" topic in the VFP Help file for a complete list of properties.

The VFP OLE DB provider doesn't support dynamic ADO cursors. However, you can create an updatable RecordSet in one of two ways. The first is to use a server-side cursor (the default) and open it with the Use command:

```
loRS.Open('use Customer')
```

The other way is to use a client-side cursor:

```
loRS.CursorLocation = 3  && adUseClient
loRS.Open('select * from Customer')  && or loRS.Open('use Customer')
```

You can then make changes to the RecordSet and use its Update() or UpdateBatch() methods to write the changes back to the source tables.

Parameterized views are a problem—if you try to open them through the OLE DB provider, you get "SQL column *parameter name* not found." Creating an ADO Parameter object with the proper name and value doesn't help. Hopefully, this will be fixed in a future release.

Stored procedures and database events

In addition to retrieving data or issuing SQL commands with the OLE DB provider, you can call stored procedures of a DBC. This is done through the ADO Command object. Here's an example of a stored procedure:

```
procedure GetTotalSalesByCustomer(tcCustID)
select sum(Order_Amt) as TotalSales ;
  from Orders ;
  where Cust_ID = tcCustID ;
  into cursor Sales
return TotalSales
```

Here's how this procedure is called using the OLE DB provider. Note that you have to set the CommandType property to 1 (the adCmdText constant) or 8 (adCmdUnknown) rather than 4 (adCmdStoredProc) and that the resulting RecordSet has a single row and a single column called "Return_Value".

```
local loConn as ADODB.Connection, ;
  loRS as ADODB.RecordSet, ;
  loCommand as ADODB.Command
loConn    = createobject('ADODB.Connection')
loCommand = createobject('ADODB.Command')
loConn.ConnectionString = 'Provider=vfpoledb;Data Source=' + ;
  addbs(_samples) + 'Data\Testdata.DBC'
loConn.Open()
loCommand.ActiveConnection = loConn
loCommand.CommandType     = 8  && adCmdUnknown
loCommand.CommandText     = "GetTotalSalesByCustomer('ALFKI')"
loRS = loCommand.Execute()
wait window 'Total sales for ALKFI: ' + ;
  transform(loRS.Fields('Return_Value').Value)
loConn.Close()
```

One thing that may not be intuitive is what happens inside the stored procedure. Can it return a VFP cursor as an ADO RecordSet? What happens if you specify a scalar return value such as a numeric value or string? The thing to remember with a stored procedure is that it's being called from within the VFP engine, so open tables and cursors aren't accessible to the outside world. That means you can't expect to do something like a SQL Select into a cursor and expect that cursor to somehow be returned by the OLE DB provider to the client code. The only thing the OLE DB provider can see is the return value of the stored procedure.

There are some serious limitations in what you can do in a stored procedure. Here are the basic rules:

- Potentially destructive commands and functions, including anything that writes to disk (with the exception of updating fields in a table), aren't allowed. Examples of these functions are StrToFile(), FOpen(), Delete File, and Set TextMerge.

- The OLE DB provider doesn't contain VFP's Object Manager, so no OOP features are supported. This means, for example, you can't use CreateObject() to instantiate an object to do the work.

- On Error isn't supported, so there's essentially no error handling.

- Macro expansion isn't permitted.

- For obvious reasons, there's no user interface support, so commands and functions that request or output values or otherwise display a user interface aren't allowed. Functions in this category include InputBox(), GetFile(), and MessageBox().

The "Supported Visual FoxPro Commands and Functions" and "Supported Visual FoxPro SET Commands" topics in the VFP Help file list the commands and functions you can use, while the "Unsupported Visual FoxPro Commands and Functions" topic lists those you can't use. Because of the limited set of commands and functions you can use, creating useful stored procedures can be a challenge, and debugging them a nightmare.

You might want to insert conditional code into your stored procedures that executes different code when they're called from the OLE DB provider. The Version() function returns "Microsoft OLE DB Provider for Visual FoxPro *version number* for Windows" when called by the provider, so you can use code like the following:

```
if 'OLE DB' $ version()
* code executed from OLE DB provider
else
* code executed from within VFP
endif
```

DBC events are fired from the OLE DB provider just as they are from within VFP, but since they're stored procedures, they have the same limited range of things you can do with them. For example, popping up a dialog asking users to log in when they try to open a table won't work, since that requires a user interface.

> *The Developer Download files at **www.hentzenwerke.com** include several programs that demonstrate the use of various OLE DB features. ADORecordSet.PRG shows how to retrieve data from VFP using the OLE DB provider. ADOProperties.PRG displays the contents of the Properties collection of the ADO Connection and RecordSet objects. ADOStoredProc.PRG shows how stored procedures can be called. ADODBCEvents.PRG demonstrates DBC events and field default values firing when tables are accessed from the provider.*

Summary

VFP 5 had only minor changes to the database engine, and VFP 6 had none. VFP 7 adds several welcome improvements to the engine that allow VFP developers to create better developer tools and better user applications.

Chapter 6
OOP Enhancements

Object orientation is one of Visual FoxPro's most powerful features. VFP 7 has a variety of improvements in this area, including new properties and methods, and even a pair of new events.

The massive changes in VFP 3 changed FoxPro from a procedural language to an object-oriented one. Each subsequent version has added new classes or enhanced existing classes. While VFP 7 doesn't include any new base classes, it does add a number of features to existing classes, as well as improving the way we work with them.

Creating classes

Creating classes in code (rather than with the Class Designer) is taking on increasing importance for several reasons.

The Session class (introduced in VFP 6 Service Pack 3), which is extremely useful for creating Automation servers, can't be subclassed in the Class Designer. In addition, some of the new features in VFP 7, such as strong typing, apply only to code classes (that is, non-visual classes). (See "Using the session class in COM servers" and "Storing VFP 7 COM classes" in Chapter 12, "Building World-Class COM Servers in VFP 7," to learn more about the importance of the Session class and strong typing.)

In VFP 6 and earlier versions, when you have a class definition in code, you have to be sure to SET PROCEDURE (or SET CLASSLIB) to the file containing the class library for the parent class before instantiating the class. VFP 7 makes it easier to write class definitions by adding an optional OF <classlib> clause to DEFINE CLASS. For example, to subclass the _form class in the FoxPro Foundation Classes, you can begin the class definition like this:

```
DEFINE CLASS frmMyForm AS _form OF HOME()+"FFC\_BASE.VCX"
```

DEFINE CLASS has another new keyword: IMPLEMENTS. See Chapter 13, "Implementing Interfaces," for an explanation of the meaning and use of this keyword.

There's another change that only affects coded class libraries. In earlier versions, when you instantiate an object from a PRG-based class, if the Name property isn't explicitly given a value in the properties section of the class definition, the Name of the object is set to the class name plus a number. Numbers are assigned sequentially, increasing each time you instantiate a new object of that class (that is, myObject1, myObject2, myObject3, and so forth). This approach to object naming is different from that used for VCX-based classes, and, more importantly, the need to determine the next available number can slow down code considerably when many objects of a single class are instantiated.

In VFP 7, this behavior is gone. All unnamed objects are assigned the name of the class they belong to rather than a unique name.

Exploring classes

The AMEMBERS() function lets you explore a class or an object. Depending on the value you pass for the third parameter, it fills an array with a list of the properties of the object, a list of all members of the object (properties, methods, and contained objects), or just a list of contained objects. In VFP 6 and earlier, AMEMBERS() works only on native VFP objects.

VFP 7 extends AMEMBERS() in several ways. First, the function now works on COM objects, as well as native objects. It also provides additional information about native objects. Passing 3 for the third parameter indicates that the function should return a four-column array—the contents of the columns are shown in **Table 1**. A third parameter of 3 is also the key to exploring COM objects.

Table 1. *What's in an object? Calling AMEMBERS() with 3 as the third parameter returns a four-column array.*

Column	Contents
1	Name of the property, event, or method.
2	Type of item. For VFP objects, the possible values are "Property", "Event", or "Method". For COM objects, the possible values are "PropertyPut", "PropertyGet", "PropertyPutRef", and "Method".
3	Empty for properties of VFP objects. For methods of VFP objects, the parameter list. For properties and methods of COM object, the member's signature, consisting of the parameter list, plus the return value.
4	The help string for the item.

For example, to get a list of the members of the Windows Scripting Host's FileSystemObject, you can use this code:

```
oWSH = CreateObject("Scripting.FileSystemObject")
nMemberCount = AMEMBERS( aWSHMembers, oWSH, 3 )
```

Here's a partial listing of the array created. (The actual array has 27 rows.)

```
(    1,    1)    C    "BuildPath"
(    1,    2)    C    "Method"
(    1,    3)    C    "(Path as String, Name as String) as String"
(    1,    4)    C    "Generate a path from an existing path and a name"
(    2,    1)    C    "CopyFile"
(    2,    2)    C    "Method"
(    2,    3)    C    "(Source as String, Destination as String,
[OverWriteFiles as Logical=.T.])"
(    2,    4)    C    "Copy a file"
(    3,    1)    C    "CopyFolder"
(    3,    2)    C    "Method"
(    3,    3)    C    "(Source as String, Destination as String,
[OverWriteFiles as Logical=.T.])"
(    3,    4)    C    "Copy a folder"
(    4,    1)    C    "CreateFolder"
(    4,    2)    C    "Method"
(    4,    3)    C    "(Path as String) as IFolder"
(    4,    4)    C    "Create a folder"
(    5,    1)    C    "CreateTextFile"
```

```
(    5,    2)     C      "Method"
(    5,    3)     C      "(FileName as String, [Overwrite as Logical=.T.],
[Unicode as Logical=.F.]) as ITextStream"
(    5,    4)     C      "Create a file as a TextStream"
```

AMEMBERS() has also acquired a cFlags parameter (the fourth parameter) that lets you specify, for native objects, which members to return. **Table 2** lists the flag characters. The flags in each filter group are mutually exclusive. However, by default, when you concatenate multiple flag characters into the cFlags parameter, they're combined with OR, so a cFlags parameter of "HP" includes all hidden and protected properties, events, and methods (PEMs). Passing "GU" includes all members that are either public or user-defined in the result. (Be aware that the "C" flag doesn't catch changes to array properties.)

Table 2. Choosing members—AMEMBERS() new, fourth, parameter lets you filter the list of members returned.

Flag character	Filter group	Meaning
P	Visibility	Protected
H	Visibility	Hidden
G	Visibility	Public
N	Origin	Native
U	Origin	User-defined
I	Inheritance	Inherited
B	Inheritance	Base
C	Changed	Changed
R	Read-only	Read-only

There are two special flags. Including the "+" anywhere in the cFlags parameter indicates that the filters should be combined with AND rather than OR. So, for example, passing "GU+" includes only members that are both public and user-defined.

The second special flag is "#", which adds a column to the resulting array. The new column shows the flags (the same values as in Table 2) that apply to each member.

This code creates an instance of the _MoverLists class from the FoxPro Foundation Classes, and then lists the Protected members of the class, including their flags:

```
oObject = NewObject( "_MoverLists",HOME()+"FFC\_CONTROLS" )
AMEMBERS( aMemberList, oObject, 3, "P#" )
LIST MEMORY LIKE aMemberList
AMEMBERLIST              Pub      A
(    1,    1)     C      "ADDTOPROJECT"
(    1,    2)     C      "Method"
(    1,    3)     C      ""
(    1,    4)     C      "Dummy code for adding files to project."
(    1,    5)     C      "CPUI"
(    2,    1)     C      "NINSTANCES_ACCESS"
(    2,    2)     C      "Method"
(    2,    3)     C      ""
(    2,    4)     C      "Access method for nInstances property."
(    2,    5)     C      "CPUI"
(    3,    1)     C      "NINSTANCES_ASSIGN"
(    3,    2)     C      "Method"
```

```
(    3,    3)    C     "vNewVal"
(    3,    4)    C     "Assign method for nInstances property."
(    3,    5)    C     "CPUI"
(    4,    1)    C     "NOBJECTREFCOUNT_ACCESS"
(    4,    2)    C     "Method"
(    4,    3)    C     ""
(    4,    4)    C     "Access method for nObjectRefCount property."
(    4,    5)    C     "CPUI"
(    5,    1)    C     "NOBJECTREFCOUNT_ASSIGN"
(    5,    2)    C     "Method"
(    5,    3)    C     "m.vNewVal"
(    5,    4)    C     "Assign method for nObjectRefCount property."
(    5,    5)    C     "CPUI"
```

This example includes all members for the class (because all three visibilities are listed), but also includes the flags. (Only a portion of the output is shown.)

```
AMEMBERS(aMemberList, oObject, 3, "GPH#")
LIST MEMORY LIKE aMemberList

AMEMBERLIST              Pub      A
(    1,    1)    C     "ACTIVECONTROL"
(    1,    2)    C     "Property"
(    1,    3)    C     ""
(    1,    4)    C     "References the active control on an object."
(    1,    5)    C     "GRNI"
(    2,    1)    C     "ADDOBJECT"
(    2,    2)    C     "Method"
(    2,    3)    C     "cName, cClass"
(    2,    4)    C     "Adds an object to a container object at run time."
(    2,    5)    C     "GNI"
(    3,    1)    C     "ADDPROPERTY"
(    3,    2)    C     "Method"
(    3,    3)    C     "cPropertyName,eNewValue"
(    3,    4)    C     "Adds a new property to an object."
(    3,    5)    C     "GNI"
(    4,    1)    C     "ADDTOPROJECT"
(    4,    2)    C     "Method"
(    4,    3)    C     ""
(    4,    4)    C     "Dummy code for adding files to project."
(    4,    5)    C     "CPUI"
(    5,    1)    C     "AOBJECTREFS"
(    5,    2)    C     "Property"
(    5,    3)    C     ""
(    5,    4)    C     "Array of object references properties."
(    5,    5)    C     "GUI"
(    6,    1)    C     "BACKCOLOR"
(    6,    2)    C     "Property"
(    6,    3)    C     ""
(    6,    4)    C     "Specifies the background color used to display text
and graphics in an object."
(    6,    5)    C     "GNI"
```

The form ShowAMembers.SCX in the Developer Downloads available at ***www.hentzenwerke.com*** *lets you experiment with AMEMBERS().*

New and enhanced PEMs

VFP 7 includes a variety of changes to the properties, events, and methods (PEMs) of its classes. There are brand-new PEMs, PEMs added to additional objects, and new values for some properties. This section looks first at the changes that affect multiple classes, and then explores those affecting only a single class.

Multi-class changes

Many of the changes to PEMs apply to more than one class, some of them to quite a few classes.

MouseEnter and MouseLeave events

Exposing new events is unusual for Visual FoxPro, but in VFP 7, all visible controls have new MouseEnter and MouseLeave events that give you the opportunity to take action as the mouse passes through the control. These events take the same parameters as MouseMove: the mouse button or buttons that are currently pressed; which, if any, of the Ctrl, Shift, and Alt keys is pressed; and the current mouse position. You can use these methods to enable and disable certain options based on the mouse position. They're also convenient for manipulating the new VisualEffect property of buttons (described in "Changes to controls" later in this chapter).

Objects collection

Every container class in VFP has a way of accessing its members, generally through a collection named for the member type. For example, PageFrame has a Pages collection and Grid has a Columns collection. However, some of the containers also offer a more generic way to access their members—the Objects collection. Objects is a COM collection complete with Count and Item properties.

In VFP 7, all container classes have an Objects collection, including those that didn't in VFP 6 (CommandGroup, DataEnvironment, Grid, PageFrame, and OptionGroup).

SpecialEffect property

Many controls have a new "Hot Tracking" setting (2) for SpecialEffect that makes them flat except when the mouse passes over them. At that point, depending on the particular control, they become either raised or depressed. For check boxes and option buttons, the Hot Tracking setting works only when Style is set to Graphical. Like the changes to menus discussed in Chapter 3, "New and Better Tools," this setting makes it easier to write applications that follow the new flat-look interface style.

 The form UIChanges.SCX in the Developer Downloads available at ***www.hentzenwerke.com*** *demonstrates the MouseEnter and MouseLeave events, as well as the Hot Tracking setting for SpecialEffect and command buttons' new VisualEffect property (discussed in "Changes to controls" later in this chapter).*

WriteMethod() method

The WriteMethod() method allows you to programmatically add code to a method. In VFP 7, it has a new (third) parameter that allows you to create methods on the fly. When the method specified by the first parameter does not exist and the lCreateMethod parameter is True, the method is created. This approach works only at design time, and the form or class must be saved after the method is added. These limitations are reasonable since WriteMethod() is intended for use in builders.

Form and toolbar changes

A couple of changes affect forms and/or toolbars. All of them help to build more standard Windows applications.

hWnd property

Every window in Windows has a "handle" that identifies it. In VFP 7, the window handle of forms and toolbars is finally directly accessible—through the new hWnd property. In older versions, you need to make a couple of function calls to get this information. **Figure 1** shows a form that passes its hWnd to an API function and changes itself to a circle. The code for the form (as exported by the Class Browser) is shown in **Listing 1**.

*The form in Figure 1 is available as MkCircle.SCX in the Developer Downloads at **www.hentzenwerke.com**.*

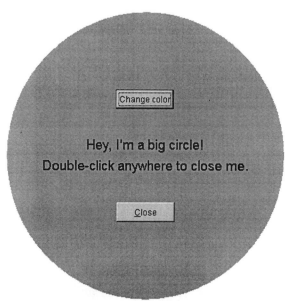

Figure 1. Getting a handle on a form. This form passes its window handle to the API function SetWindowRgn in order to change the form into a circle. Double-click anywhere on the form to close it.

Listing 1. *Using a form handle—this code creates the form shown in Figure 1.*

```
PUBLIC ofrmcircle

ofrmcircle=NEWOBJECT("frmcircle")
ofrmcircle.Show
RETURN

DEFINE CLASS frmcircle AS form


    Height = 400
    Width = 400
    DoCreate = .T.
    AutoCenter = .T.
    BorderStyle = 0
    Caption = "Form"
    Movable = .F.
    TitleBar = 0
    WindowType = 1
    BackColor = RGB(128,128,255)
    Name = "frmCircle"


    ADD OBJECT lblcircle AS label WITH ;
        AutoSize = .T., ;
        FontSize = 14, ;
        BackStyle = 0, ;
        Caption = "Hey, I'm a big circle!", ;
        Height = 25, ;
        Left = 113, ;
        Top = 173, ;
        Width = 173, ;
        Name = "lblCircle"


    ADD OBJECT lbldblclick AS label WITH ;
        AutoSize = .T., ;
        FontSize = 14, ;
        BackStyle = 0, ;
        Caption = "Double-click anywhere to close me.", ;
        Height = 25, ;
        Left = 50, ;
        Top = 202, ;
        Width = 300, ;
        Name = "lblDblClick"


    ADD OBJECT cmdcolor AS commandbutton WITH ;
        Top = 108, ;
        Left = 156, ;
        Height = 27, ;
        Width = 84, ;
        Caption = "Change color", ;
        Name = "cmdColor"
```

```
ADD OBJECT cmdclose AS commandbutton WITH ;
    Top = 264, ;
    Left = 158, ;
    Height = 27, ;
    Width = 84, ;
    Caption = "\<Close", ;
    Name = "cmdClose"


PROCEDURE DblClick
    ThisForm.Release()
ENDPROC


PROCEDURE Init
    LOCAL nhWnd, nWidth, nHeight, nRegion

    DECLARE INTEGER CreateEllipticRgn IN gdi32 ;
            INTEGER X1 , INTEGER Y1 , INTEGER X2 , INTEGER Y2
    DECLARE INTEGER SetWindowRgn IN user32 ;
            INTEGER HWND, INTEGER hRgn , INTEGER bRedraw

    nhWnd = This.HWnd
    nWidth = This.WIDTH / 1 && change ratio
    nHeight = This.HEIGHT / 1 && change ratio
    * Call API to convert an otherwise regular form into a circular one.
    nRegion = CreateEllipticRgn(0, 0, nWidth, nHeight)
    SetWindowRgn(nhWnd, nRegion, 1)
ENDPROC


PROCEDURE lblcircle.DblClick
    ThisForm.DblClick()
ENDPROC


PROCEDURE lbldblclick.DblClick
    ThisForm.DblClick()
ENDPROC


PROCEDURE cmdcolor.Click
    nColor = GETCOLOR(ThisForm.BackColor)
    IF nColor <> -1
       ThisForm.BackColor=nColor
    ENDIF
ENDPROC


PROCEDURE cmdclose.Click
    ThisForm.Release()
ENDPROC


ENDDEFINE
```

The main VFP window, accessed through the system variable _VFP, and its client area, accessed using _Screen, also have the hWnd property. Each has a different value for it. See

Chapter 8, "Resource Management," for more about the differences between _VFP and _Screen in VFP 7.

ShowInTaskBar property
Forms have a new ShowInTaskBar property that determines whether top-level forms appear in the Windows taskbar. By default, the property is True and any top-level form has an independent presence in the taskbar. When ShowInTaskBar is set to False, there's no taskbar item for the form and it minimizes to the desktop, rather than to the taskbar.

Style property
The Style property has been added to Separators, the objects that let you space items in a toolbar. By default, Style is set to 0-Normal. But you can set Style to 1-Vertical Rule. This new setting allows you to create toolbars that look like those in commercial applications—with a sunken vertical bar between groups of buttons. Note that the vertical line shows up only at run time, not at design time.

Figure 2 shows a "standard" toolbar where the Separators have their Style set to 0. **Figure 3** shows the same toolbar with the Separators' Style property set to 1.

Figure 2. Invisible separators—the Style property for the separators in this toolbar is set to 0-Normal.

Figure 3. Visible separators—in this version of the toolbar, the Style property for the separators is set to 1-Vertical Rule, and thus they have a visual presence at run time.

 The toolbar class shown in Figure 2 and Figure 3 is in the Chapter6.VCX class library in the Developer Downloads available at www.hentzenwerke.com.

To test the example toolbar class, instantiate it to a variable and set Visible to True. If you pass False or no parameters to the object, you get the toolbar in Figure 2 (invisible separators):

```
oToolbar = NewObject("tbrStandard", "chapter6.vcx")
oToolbar.Visible = .T.
```

To see the version with the vertical rules, pass True to the Init() method:

```
oToolbar = NewObject("tbrStandard", "chapter6.vcx", "", .T.)
oToolbar.Visible = .T.
```

Changes to controls

Finally, there are a few items that affect individual controls. As with the others, many of these respond to long-time developer requests.

Buttons

Command buttons have a new property, VisualEffect, that lets you raise or depress the button at run time. VisualEffect is read-only at design time. VisualEffect has three available settings: 0-None, 1-Raised, and 2-Depressed.

Setting VisualEffect to 1-Raised in MouseEnter and restoring it to the default setting of 0-None in MouseLeave gives the same results as setting SpecialEffect to the new 2-Hot Tracking setting.

 The Close *button on the form UIChanges.SCX in the Developer Downloads available at **www.hentzenwerke.com** demonstrates the VisualEffect property.*

Grids

Since Visual FoxPro 3.0 was first released, developers have wondered why the BeforeRowColChange and AfterRowColChange events weren't divided into separate BeforeRowChange, BeforeColChange, AfterRowChange, and AfterColChange events. While VFP 7 doesn't go quite that far, the new RowColChange property does make it easy to know why the two events fired. It contains a value that indicates what changed: the row (1), the column (2), both (3), or neither (0). (You get the "neither" value when the grid is first displayed and when it's refreshed.) Your code can check that value and act accordingly.

The new HighlightRowLineWidth property indicates how many pixels should be used to create a highlight around the current row. This setting is only used when HighlightRow is set to its default value of True.

Headers

A WordWrap property has been added to the Header object in grids, so that headers can occupy more than one line. This may be the single most requested grid-related feature.

ProjectHook changes

When project hooks were added in VFP 6, developers immediately found uses for them. But a few features were missing. VFP 7 plugs those holes with three new events: QueryNewFile, Activate, and Deactivate.

QueryNewFile fires when you begin the process of adding a file to a project. That happens when you click the **New** button in the Project Manager. Previously, no event fired when a new file was added.

The Activate and Deactivate events for the ProjectHook object are like those of other classes—they fire when the object becomes active and when it loses focus, respectively. In the case of project hooks, however, that's when the project associated with the project hook is activated or deactivated. This means you now have the ability to modify the VFP environment as you switch between projects, offering the chance to change things like the VFP PATH, field mappings, and other project-specific settings.

Summary

VFP 7's changes to the OOP part of the language make it easier to create classes and work with them, as well as giving forms and controls more of the behaviors developers and users want. VFP 7 also provides the tools needed to create interfaces in the Windows 2000 style.

Chapter 7
Strings

Visual FoxPro has always had good facilities for string manipulation, but VFP 7 includes a number of improvements. Among the areas enhanced are the ability to merge text with data, parsing of strings, and changing text within a string.

Working with strings has become increasingly important in the past few years, thanks to the World Wide Web. Since HTML and XML are just text with tags, the ability to manipulate text rapidly and easily has taken on new significance. FoxPro has always had good string-handling tools, and with VFP 7, they continue to improve.

Text-merge improvements

FoxPro's text-merge facility is one of those tools whose time came and went and has now come back. It was added in FoxPro 2.0 to make code generation easier for GENSCRN and GENMENU, the screen and menu generating programs. In a Web-oriented world, text-merge provides an easy way to generate HTML and XML strings that contain data.

Text-merge combines low-level file handling with run-time evaluation of expressions and type conversion to provide an easy mechanism for generating complex text. In VFP 7, text-merge has been enhanced in several ways.

First, it's now possible to send text-merge output to a variable rather than a file. SET TEXTMERGE TO has a new MEMVAR clause that lets you specify a variable as the output destination, like this:

```
SET TEXTMERGE TO MEMVAR cContents
```

The SET("TEXTMERGE") function that lets you find out how text-merge is configured has several new options. Pass 2 as the second parameter to find out what file you're merging to and 3 to check the SHOW/NOSHOW setting. Passing 4 lets you determine the stack level of the routine in which a text-merge sequence is executing. Unfortunately, there's no way to find out the name of the variable to which text-merge output has been sent.

In addition, the TEXT … ENDTEXT command has been enhanced. The TEXT line now has several options, where in previous versions, it had none. Here's the new syntax:

```
TEXT [ TO VarName [ ADDITIVE ] [ TEXTMERGE ] [ NOSHOW ] ]
   Text lines
ENDTEXT
```

The new syntax lets you perform text-merge to a variable with just a TEXT … ENDTEXT sequence, without using SET TEXTMERGE. For example, this block of code sends a string plus the current date to the variable cDate, without echoing it to the screen:

```
TEXT TO cDate TEXTMERGE NOSHOW
Today is <<DATE()>>
ENDTEXT
```

The biggest change on the text-merge front is the addition of a new TextMerge() function that accepts an expression to be evaluated, a flag that indicates whether the evaluation is recursive, and a set of text-merge delimiters, and returns the result of the evaluation. This line of code is equivalent to the preceding example:

```
cDate = TextMerge("Today is <<DATE()>>")
```

 The form TextMerge.SCX in the Developer Download files at **www.hentzenwerke.com** *demonstrates all three ways of merging text.*

Parsing strings

A new function, StrExtract(), has been added to aid in breaking strings into their component parts. Although this function was probably added to simplify handling of XML, it can be used in other processing as well.

StrExtract() takes a string and a pair of delimiters and extracts the portion of the string that occurs between those delimiters. The key aspect of this function is that the beginning and ending delimiters can be multiple characters. So you can apply the function to an XML string, passing beginning and ending tags. For example:

```
cXML = "<customer><custid>37</custid>" + ;
       "<name>Fred's Auto Parts</name></customer>"
? StrExtract( cXML, "<name>", "</name>")
```

displays:

```
Fred's Auto Parts
```

The full syntax of StrExtract() is:

```
cResult = STREXTRACT( cSource, cBeginDelim [, cEndDelim
                    [, nOccurrence [, nFlags ] ] ] )
```

You can extract any occurrence between the specified delimiters by passing the optional nOccurrence parameter. The optional nFlags parameter lets you make the search case-insensitive and indicate whether the ending delimiter is optional—in that case, the function returns everything from the beginning delimiter to the end of the string. (That's also what happens when the ending delimiter is omitted.)

For example, using the cXML string defined previously:

```
? StrExtract( cXML, "<NAME>", "</NAME>")
```

returns the empty string because the search is case-sensitive, while:

```
? StrExtract( cXML, "<NAME>", "</NAME>", 1, 1)
```

returns:

```
Fred's Auto Parts
```

The fourth parameter (1) indicates that extraction begins at the first occurrence of <NAME> in the string. The fifth parameter (also 1) makes the search case-insensitive.

A couple of other changes also relate to parsing. Two functions have been promoted from the FoxTools library of utility functions (FoxTools.FLL in the main VFP directory) to the core VFP language. GetWordCount() returns the number of words in the text you pass as the first parameter. GetWordNum() returns a specified word in the text—the text from which to extract a word is the first parameter and the word number is the second. (Note that these functions are called Words() and WordNum(), respectively, in FoxTools.) Each accepts an optional parameter to indicate where one word ends and another begins—if it's omitted, a space, tab, or return separates words. This function outputs the words in a string (cInputString) one per line:

```
LPARAMETERS cInputString
LOCAL nWordCount, nWordNum
nWordCount = GetWordCount(cInputString)
FOR nWordNum = 1 TO nWordCount
    ? GetWordNum(cInputString, nWordNum)
ENDFOR
```

However, that example isn't the best way to do this task. It turns out that while the new GetWord... functions are fast enough for pulling out a word here and there, they're really not intended for heavy-duty parsing.

In fact, the fastest way to do this parsing task in VFP 7 shows off a change to the ALINES() function. This function, which breaks a string up into lines and puts each line into an array element, has a new parameter in VFP 7 that specifies additional characters that indicate the end of the line (other than the default CHR(13) and CHR(10)—carriage return and line feed, respectively).

Here's another version of the function to output each word in a string onto a separate line, using ALINES()'s new functionality:

```
LPARAMETERS cInputString
LOCAL nWordCount
LOCAL ARRAY aWords[1]
nWordCount = ALINES(aWords, cInputString, " ", CHR(9))
FOR nWordNum = 1 TO nWordCount
    ? aWords[nWordNum]
ENDFOR
```

The form WordsOut.SCX in the Developer Downloads available at **www.hentzenwerke.com** *shows four approaches to parsing words from a string, and runs timing tests on them.*

Miscellaneous string changes

Several other string-related functions have been enhanced in VFP 7. First, STRTRAN() has a new flags parameter that indicates whether the search and replacement it performs should be case-sensitive or not. If the parameter is entirely omitted, the search is case-sensitive, as in older versions of FoxPro. When included, the parameter has three possible values, shown in **Table 1**.

Table 1. *STRTRAN() can now do case-sensitive searching and replacement.*

Value	Meaning
0	Case-sensitive search
1	Case-insensitive search with no case change in the replacement string
3	Case-insensitive search with case change in the replacement string

While 2 is an acceptable value for this parameter, it gives the same results as 0. You can't combine case-sensitive search with changing case in the replacement string.

The new syntax for STRTRAN() is:

```
cResult = STRTRAN( cOriginal, cFind, cReplace
                [, nStartOccurrence [, nNumberOfOccurrences [, nFlags ] ] ] )
```

For example, without the new parameter, this call:

```
? STRTRAN("Now is the time", "now", "then")
```

returns the original string "Now is the time". With the new parameter, you can call the function like this:

```
? STRTRAN("Now is the time", "now", "then", -1, -1, 1)
```

and it returns:

```
"then is the time"
```

To maintain the original case, make this call:

```
? STRTRAN("Now is the time", "now", "then", -1, -1, 3)
```

and you see:

```
"Then is the time"
```

In this last example, if the string passed to STRTRAN() was "NOW is the time", the return value would be "THEN is the time".

Most English speakers are familiar only with the ASCII character set that encodes 256 characters using 8 bits. But that's not sufficient for all languages. Double-byte character sets use 16 bits (2 bytes) to encode characters—they're used primarily for Asian languages, which are pictograph-based and have extremely large character sets. The Unicode character set was created to include all the characters from virtually every known language. The STRCONV() function was added in VFP 3.0b to convert strings from one character set to another. VFP 7 adds support for another character set, UTF-8. This character set takes a different approach to encoding characters—it uses variable size numbers, so that common characters (like the ones in the ASCII character set) can be represented by a single byte, while less common characters take more storage.

StrToFile() copies a string to a file. Together with its inverse function, FileToStr(), it's made moving text in and out of files much easier. In VFP 7, a new nFlags parameter (that replaces the lAdditive parameter used in VFP 6) lets you specify that the string being copied is in Unicode or UTF-8 format. Unlike other nFlags parameters, you don't add bits to create this parameter—the values are mutually exclusive. The first bit is for overwrite/additive—pass 0 to overwrite (the default) or 1 to append the string to the existing file. The next bit is for Unicode—pass 2. The bit after that is for UTF-8—pass 4 for the parameter. When you specify either Unicode or UTF-8, the file is automatically overwritten using the appropriate encoding method.

Summing up

While the number of string-related changes in VFP 7 isn't huge, these enhancements add welcome functionality that makes it easier than ever to manipulate textual data.

Chapter 8
Resource Management

This chapter focuses on changes in VFP 7 related to managing resources, such as files and directories, network resources, DLL functions, memory, support for languages other than English, and so forth.

A lot of the commands and functions in VFP fall in the category of "resource management." Resources can be anything an application needs to access, such as file system resources (files, directories, and drives, whether local or network resources), printers, functions in Windows or other DLLs, dialogs, Help files, language support, fonts, memory, and so on. Commands and functions in this category include ADir(), which fills an array with information about files in a specific directory; AGetFileVersion(), which fills an array with version information for a file; Declare, which tells VFP how to access a function in a DLL; DiskSpace(), which returns the amount of free space in a volume; and MD, which creates a new directory.

This chapter describes the changes made in VFP 7 related to resource management, both in language elements and other behavior.

Compiler and variable management

VFP 7's compiler treats Include files much better than previous versions, plus it gives you control over the compiler display in a run-time environment. Also, you can now detect when undeclared variables are used in your code.

#Include

Finally, the solution to something that's been a problem since VFP 3 was released. First, some background.

Suppose you like to keep source code files organized in different directories by usage and origin. For example, files used in every project, such as base classes and certain utilities, go in a "Common" directory. Files used regularly but not in every project, such as application framework files, go in a "Library" directory (see **Figure 1** for the directory structure). There are obviously dependencies between these directories. For example, since it's a good practice to create classes based on your base classes rather than VFP's base classes, all class libraries in the Library directory reference the base class VCX in the Common directory. This isn't a problem, because VFP uses relative paths to reference a VCX; for example, a class in the Library directory may reference its parent class in "..\Common\MyBaseClasses.VCX" since the Library and Common directories share the same parent directory. Even if you create a project on a different drive and add files from both types of directories, VFP properly finds all the dependencies and compiles everything correctly. Well, all except one thing: Include files.

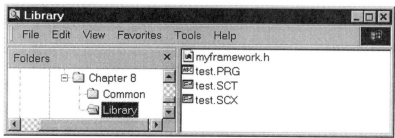

Figure 1. The directory structure illustrating the problem with Include files in earlier versions of VFP.

VFP developers typically use Include files to define constants for two things: fixed or non-obvious values (such as ccCR for Chr(13), a carriage return, and cnERR_FILE_NOT_FOUND for 1, the error number for the "file not found" error) and strings displayed to the user that may have to change in the future, either to reword a phrase or provide it in a different language (such as ccMSG_WANT_TO_QUIT for "Are you sure you want to quit?"). Suppose your base classes use one Include file, utilities programs and classes use their own Include files, files in the Library directory use a different set of Include files, and so on. As you may imagine, some constants may be used in lots of places; ccCR is one that may be used in many different functions and classes. It'd be a shame to have to define ccCR in every Include file; fortunately, Include files can themselves use #Include to include the contents of another Include file. If an Include file in one directory is referenced in an Include file in a different directory (for example, Library\MyFramework.H includes Common\MyBaseClasses.H), obviously you should use a relative path in the #Include statement to avoid hard-coding the path:

```
#include ..\Common\MyBaseClasses.H
```

Unfortunately, when you add a VCX or PRG using MyFramework.H to a project in a project-specific directory and then build an EXE from that project, VFP versions prior to 7.0 don't compile the VCX or PRG properly. When you run the application, you get "variable ccCR not defined" errors wherever ccCR is used in code because VFP left "ccCR" in the compiled code rather than replacing it with "Chr(13)". Why? Because when VFP saw the relative path in the #Include statement in MyFramework.H, it assumed the path was relative to *the current directory* (that is, the project directory), not to the location of MyFramework.H. It does the same thing with PRG files. Interestingly, it works just fine with classes in a VCX or SCX that reference an Include file with a relative path. This pretty much forces you to redefine the same constants again and again in different Include files. Hmm, wasn't VFP supposed to eliminate the need to copy and paste the same thing over and over?

Okay, that's a lot of background, but here's the improvement in VFP 7: Relative paths in #Include statements in Include and PRG files are now considered relative to the location of the source file, not the current directory, when they're compiled. In addition, VFP 7 now searches more extensively to find an Include file. For a VCX or SCX, any relative path in the Include file specification is applied in the following search order:

1. The directory the VCX or SCX is in

2. The current directory

3. The VFP path

For PRGs, the search order is:

1. The current directory (including relative path)

2. The VFP path (including relative path)

3. For compilation done from a project build, the project directory (including relative path)

4. For compilation done from a project build, the directory the PRG is in (including relative path)

5. The directory the PRG is in (no relative path)

6. VFP home directory (no relative path)

To demonstrate both the problem and the fix, the example files for this chapter have the directory structure (Common and Library subdirectories of the same directory) and Include files (Common\MyBaseClasses.H and Library\MyFramework.H) described earlier.

 Download the source code from the Developer Download files at ***www.hentzenwerke.com*** *and preserve the directory structure in the ZIP file for this chapter when you unzip it.*

Library\Test.PRG includes Common\MyBaseClasses.H using a relative path. In VFP 6, CD to the directory in which you unzipped the ZIP file for this chapter (that is, the parent directory of Library and Common) and type the following in the Command Window:

```
compile Library\Test
do Library\Test
```

You get a "variable ccCR not defined" error, indicating that VFP 6 didn't compile the PRG properly. Now do the same thing in VFP 7; no error message means it worked correctly.

Library\Test.SCX shows the problem with Include files referenced in Include files. It includes MyFramework.H, which includes Common\MyBaseClasses.H using a relative path. In VFP 6, type the following in the Command Window:

```
compile form Library\Test
do form Library\Test
```

Click the **Click Me** button; as with Test.PRG, you get a "variable ccCR not defined" error. Again, doing this in VFP 7 shows that it now works correctly.

Compile

In VFP 7, the Compile commands (Compile, Compile Classlib, Compile Report, and so forth) respect the setting of Set Notify. With Set Notify Off, no "compiling" dialog is displayed. This obviously isn't an issue in a development environment, but VFP 6 Service Pack 3 added the ability to compile files in a run-time environment. In that case, this improvement is important for two reasons: In-process COM servers can't display any user interface, and you likely don't want your users to see such a dialog.

_VFP.LanguageOptions

Using undeclared memory variables can lead to some of the thorniest bugs in VFP. A variable can suddenly take on an unexpected value after a subroutine has been called if that subroutine uses the same variable. This often doesn't cause an error, which would be easy to debug, but incorrect behavior instead, which is much harder to detect. Consider the following code:

```
for lnI = 1 to 10
   do MyRoutine
next lnI

procedure MyRoutine
for lnI = 1 to 5
* some code
next lnI
return
```

How many times does the first loop execute? If you said 10, you need a refresher course in variable scoping. If you said five (figuring the first call to MyRoutine causes lnI to be set to 6, eliminating iterations two through five in the first loop), you're warmer. The correct answer is an infinite number of times (or however many can execute until you press Esc or use the Windows Task Manager to end the VFP session). That's because each call to MyRoutine ends with lnI being 6, so the loop never hits its terminating value of 10.

To help track this problem down, the _VFP system variable has a new LanguageOptions property. Setting this property to 1 sends information to the debugger output (either the Debug Output window or a file if you use the Set DebugOut command) when any code references a variable that hasn't been declared as Public or Local. Since Private doesn't actually create a variable, any variables declared as Private are considered undeclared. Also, variables created on the fly by a command or function, such as arrays created with functions like ADir() or variables created with Scatter, are considered Private and therefore undeclared. Note that this only works in the development environment (it's ignored at run time) and only when you run the code (it's not handled at compile time, which would have been even better).

 To see this setting in action, run the following code (TestLangOptions.PRG, included with the Developer Download files you can download for this chapter from **www.hentzenwerke.com**).

```
_vfp.LanguageOptions = 1
activate window 'Debug Output'

a = 1
private b
```

```
b = 1
public c
c = 1
local d
d = 1
adir(e, '*.*')
do TestVars

_vfp.LanguageOptions = 0

procedure TestVars
f = 2
```

It produces the following in the Debug Output window (the path for the file shown in the fifth item in each line has been removed for brevity):

```
LangOptionsErr,4/7/2001 9:58:15 AM,4,TESTLANGOPTIONS,TESTLANGOPTIONS.FXP,A
LangOptionsErr,4/7/2001 9:58:15 AM,6,TESTLANGOPTIONS,TESTLANGOPTIONS.FXP,B
LangOptionsErr,4/7/2001 9:58:15 AM,11,TESTLANGOPTIONS,TESTLANGOPTIONS.FXP,E
LangOptionsErr,4/7/2001 9:58:15 AM,17,TESTVARS,PROCEDURE TESTVARS
   TESTLANGOPTIONS.FXP,F
```

The first and second comma-delimited items indicate what the output is for and when the code was executed. The third, fourth, and fifth items are the line number, routine (method, function, or procedure) name, and source code file where the variable was used. The sixth item is the name of the undeclared variable.

File system management

VFP 7 has improvements in four functions related to file system resources: ADir(), ANetResources(), DiskSpace(), and GetDir().

ADir()

ADir() now accepts a fourth parameter, nFlag. A setting of 0 forces file names to uppercase. This is the behavior of previous versions of VFP and the default behavior if the fourth parameter isn't passed. A setting of 1 preserves file name case, and 2 shows names in DOS 8.3 format (so MyLongFileName.Txt would appear as MYLONG~1.TXT).

ANetResources()

This function, which fills an array with the share or printer resources on a specific server, now accepts 0 for the third parameter, nResourceType, to fill the array with both share and printer resources. Previously, you had to call it twice, first passing 1 for shares and then 2 for printers, to get both types of resources. Also, you can now pass a domain name as well as a server name for the second parameter. Here's an example (substitute your server or domain name for "MyServer"):

```
anetresources(laAll, '\\MyServer', 0)
display memory like laAll
```

DiskSpace()

In previous versions of VFP, DiskSpace() returned incorrect values when there was more than 2GB of free disk space (this wasn't a bug in VFP, but in the Windows API function DiskSpace() calls). This has been fixed in VFP 7, as long as the operating system is newer than the first release of Windows 95 (Win95 OSR2 or later). In addition, you can pass a new second parameter to determine what DiskSpace() should return: the total amount of space on the volume (1), the amount of free space (2 or no second parameter), or the amount of free space available to the current user (3).

GetDir() and CD ?

GetDir() has three new parameters: cCaption, the caption of the dialog (the default is "Browse for Folder"), nFlags to indicate the behavior of the dialog, and lRootOnly that allows you to treat the starting directory as the root so the user can't navigate above it. If any of the new parameters are passed, this function uses the SHBrowseForFolder Windows API function, so the dialog has the same user interface as other Windows applications.

The VFP Help topic for GetDir() includes a list of some of the values for the flags parameter; the SHBrowseForFolder topic in the MSDN Help file has a complete list. Like other functions that support a similar parameter (such as the MessageBox() function), you can add together different values to provide the behavior you want. Not all of the flags values are available in all operating environments. Including an edit box in the dialog (16) and displaying files as well as folders (16384) requires version 4.71 of Shell32.DLL, so it's available with Windows 98 and later versions or with Internet Explorer 4.0 or higher with Shell Integration turned on. Using Windows Explorer-like features (64), shown in **Figure 2**, requires version 5.00 of Shell32.DLL, so it's available in Windows 2000 and above.

This example has "Import From" as the caption, displays "Select directory" and an edit box (the "16" in the flags parameter), only allows physical locations to be selected (the "1" in the flags parameter), and doesn't allow the user to navigate above the current directory. **Figure 3** shows the resulting dialog.

```
lcDir = getdir('', 'Select directory', 'Import From', 16 + 1, .T.)
```

The dialog displayed when you type CD ? is the same one you see if you specify 64 as the flags parameter for GetDir().

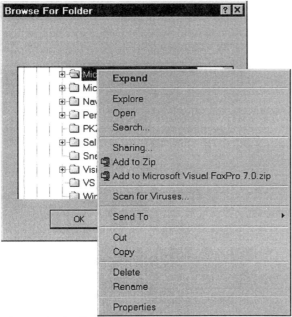

Figure 2. Adding 64 to the flags parameter of GetDir() displays a dialog with features similar to Windows Explorer, such as context menus.

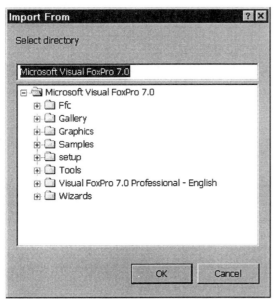

Figure 3. The user can only select physical locations, can't navigate above the current directory, and can enter the desired directory name into the edit box.

DLL management

The new ADLLS() function and improvement in Clear DLLS make DLL resource management easier. In addition, Declare DLL can now accept a new data type.

ADLLS()

This new function fills an array with declared DLL functions. The array contains the name of the function, the alias name it was given, and the DLL in which it exists. The following code shows the DLL functions loaded by the FoxPro Foundation Classes (FFC) Registry class:

```
oRegistry = newobject('Registry', home() + 'FFC\Registry.vcx')
oRegistry.LoadRegFuncs()
adlls(laDLLs)
display memory like laDLLs
```

Here are the contents of the first row of the array created by this code:

```
laDLLs[1, 1]    RegCloseKey
laDLLs[1, 2]    RegCloseKey
laDLLs[1, 3]    C:\WINNT\system32\ADVAPI32.DLL
```

Clear DLLS

This command can now accept a list of function aliases to clear from memory; in earlier versions, it cleared all DLL functions from memory. Here's an example:

```
clear dlls GetSaveFileNameA, GetOpenFileNameA
```

Declare DLL

In addition to the usual data types (such as Integer and String), Declare now accepts a new Object type, both for parameters and the function return value.

Language management

FoxPro has long provided support for non-English languages. FoxPro 2.x added support for code pages and collate sequences, and VFP added support for languages read right-to-left, such as Hebrew. VFP 7 has additional improvements in this area.

GetFont()

GetFont() has a new optional fourth parameter, nFontCharSet, to specify the default language script. Passing a value for this parameter (see the VFP Help topic for this function for details) enables the Script combo box in the dialog and includes the code for the selected language script in the return string. The following code creates the dialog shown in **Figure 4**:

```
? getfont('Arial', 8, '', 161)   && displays "Arial,8,N,162" if Turkish chosen
```

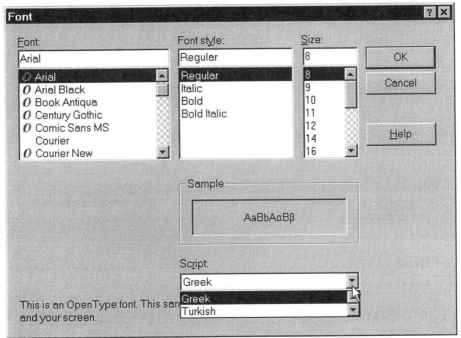

Figure 4. GetFont() now supports the Script *combo box.*

Language resource files

Because users can switch locale IDs on the fly in Windows 2000, VFP 7 now installs resource files for other languages (VFP7CHS.DLL, VFP7CHT.DLL, VFP7DEU.DLL, VFP7ESP.DLL, and VFP7KOR.DLL) with the English version of VFP 7. Note that this only affects development systems; see the "Distributing applications" section of this book's Chapter 3, "New and Better Tools," and the "Managing Files in an International Application" topic in the VFP Help file for information on installing language resource files with applications you create in VFP.

SYS(2300)

VFP has an internal list of code pages it supports, called the "national language support," or NLS, list. The following code pages are in the default list: 874 (Thai Windows), 932 (Japanese Windows), 936 (Chinese [PRC, Singapore] Windows), 949 (Korean Windows), 950 (Chinese [Hong Kong SAR, Taiwan] Windows), 1255 (Hebrew Windows), and 1256 (Arabic Windows). SYS(2300) is a new function that allows you to add or remove support for code pages. Pass it the code page number and either 0 to remove the code page from the NLS list or 1 to add it. If you omit the third parameter (0 or 1), the function just tells you whether the code page is in the list (1, if it is; 0, if not).

Input and display

VFP 7 has three new functions in this category.

DisplayPath()

This new function is useful when you want to display a file name but don't have a lot of space to do so. You specify the file name and maximum length, and DisplayPath() returns a string up to that many characters with an ellipsis (…) in place of some of the characters if necessary. The following code, run from the VFP 7 home directory ("D:\Program Files\Microsoft Visual FoxPro 7.0" in this case), displays the indicated results:

```
lcFile = fullpath('this is a very long filename.txt')
? displaypath(lcFile, 15)   && "this is a ve..."
? displaypath(lcFile, 25)   && "this is a very long fi..."
? displaypath(lcFile, 35)   && "this is a very long filename.txt"
? displaypath(lcFile, 40)   && "d:\...\this is a very long filename.txt"
? displaypath(lcFile, 75)
&& "d:\...\microsoft visual foxpro 7.0\this is a very long filename.txt"
? displaypath(lcFile, 85)
&& "d:\program files\microsoft visual foxpro 7.0\this is a very long
   filename.txt"
```

InputBox()

This new function displays a dialog in which the user can enter a single string; **Figure 5** shows an example of its appearance. If it looks familiar, that's because this dialog has existed since VFP 3 but wasn't directly accessible before. It's the same dialog displayed to get values for parameterized views. You can specify the prompt, the dialog caption, a default value, a timeout value, and a value to be returned if the dialog times out. It uses the current _Screen icon for its icon. The following code opens the VFP sample Customer table, asks you for a city (the default is "San Francisco"), and shows how many customers were found in that city:

```
use _samples + 'Data\Customer'
lcCity = inputbox('Enter the city to search for:', 'Find City', ;
  'San Francisco', 5000)
select count(*) from Customer ;
  where City = lcCity ;
  into array laFind
wait window transform(laFind[1]) + ' customers were found in ' + lcCity
```

Because you have no control over the appearance of the dialog other than the prompt, caption, and icon, it's hard to say whether this function will be used much in real applications. However, for developer tools or simple applications, it saves you from having to create a form just so the user can enter a single string.

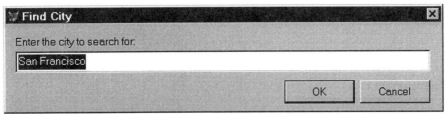

Figure 5. The InputBox() function is a quick and dirty way to prompt the user for a single string.

SYS(602)
VFP 6 Service Pack 5 added a new setting configurable only in Config.FPW: Bitmap. Normally, VFP updates the screen by drawing a bitmap in memory, and then moving the entire bitmap to the screen at once. While this provides better video performance for normal applications, it slows down applications running under Citrix or Windows Terminal Server. Those environments look for changes to the screen and send them down the wire to the client system. Because every change causes the entire screen to be sent to the client, rather than just the changes made, this results in a lot of data being sent. Adding Bitmap = Off turns off this screen drawing behavior.

Okay, that's the background. What's new to VFP 7 is SYS(602), which allows you to determine the value of this setting.

Windows setting management
VFP 7 makes it easier to make your applications respect the user's Windows Control Panel settings.

_DblClick and _IncSeek
There are two changes to _DblClick in VFP 7. First, rather than a default value of 0.5 second, it now respects the double-click speed setting in the Mouse applet of the Windows Control Panel, a welcome change to those developers trying to make their applications respect the user's Windows settings. Second, _DblClick is now used only as the double-click rate and not for incremental searching in controls such as combo boxes and list boxes. The new _IncSeek system variable, which supports the same range of values as _DblClick (0.05 to 5.5 seconds), is used as the incremental search interval.

Set('Century')
Passing 3 as the second parameter returns the rollover date setting in the Regional Options applet of the Control Panel in Windows 98, Windows ME, and Windows 2000 (for example, on a Windows 2000 system with the default setting, it returns 2029). In Windows 95 and NT, it returns −1.

Memory management

Unlike C programmers, VFP developers don't usually worry about memory management. However, VFP 7 now has two functions related to this topic.

SYS(1104)

Technically, SYS(1104) isn't new, but in VFP 7, it finally appears in the VFP Help file. This function purges memory cached by programs and data. Since the amount of memory available to VFP can make a huge difference in performance, calling this function after executing commands that make extensive use of memory buffers (such as SQL Select statements) can help your application's speed.

SYS(2600)

SYS(2600) either copies the contents of a specified range of memory addresses to a string or copies the contents of a string to memory. Readers familiar with the BASIC programming language will recognize these features as the equivalent of the Peek() and Poke() functions. To see an example of this function, type "Getenv" and an open parenthesis in the Command Window and notice the list of environment variables that IntelliSense displays (see Chapter 1, "IntelliSense," for a detailed description of IntelliSense). That list is read from memory using SYS(2600). To see exactly how that's done, do the following:

```
use (_foxcode) again shared
locate for Expanded = 'GetEnv'
browse
```

Open the Data memo field and peruse the code. The Peek() function in this code uses SYS(2600).

Writing to memory without due caution can be dangerous to your system's health, so be careful if you use that behavior of this function.

Other changes

The rest of the improvements in VFP 7 related to resource management don't fall into any one specific category.

_Screen and _VFP

In previous versions of VFP, there was no way to determine the exact coordinates of the main VFP window, _Screen. While menu bars and docked toolbars obviously reduce the amount of usable space in _Screen, its Top, Left, Height, and Width properties reflected the values of the entire VFP application window. In VFP 7, these properties of _Screen now apply only to the VFP "client" area, while those in _VFP apply only to the entire VFP application window.

For example, **Table 1** shows the values of these properties in VFP 6 and 7 on a system using 1280x1024 resolution and running VFP in a maximized window with the Standard toolbar docked at the top and the status bar turned on. The reason the Top and Left properties of _VFP are negative is that the border of the window is by default moved outside the viewable area of the screen. Notice in VFP 7 that the Top and Height properties of _Screen show the effects of the menu bar, docked toolbar, and status bar. Removing any of these or docking additional toolbars or windows at any edge alters the size of the client area, so the properties of _Screen change appropriately but those of _VFP do not.

Table 1. *The differences between the Top, Left, Height, and Width properties of _Screen and _VFP in VFP 6 and 7.*

Property	VFP 6		VFP 7	
	_Screen	_VFP	_Screen	_VFP
Top	-4	-4	69	-4
Left	-4	-4	0	-4
Height	899	899	902	1003
Width	1280	1280	1280	1288

Another change is that both of these system variables now have an hWnd property (the Form and Toolbar base classes also have this new property; see Chapter 6, OOP Enhancements"), which contains the handle of the appropriate window. Window handles are used by many Windows API functions to do something with a window, such as sending a message to it. Obtaining the window handle for VFP in previous versions meant calling a Windows API function such as GetDesktopWindow(). Now, you simply refer to the hWnd property.

In addition to hWnd and LanguageOptions (discussed in the "Compiler and variable management" section of this chapter), _VFP has two other new properties: EditorOptions and VFPXMLProgID. EditorOptions affects the new IntelliSense and editor enhancements, so it is discussed in detail in Chapter 1, "IntelliSense," and Chapter 2, "Editor Enhancements." VFPXMLProgID provides a way to override the functionality of the new XML functions; see Chapter 15, "Working with Web Services," for more information.

Like the Form base class, _Screen has a new ShowInTaskBar property (see Chapter 6, "OOP Enhancements," for a discussion of this property). Because it's read-only for _Screen, it doesn't really serve a useful purpose.

AStackInfo()

This new function is a welcome addition to any error handling scheme or any other code using the SYS(16) function (which returns the name of the executing program at any level in the call stack). AStackInfo() fills an array with information about the entire call stack; see **Table 2** for the columns in the array. Some of this information isn't available any other way. For example, there's no other way to get the line number or source code for different levels of the call stack. Also, the information SYS(16) gives for PRG files in an EXE is incomplete.

Table 2. *Columns in the array filled by AStackInfo().*

Column	Description
1	The call stack level
2	The executing file name
3	The module or object name
4	The source file name
5	The line number
6	The source code (if available)

*The Developer Download files at **www.hentzenwerke.com** include example files that demonstrate how AStackInfo() works.*

To see AStackInfo() in action, run Test.EXE from the Windows Explorer (so it's running under the VFP run time, not the development environment). The main program is TestAStackInfo.PRG. It calls the ShowForm function (also in TestAStackInfo.PRG), which runs the Test form. Clicking on the Click me button instantiates a form class. Clicking on the Click me too button in that form displays the contents of the array filled by AStackInfo(). Here are the results on one system (the paths on yours will obviously be different):

```
laStack[1, 1]    1
laStack[1, 2]    "d:\book\chapter8\test.exe"
laStack[1, 3]    "testastackinfo"
laStack[1, 4]    "d:\book\chapter8\testastackinfo.prg"
laStack[1, 5]    5
laStack[1, 6]    "do ShowForm"

laStack[2, 1]    2
laStack[2, 2]    "d:\book\chapter8\test.exe"
laStack[2, 3]    "showform"
laStack[2, 4]    "d:\book\chapter8\testastackinfo.prg"
laStack[2, 5]    11
laStack[2, 6]    "do form test"

laStack[3, 1]    3
laStack[3, 2]    "d:\book\chapter8\test.sct"
laStack[3, 3]    "frmtest.cmdclickme.click"
laStack[3, 4]    "d:\book\chapter8\test.sct"
laStack[3, 5]    2
laStack[3, 6]    "loForm.Show()"

laStack[4, 1]    4
laStack[4, 2]    "d:\book\chapter8\test.vct"
laStack[4, 3]    "testform.cmdclickme.click"
laStack[4, 4]    "d:\book\chapter8\test.vct"
laStack[4, 5]    2
laStack[4, 6]    "astackinfo(laStack)"
```

Notice the difference in the third column in each row. The first row is from code in the main program, so it shows the main program name as the module. The second row is from the ShowForm function in TestAStackInfo.PRG, so it shows that function name as the module. The other two rows show the complete object method hierarchy for the executing code. The fact that the second column doesn't show the EXE name for rows three and four is a bug that hopefully will be fixed in a service pack.

Home()

To meet Windows 2000 requirements, applications should store user-specific files in a user application data directory. In VFP 7, this directory is something like C:\Documents and Settings\<user name>\Application Data\Microsoft\Visual FoxPro. By default, VFP stores tables such as the FoxUser resource file, the IntelliSense FoxCode table, and the Task List FoxTask table in this directory. You can now determine the location of this directory by passing 7 to the Home() function.

Set Help
The Set Help command has been enhanced to support new features in HTML Help 2. Unfortunately, with very little information on this unreleased version (as of this writing) being available, we can't tell you any more about the enhancements to Set Help than the topic in the VFP Help file does.

Splash screen
The splash screen displayed when VFP is passed the "B" command line switch can now display GIF and JPG images (previously, only BMP files were supported), and you can specify the duration in milliseconds. Here's an example that displays the specified image for three seconds:

```
VFP7.EXE -b\Images\MyImage.GIF,3000
```

Run time files
VFP no longer installs its run time files (VFP7R.DLL, VFP7T.DLL, VFP7RUN.EXE, FoxHHelp7.DLL, FoxHHelpPS7.DLL, and the VFP7Rxxx.DLL language resource files) in the Windows System directory. Instead, they're installed in C:\Program Files\Common Files\Microsoft Shared\VFP.

Version()
The build number for VFP 7 now appears in the final section of the version number (for example, "07.00.0000.9147") rather than the third section (such as "06.00.8862.00"). Why would you care? Because VFP 6 Service Pack 3 had way more changes than you'd expect in a service pack, such as support for the Compile command in a run-time environment, some developers relied on the build number (Service Pack 3 was build number 8492), parsed from the version number, to determine whether they could use certain features or not. Here's an example of how they determined that:

```
lcVersion = substr(version(4), at('.', version(4), 2) + 1)
lcVersion = left(lcVersion, at('.', lcVersion) - 1)
if lcVersion >= 8492
* use some feature added in VFP 6 Service Pack 3
endif lcVersion >= 8492
```

Of course, this code doesn't work in VFP 7 because the position of the build number in the version string has moved. GetVFPVersion.PRG solves this problem: It returns the build number regardless of its position. Now you can simply call GetVFPVersion and check its return value to see whether you can use some feature. Here's the code:

```
function GetVFPVersion
local lcVersion
lcVersion = version(4)
if version(5) < 700
```

```
  lcVersion = substr(lcVersion, at('.', lcVersion, 2) + 1)
  lcVersion = left(lcVersion, at('.', lcVersion) - 1)
else
  lcVersion = substr(lcVersion, at('.', lcVersion, 3) + 1)
endif version(5) < 700
return lcVersion
```

 *The Developer Download files at **www.hentzenwerke.com** include GetVFPVersion.PRG. The download version can also be used in versions of VFP earlier than 6.0; it returns "0000" for those versions.*

Summary

VFP 7 has extensive improvements in the area of resource management. These improvements fix bugs in earlier versions, make it easier to respect the user's Windows settings, help track down variable declaration and scoping problems in your applications, provide better file system resource management, and benefit VFP developers in many other ways.

Chapter 9
Arrays

Array support in Visual FoxPro has always been strong. In VFP 7, a few key changes make arrays an even better tool than in earlier versions.

Visual FoxPro offers arrays as another way to work with data. There's a group of functions (such as ALEN() and ACOPY()) to manage arrays, as well as a large number of functions that put information about the system or the current environment into an array.

VFP 7 adds to both groups by enhancing two key array manipulation functions and adding several new functions to put information into arrays. Many of the existing functions that store data into arrays have also been enhanced. In addition, VFP 7 offers the ability to return an array from a subroutine in certain situations.

The new and enhanced functions that store system or environment information are discussed in the chapters that cover the relevant information. This chapter focuses on changes to core array functionality.

Returning arrays from functions

In older versions of VFP, the return value from a function had to be a scalar (non-array). In VFP 7, a function can return an array, provided the array is still in scope when the function is done. In practice, this ability is limited to methods returning array properties.

This example uses the functionality to expand VFP's array-handling capabilities. The built-in ASUBSCRIPT() function returns either the row or the column for a given array element, depending on the parameters you pass. The AGetBothSubscripts() method returns an array containing both subscripts:

```
DEFINE CLASS cusArrayFns AS Custom

DIMENSION aReturn[2]

FUNCTION AGetBothSubscripts
* Return both subscripts of an array
* in an array

LPARAMETERS aInArray, nElement

* First, check parameters
DO CASE
CASE PCOUNT() < 2
   * Did we get two params?
   ERROR 1229 && Too Few Arguments.
   RETURN .F.

CASE VARTYPE(aInArray) = "U"
   * Does the array variable exist? This case
   * should never occur because the
   * LPARAMETERS line should catch it.
```

```
      ERROR 225 && "Name" is not a variable.
      RETURN .F.

CASE TYPE("aInArray[1]") = "U"
      * Is it an array?
      ERROR 232, "aInArray" && "Name" is not an array.
      RETURN .F.

CASE ALEN( aInArray, 2 ) = 0
      * Is it a 2-D array?
      ERROR 1234 && Subscript is outside defined range.
      RETURN .F.

CASE VARTYPE(nElement) <> "N"
      * Did we get an element number?
      ERROR 11 && Function argument, value, type, or count is invalid.
      RETURN .F.

CASE NOT BETWEEN( nElement, 1, ALEN(aInArray))
      * Is the subscript valid for this array?
      ERROR 1234 && Subscript is outside defined range.
      RETURN .F.

OTHERWISE
      * So far, so good

ENDCASE

* Use the built-in functions to get the information
* and put it into the array.
This.aReturn[1] = ASUBSCRIPT( aInArray, nElement, 1 )
This.aReturn[2] = ASUBSCRIPT( aInArray, nElement, 2 )

RETURN @This.aReturn

ENDDEFINE
```

The method first checks its parameters thoroughly, using the built-in ERROR command to trigger the appropriate Visual FoxPro error if there are problems. Once the parameters have been cleared, ASUBSCRIPT() is called twice, once for the row and once for the column of the specified element, and the results are stored in the array property aReturn. Finally, the method returns the array, using the same "@" notation used for passing parameters by reference.

To use the method, you need to instantiate the object, and then pass the AGetBothSubscripts() method an existing array and an element number. This example populates an array with data from the TasTrade database, and then lets the user specify a series of element numbers, showing the row and column for each.

```
LOCAL aSb[2], aEmps[1], lDone, oAFns AS cusArrayFns

* Populate an array

SELECT First_Name, Last_Name, Title ;
   FROM _SAMPLES + "TasTrade\Data\Employee" ;
```

```
        INTO ARRAY aEmps

oAFns = CREATEOBJECT( "cusArrayFns")

DO WHILE NOT lDone
    nElement = INT(VAL(INPUTBOX("Element number", "Choose an element", "0")))
    IF nElement = 0
        lDone = .t.
    ELSE
        aSb = oAFns.AGetBothSubscripts( @aEmps, nElement )
        MESSAGEBOX( "Element " + TRANSFORM( nElement ) + ;
                    " is in position (" + TRANSFORM(aSb[1]) + ;
                    "," + TRANSFORM(aSb[2]) + ")",64 + 0)
    ENDIF
ENDDO

RETURN
```

 Both AGetBothSubscripts() and the code to test it are included in ArrayFns.PRG in the Developer Downloads available at **www.hentzenwerke.com**.

In addition to having to call it as a method, one feature makes AGetBothSubscripts() clearly different from a built-in array function: You have to explicitly pass the array by reference, as in the example.

Because the array must be in scope after the call, using this new capability with functions results in bad code. Here's an example:

```
DIMENSION laTest[1]
LOCAL laArray[1]
laArray = FillArray()
CLEAR
DISPLAY MEMORY LIKE la*

FUNCTION FillArray
DIMENSION laTest[2]
laTest[1] = 'howdy'
laTest[2] = 'doody'
RETURN @laTest
```

Even though it's not receiving the return array, laTest must be dimensioned in the calling routine because that's the name of the array in the FillArray function and in order for this to work, it must be in scope in the calling routine. Also, laTest can't be declared LOCAL anywhere or scoping problems occur. You must also avoid declaring any array properties in your classes as PROTECTED if you plan to return them as method results.

Using this feature requires a lot of coupling between the caller and called routines, and coupling is normally something to be avoided like the plague.

Better searching and sorting in arrays

Modifications to two of FoxPro's array-handling functions make them more useful in VFP 7. Both ASCAN() and ASORT() now have the ability to ignore case. ASCAN() has several other new features, as well: You can choose whether it does an exact search (in the SET EXACT sense); you can limit the search to a specific column; and you can tell it to return the row number rather than the element number in a two-dimensional array. The VFP developer community has requested all of these changes over the years.

Improved searching

ASCAN() has two new parameters. The new fifth parameter is nSearchColumn for indicating which column to search. You can combine it with the parameters for start position and number of elements to search only particular elements within a specific column. Alternatively, you can specify –1 for both the start position and number of elements to search the entire specified column.

To set up an example, this code creates an array containing information about the persistent relations in the TasTrade database:

```
OPEN DATABASE HOME(2)+"TasTrade\Data\TasTrade"
ADBOBJECTS(aRelns,"RELATION")
```

The resulting array has five columns. The first is the name of the child table in the relation and the second is the name of the parent table. The third and fourth columns contain the names of the tags used to maintain the relation in the child and parent tables, respectively. The final column indicates the type of relational integrity for that relation.

To find relations involving a particular table as a child, you need to search the first column. For example, this call finds the first relation involving the Products table as a child:

```
? ASCAN( aRelns, "PRODUCTS", -1, -1, 1) && displays 16 (row 4, column 1)
```

To find the first relation involving Products as a parent, search only the second column, like this:

```
? ASCAN( aRelns, "PRODUCTS", -1, -1, 2) && displays 2 (row 1, column 2)
```

The new sixth parameter in ASCAN(), nFlags, improves the search in several ways. There are four, additive, bit values for nFlags, as shown in **Table 1**. Consider defining a set of constants for these values, so you don't have to remember them.

Table 1. *ASCAN() flags—add together the values shown to create the nFlags parameter.*

Bit	Add to nFlags	Meaning
0	0	Search is case-sensitive. Default.
0	1	Search is case-insensitive.
1	0	EXACT is off. Effective only when Bit 2 is set (4).
1	2	EXACT is on. Effective only when Bit 2 is set (4).
2	0	Current SET EXACT setting applies.
2	4	Use the exactness setting from Bit 1.
3	0	Return the element number of the matching item.
3	8	Return the row number of the matching item, if this is a two-dimensional array.

Using the previous example, you can try several changes. The most useful is getting the row number rather than the element number:

```
? ASCAN( aRelns, "PRODUCTS", -1, -1, 1, 8) && displays 4
```

If you don't want to worry about the case of the data in the array, add the flag for case-insensitivity to the flag for returning the row number:

```
? ASCAN( aRelns, "products", -1, -1, 1, 9) && displays 4
```

The flags for dealing with exact matches are a little confusing. The value of bit 2 determines whether the function pays any attention to the value of bit 1. This gives you the option of either following the current SET EXACT setting or overriding it for the search. Add 4 (4 for bit 2 and 0 for bit 1) to nFlags to make sure you search with EXACT off; add 6 (4 for bit 2 and 2 for bit 1) to force ASCAN() to search with EXACT on. No matter which value you pass, it doesn't affect anything outside the single ASCAN().

 *The form ShowAScan.SCX, in the Developer Downloads available at **www.hentzenwerke.com**, lets you experiment with the changes to ASCAN().*

Case-insensitive sorts

ASORT(), which sorts the data in an array, has a new (fifth) parameter, nFlags, used to specify whether or not the sort is case-sensitive. If this parameter is omitted or 0, the sort is case-sensitive, as in older versions of FoxPro. If the parameter is 1, the sort is case-insensitive. (Of course, since this parameter is called nFlags, it's possible that additional flags will be added to this function in the future.)

Suppose you have an array, aSortMe, containing the following data:

```
"Files"
"boxes"
"file cabinet"
"PAPERCLIPS"
```

```
"Paper"
"Stapler"
```

If you call ASORT() without the new parameter, like this:

```
ASORT( aSortMe )
```

the results look like:

```
"Files"
"PAPERCLIPS"
"Paper"
"Stapler"
"boxes"
"file cabinet"
```

By adding the nFlags parameter, like this:

```
ASORT( aSortMe, -1, -1, 0, 1 )
```

you get a list in the order that most people would expect:

```
"boxes"
"file cabinet"
"Files"
"Paper"
"PAPERCLIPS"
"Stapler"
```

Note that, as with ASCAN(), you can pass –1 for the first element and number of elements parameters to sort the entire array based on the contents of the first column.

Summing up

Arrays have always provided a handy way to manipulate data in memory. With these changes, they're more useful than ever.

Chapter 10
Bits and Pieces

This is the "what's left over" chapter for new and enhanced language elements. It discusses improvements that don't fit into a specific category.

Although the new and enhanced functions described in this chapter don't fit neatly into one of the categories covered in earlier chapters, they're still useful improvements. For example, how many times have you used MessageBox() to display the result of a calculation, only to get a "function argument value, type, or count is invalid" error because the value isn't a string? How long have you wanted a run-time equivalent of the VFP Command Window so you can tweak the contents of a table or help debug a problem at your client's office? The improvements described in this chapter help with those tasks and more.

BitOr(), BitXor(), and BitAnd()

These functions can now accept more than the two parameters they do in VFP 6; they'll accept up to 26 parameters in VFP 7. This is useful in cases (such as some API functions and COM objects) where several flags have to be ANDed or ORed together, such as BitOr(expr1, expr2, expr3, expr4). In VFP 6, you have to use something like BitOr(BitOr(BitOr(expr1, expr2), expr3), expr4) to do this.

CToT()

In VFP 7, CToT() supports the XML date format YYYY-MM-DDTHH:MM:SS.SSS (such as 2001-03-22T14:35:49), which is returned by XML queries against SQL Server and other databases that support it. One quirk, however, is that you have to Set Date YMD for this to work. Hopefully, that'll be fixed in a service pack.

ExecScript()

This new function accepts a string, which should be VFP code, as a parameter and executes it. Why is this capability useful? That's like asking why macro expansion in VFP is useful—it gives you the ability to define behavior at run time rather than development time. You can generate some code that depends on certain run-time conditions, and then execute that code. One use is giving more advanced users the ability to script new behavior in your application. For example, consider an accounting system that gives its users the ability to perform additional tasks for key operations. Perhaps a user wants to send an e-mail to a client when an order from that client is posted. He could write some code to send the e-mail and tell the accounting system to execute that code when an order is posted. Even if you don't provide such advanced capabilities in your applications, here's a simple one you'll want to use: a run-time command interpreter you can hook into your application so you can have the equivalent of the VFP Command Window in a run-time environment.

*The Developer Download files at **www.hentzenwerke.com** include Console.VCX, which contains the ConsoleForm class described in the next paragraph, and TestConsole.PRG, which shows how to use ConsoleForm.*

ConsoleForm is a simple command interpreter that acts like the VFP Command Window but in a run-time environment. It's just a form with an edit box for entering code and a command button to execute the contents of the edit box using ExecScript(). However, it has a few bells and whistles, including the ability to either emulate the Command Window (that is, each line of code is executed when you press Enter) or execute an entire block of code at once (uncheck the **Emulate Command Window** check box), load code from a file, and scroll through a code "history" so you can re-execute code. This class can be called from an error handler to assist with debugging or from a menu item only available to developers at run time to allow you to perform tasks that would normally require a development copy of VFP at the client site. To see ConsoleForm in action, run TestConsole.PRG. **Figure 1** shows an example where a table is opened, a calculation performed, and the result displayed (sharp-eyed readers will note that this example also shows the new automatic transformation feature of the MessageBox() function, discussed next).

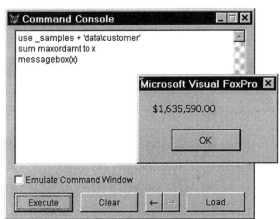

Figure 1. *The ConsoleForm class is a useful example of the new ExecScript() function.*

MessageBox()

MessageBox() has two new features: a new fourth parameter to specify the timeout value in milliseconds (after the timeout expires, the dialog automatically closes and the function returns –1) and auto-transformation of non-character values. Of course, you'll still have to use Transform() or some other function to convert non-character values to character if you want to concatenate multiple values, such as "Today's date: " + Transform(Date()).

Here's an example that displays the current date (showing how the value is automatically transformed) and automatically closes after two seconds:

```
messagebox(date(), 'Current Date', 0, 2000)
```

OS()

OS() now accepts many new parameters to determine different things about the operating system, such as the major and minor version numbers and build number, which service pack is installed (including major and minor version numbers), and which additional products may be installed (such as BackOffice or Terminal Server). For example, on Doug's system (Windows 2000 Server with Service Pack 1 installed), OS(1) returns "Windows 5.00", OS(7) returns "Service Pack 1", and OS(11) returns 3 (indicating Windows 2000 Server). See the VFP Help topic for this function for a complete list of parameter values.

Quarter()

This new function returns the quarter in which the specified Date or DateTime expression falls. You can specify the starting month for the year (the default is 1) so it can be used for either calendar or fiscal years. The following code demonstrates this function (the InputBox() function also used in this code is described in Chapter 8, "Resource Management"):

```
lcDate = inputbox('Date:', 'Enter Date', dtoc(date()))
ldDate = ctod(lcDate)
wait window lcDate + ' is in quarter ' + transform(quarter(ldDate)) + ;
   ' of the calendar year and quarter ' + transform(quarter(ldDate, 4)) + ;
   ' of a fiscal year starting on April 1.'
```

Summary

So far, this book has focused on the improvements in the IDE, the new and improved tools, and the new and enhanced commands and functions in VFP 7. These improvements make VFP developers more productive and the applications they develop more powerful and easier to use. The next section of the book concentrates on the new features in VFP 7 related to building component-based software.

Section 3
Developing Components

Chapter 11
Building Component-Based Software

For several years now, Visual FoxPro has provided developers with the ability to create component-based software applications. Although previous versions of VFP allowed you to wade in the waters of COM component development, VFP 7 allows you to dive in headfirst. If you have not yet made the transition to components, this chapter invites you to "come on in, the water's fine!" It not only presents the basics of component development, but also provides *compelling reasons* for creating component-based applications. In addition, you will also learn what Microsoft's .NET initiative means to the future of COM components.

The Fox team has spent a great deal of time and energy improving Visual FoxPro's ability to create world-class software components. In fact, many of the major enhancements in Visual FoxPro 7 relate to the creation of COM components.

Unfortunately, many Visual FoxPro developers have never taken advantage of VFP's component capabilities. Instead, they continue to create monolithic applications similar to the applications they created using FoxPro 2.x.

This brings up some questions. Why should you create component-based applications? How do you create them? What does the advent of Microsoft's .NET Framework mean for the future of COM components?

Creating monolithic applications

What is a monolithic application? It is an application with its user interface, business logic, and data services inextricably bound to each other. For example, in a monolithic application, the majority of application code is tucked away inside the methods and events of user interface controls—the Click() event of command buttons, the Valid() event of text boxes and other controls, the InteractiveChange() event of combo boxes, as well as custom methods of controls and forms.

What happens, however, if you want to replace your Visual FoxPro front end with a thin-client Web interface?

In a monolithic application, taking the Visual FoxPro user interface out of the picture takes all of the application code with it, making it impossible to access your application from a Web browser front end. Many times developers address this issue by leaving the code in the VFP user interface and creating a completely separate Web application. This results in two code bases—one for the desktop and one for the Internet, therefore creating a maintenance nightmare!

In certain respects, Visual FoxPro actually encourages developers to create monolithic applications. One example of this is the use of data environments in forms and reports. As shown in **Figure 1**, the "Client" form's data environment is set to load the "clients" table when the form instantiates. However, this binds the user interface directly to the data. What happens if you want to upsize your application to a client/server database such as SQL Server or Oracle? It would be extremely difficult because the user interface is inextricably and directly bound to the data.

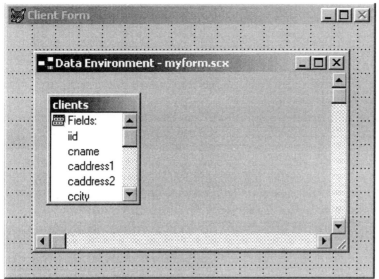

Figure 1. *Using Visual FoxPro's built-in data environments results in the creation of monolithic software applications.*

Monolithic applications are a "rock in the river of change." When the inevitable changes in end-user requirements or in the software industry itself occur, monolithic software architecture usually requires that you completely rewrite large portions of your application in order to integrate these changes.

What is the alternative to creating monolithic applications? The answer is component-based applications.

Creating component-based, n-tier applications

Component-based applications stand in stark contrast to monolithic applications. While monolithic applications are inflexible and difficult to change, component-based applications are flexible and adaptive.

An "n-tier" software architecture specifies that an application should be segregated into at least three separate sections or tiers—the user interface (tier 1), business logic (tier 2), and data services (tier 3). These three tiers can be divided down further into subtiers—thus the designation "n-tier."

Dividing an application into different tiers allows you to change its user interface, business logic, or data services without having a tremendous impact on the other tiers. For example, you can easily replace your Win32 Visual FoxPro interface with a thin-client browser without affecting the application's middle-tier business logic or back-end data services. You can also change your application's back-end data from Visual FoxPro to SQL Server without changing its business logic or user interface.

Of all the different tiers in an n-tier application, the most challenging to create is the business tier. If you do not place business logic inside user interface elements, where should the code be located? Your application business logic should reside within business objects.

An introduction to business objects

What is a business object? A business object is a high-level object that usually represents a real-world person, place, event, or business process. For example, in a point-of-sale invoicing application you could create business objects such as:

- Customer

- Inventory

- Payment

As shown in **Figure 2**, business objects allow you to encapsulate all of the characteristics and behavior of a real-world entity in a single class rather than spreading the code throughout the four corners of your application's user interface. For example, all the code that has something to do with invoicing is in the Invoice object. All the code that has something to do with inventory is in the Inventory object and so on.

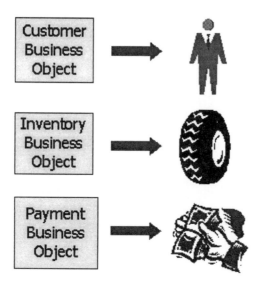

Figure 2. Business objects encapsulate characteristics and behavior of real-world entities into a single class.

Visual FoxPro does not have a business object base class. However, you can create your own business object base class from any of Visual FoxPro's non-visual classes such as the Container, Custom, or Session class. The Visual FoxPro documentation recommends using the Session class because of its ability to isolate data with a private data session.

The use of business objects is common in object-oriented languages such as SmallTalk, Java, and C++. For more information on the use of business objects and for a larger view of the OOP community in general, check out Object Management Group's Web site at **www.omg.org**.

Benefits of using business objects

As already mentioned, the biggest benefit of using business objects in your applications is the flexibility and scalability they provide. However, there are additional benefits that you should also consider.

Bridging the semantic gap

In the world of structured programming, there exists something called the "semantic gap." This is the gap between a software application and the real world. In the real world, there are customers, invoices, inventory, taxes, and orders. However, if you peek under the hood of a procedural program, you won't find an invoice or any other entity. You might find an invoice form, an invoice report, and various functions and procedures related to invoicing—but there is no single entity that represents the real-world invoice.

Business objects make complex software systems easier to understand, create, and maintain because they bridge the semantic gap. They provide a one-to-one correspondence between objects in the real world and objects within your software application.

Although at first the concept of business objects may be difficult to grasp, once you understand it, you'll never want to go back! The use of business objects makes the job of analysis, design, software construction, and maintenance far easier than procedural techniques.

Beating the "where's the code" problem

One of the most difficult aspects of software development is the problem of figuring out "where's the code." In monolithic software applications, code can be hiding just about anywhere! It can be very frustrating and time-consuming to track down code that is tucked inside a user interface control buried deep within the container hierarchy of a form.

In contrast, it's much easier to locate code in an application that uses business objects. For example, if there's a bug in an application's invoicing logic, the problem code is probably in the Invoice object. If you need to change the algorithm of a tax calculation, you need look no further than the Tax Strategy object.

Normalizing application logic

Visual FoxPro developers are usually very particular about properly normalizing application data. However, this penchant for normalization doesn't usually carry over to application logic—especially when working with a team of developers. Often, you can find the same or similar application logic repeated several times throughout an application. This is a by-product of having application logic scattered throughout the user interface.

In contrast, when using business objects, it's less likely that you will create two methods on a business object that do the exact same thing. Business objects surface your application logic into logical entities that are easy to create, debug, and maintain.

Business objects in COM servers

Typically, the only tool that can run Visual FoxPro code is Visual FoxPro—and if you store your application logic in functions and procedures, this is still true. However, if you place your application logic in the methods of business objects, it throws open the doors of reuse.

The magic that allows a wide variety of tools to access the code in your business objects is Microsoft's Component Object Model (COM). COM allows you to create software components that are programming language-independent. Not only can you *create* COM components using a wide variety of tools (Visual FoxPro, Visual Basic, C++, Delphi, Java, and so on), you can *use* them from an even wider collection of tools and technologies including Visual Basic for Applications, Active Server Pages, and the new Visual Studio.NET tools.

> *The key to making your applications accessible from Visual Studio.NET is to create component-based applications!*

How does COM make it possible for components written in different languages to communicate with each other? COM defines a software interface standard that specifies, at the binary level, how software components interact. COM acts as a common layer through which all COM-capable tools can communicate.

Visual FoxPro does all of the hard work involved in creating COM interfaces for your business objects. For details see Chapter 12, "Building World-Class COM Servers in VFP 7."

Location transparency with DCOM

As you have seen so far, COM enables software components written in different languages to communicate with each other. However, another extremely important feature of COM is its *location transparency*—the ability to access a component in a similar fashion regardless of its location. A COM component can reside just about anywhere—on your local computer, on a computer within your local area network, or across the world on a computer attached to the Internet.

The technology that gives COM its location transparency is Distributed COM (DCOM). Although you may hear DCOM discussed as if it were a technology that is separate from or in addition to COM, it isn't! DCOM is simply a term used to describe the location transparency feature of COM itself.

The ability to access components that reside on different computers opens up the world of enterprise-class distributed applications.

> *Microsoft's Component Object Model is not the only component standard in town! The majority of the non-Microsoft world adheres to the Common Object Request Broker Architecture (CORBA) binary standard. CORBA also provides language independence and location transparency. However, in contrast to COM, which is mostly a Windows-only technology, CORBA is a cross-platform standard (CORBA objects cannot be created in Visual FoxPro).*

Understanding MTS and COM+

With the advent of distributed computing, the need for an environment in which components running on remote computers could exist became apparent. Although DCOM made it possible to instantiate and access components on remote computers, you had to create homegrown solutions for implementing security, scalability, managing resources and data transactions on the remote computer.

Microsoft responded by creating Microsoft Transaction Server (MTS). MTS provided all of these services, freeing you from creating operating system-level services and allowing you to concentrate on building components that contain logic specific to your application.

COM+ is the next generation of COM and MTS—it is a runtime environment in which your COM components can run. Unlike MTS, which was an add-on for Windows NT, COM+ services are built directly into the Windows 2000 operating system. COM+ improves on the abilities of MTS and also provides new features such as loosely coupled events, queued components, and component load balancing.

What does .NET mean for COM?

Unless you've been living in a cave, you know that Microsoft has reinvented itself again. In a bid to maintain its status as the No. 1 software development tool vendor in the world, Microsoft has created the .NET development platform. The intent of .NET is to provide an integrated development environment in which you can more easily create world-class Internet applications. While other Microsoft tools have been retrofitted to integrate with the Internet, .NET was designed from its inception with the Internet in mind.

As part of its .NET initiative, Microsoft is creating Visual Studio.NET, which will include Visual Basic.NET, C++, and the new C# programming language. Although Visual FoxPro can be used in conjunction with .NET technology, it is not specifically a .NET language and will not be included in Visual Studio.NET. It will once again be distributed as a stand-alone Microsoft product.

> *This discussion is a high-level overview focused on .NET's impact on component development. For more details on .NET, check out Microsoft's .NET SDK documentation.*

The Common Language Runtime

One of the biggest changes in Visual Studio.NET is the introduction of the Common Language Runtime (CLR). A runtime is an environment in which programs are executed. In Visual Studio 6, each programming language has its own runtime. For example, when you create a COM component in Visual FoxPro 6, you must install the Visual FoxPro runtime on the machine on which the component runs. In contrast, all Visual Studio.NET languages share a common runtime, the CLR. The CLR only needs to be installed on a machine once, and then any .NET component can be installed without worrying about installing additional runtimes.

The CLR contains many features that are designed to make it easier to create components using .NET languages. For example, although it has been very easy to create components in Visual FoxPro and Visual Basic, it's been very difficult to do so in C++. The new CLR contains most of the "plumbing" necessary to create and manage software components, allowing you to concentrate on building the business logic for your components. The CLR also provides a far simpler model for deploying components. Rather than having to wrangle with DLL registration and version clashing, the CLR allows you to deploy a component simply by copying it to a computer and running it.

Regardless of which .NET programming language you use to create your components (also known as *assemblies*), when you compile .NET components rather than compiling down to machine code, they compile into an interpreted language called Microsoft Intermediate Language (MSIL, usually referred to as IL). As a secondary process (which can occur as late as when a component is executed), the IL code is compiled down to machine code and is passed on to the .NET runtime manager. The fact that components are initially stored in the IL format allows all .NET languages to use components created by other .NET languages.

The .NET component standard

What's important to note about all of this is that .NET has its own binary component standard that is completely different from the COM binary standard! What does this mean for the future of COM/COM+? What about Visual FoxPro, which isn't a .NET language and can't create .NET components?

Many believe that Microsoft's release of the .NET component standard means the immediate end of COM/COM+. Fortunately, this is not true. Microsoft realizes that most software companies (itself included) have a *major* investment in COM/COM+. For example, Microsoft's .NET Enterprise servers such as SQL Server 2000, BizTalk Server 2000, and Commerce Server 2000 are founded on COM/COM+—not on the .NET Framework (although they will eventually be updated to true .NET servers)! There is no compelling reason to spend a tremendous amount of time re-creating COM components as .NET components.

Based on this, rather than dropping support for COM/COM+ Microsoft is making it easy for both component standards to coexist peacefully. They have made it easy to treat a .NET component as a COM component and a COM component as a .NET component. See the section titled "Accessing COM components from .NET" in Chapter 12, "Building World-Class COM Servers in VFP 7," for details.

Summary

In this chapter, you have learned about the difference between monolithic and n-tier applications. You have also learned what business objects are and the benefits of using them in your applications. Finally, you saw how the COM binary standard allows reuse of software components and how COM fits into the .NET initiative. In the next chapter you will learn the details of building world-class COM servers in Visual FoxPro 7.

Chapter 12
Building World-Class COM
Servers in VFP 7

COM servers are the ticket for providing access to your Visual FoxPro applications from a wide variety of tools including COM+ Services, Internet technologies, and the new .NET Framework. This chapter shows how to use the new language enhancements in Visual FoxPro 7 to build COM servers that can easily be used from all of these technologies.

Originally, the creation of COM servers was a difficult process that was the sole domain of hardcore C++ developers. Eventually, Microsoft enhanced tools such as Visual FoxPro to make it easy to create COM servers. But this ease-of-use came with a price—loss of power. There were features available in the COM/COM+ standard that were not available in Visual FoxPro.

Fortunately, each release of Visual FoxPro continues to give more power back to you, and Visual FoxPro 7 is no exception. The enhancements described in this chapter provide a quantum leap in your ability to create world-class COM servers with Visual FoxPro!

Building a COM server

Visual FoxPro makes it very easy to create COM servers. All you need is a Visual FoxPro project that contains one or more classes marked as "OLEPUBLIC" (see the Visual FoxPro Help file topic "Creating Automation Servers" for details). As this implies, a single COM server can contain multiple COM objects.

In-process and out-of-process servers

COM servers come in two main flavors—*in-process* and *out-of-process*. Although this isn't new for Visual FoxPro 7, there are new reasons why you should choose to build one type of server or the other.

In Windows, each executing program runs in its own process or address space. COM objects in an in-process server (DLL) run in the same process as the client. COM objects in an out-of-process server (EXE) run in a process separate from the client. In-process servers run faster than out-of-process servers because there is no overhead required for cross-process marshalling (passing parameters to and from the address space of a client to the address space of a component). However, in-process servers can be "dangerous" because if the server dies, it can take the client down with it! In contrast, out-of-process servers run a bit more slowly, but they are safer because they run in a process separate from the client.

Which type of server should you create? That depends on how you want to use it. If you want to create an Automation server that has a user interface (as do Microsoft Office Automation servers), you must create an out-of-process COM server. This is because in-process servers cannot have a user interface or interact with the user interface in *any way*.

If you plan to use your COM servers with COM+, you *must* implement your server as an in-process DLL. COM+ provides a run-time environment in which your COM components are run, and it needs your server to be in-process so that it can exercise control over your components.

What about the safety issue with in-process servers? Fortunately, as shown in **Figure 1**, COM+ allows you to run an in-process server in a COM+ surrogate process that is separate from its client.

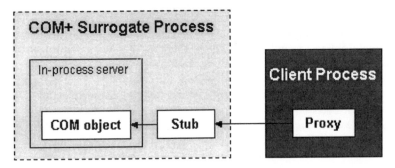

Figure 1. COM+ surrogate processes provide the fault-tolerance of an out-of-process server for in-process servers.

Since the release of Visual FoxPro 6 Service Pack 3, you can also choose between single-threaded and multi-threaded COM servers. Check the VFP 7 Help file topic "Selection of a Run-Time Library" for details.

Storing VFP 7 COM classes

You can store your OLE Public classes in either program files (PRG) or visual class libraries (VCX). However, be aware that certain VFP 7 enhancements are only available to COM classes stored in program files. Features not available to classes stored in visual class libraries include:

- Strong typing

- Implementing interfaces

- Case preservation in method and property names

- Specifying COM attributes

This is unfortunate because many Visual FoxPro developers find it easier to create classes using the visual class designer rather than creating them in procedure files. However, you can get around this limitation as follows:

1. Create your COM classes using the visual designers.

2. Create subclasses of your COM classes in program files.

3. Add the desired VFP 7 enhanced features (strong typing, interfaces, and so on) to the subclasses in the program files.

For example:

```
DEFINE CLASS ClientX AS Client FROM MyClasses.VCX OLEPUBLIC
   PROCEDURE GetCreditLimit(ClientID AS Integer) AS Currency
      RETURN DODEFAULT(ClientID)
   ENDPROC
ENDDEFINE
```

This can get tiresome pretty quickly, so hopefully the Fox team will address this issue in a future release of Visual FoxPro.

Understanding type libraries

Once you create a COM server, how can developers using other tools such as Visual Basic, C++, and Active Server Pages know how to use it? The answer is: by means of its *type library*.

A type library is a binary file that lists all the published classes in your COM server as well as their *interfaces*. A COM interface is a collection of public properties, events, and methods grouped together under one name. For more information on COM interfaces, see Chapter 13, "Implementing Interfaces."

When you compile a COM server, Visual FoxPro automatically creates a type library for you. It gives your type library the same name as your COM server, but with a TLB extension. A Visual FoxPro type library can be a stand-alone binary TLB file or can be included in a COM server DLL or EXE file. Type libraries can also be embedded in an ActiveX control (OCX). In addition to the information stored in the type library, each public class in your COM server is also added to the Windows Registry so COM services can locate them.

> If you compile a COM server on a Windows 9x machine, Visual FoxPro creates a separate type library file. If you compile a COM server on a Windows NT or Windows 2000 machine, Visual FoxPro still builds a separate type library file, but also includes the type library in the DLL or EXE.

In Visual FoxPro 6 you had very little control over the contents of the resulting type library. Many of the enhancements in Visual FoxPro 7 such as "strong typing" and "COM attributes" were added to allow you to create more descriptive type libraries.

Registry files

In addition to creating a type library file, Visual FoxPro automatically creates a Windows Registry file when you compile a COM server. The Registry file is given the same name as your COM server, but with a VBR extension.

The Registry file lists the global unique identifiers (GUIDs) for the classes in your server. A VBR Registry file is similar to a REG Registry file, except the VBR file does not contain hard-coded paths. VBR files can be used to register a COM server EXE remotely. For more information, see the VFP 7 Help topic "Clireg32.exe Remote Automation Utility."

Introducing the Object Browser

At long last, Visual FoxPro 7 gives FoxPro developers their own Object Browser! In previous versions of VFP, you had to use another tool's Object Browser (such as Visual Basic or Visual InterDev, or even Microsoft Word) to view your COM components.

The VFP 7 Object Browser's searching capabilities and its ability to view interface information make it one of the best Object Browsers available. As shown in **Figure 2**, the Web browser-like interface—complete with Back, Forward, Refresh, and Find buttons—also makes it a pleasure to use.

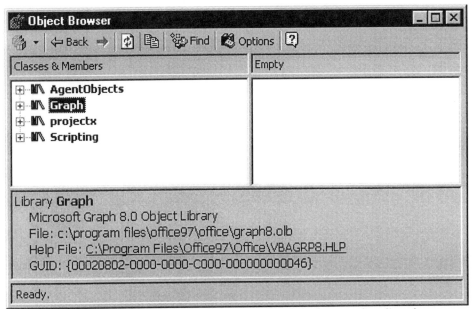

Figure 2. The Object Browser's Web browser-like interface makes it a pleasure to use.

The _OBJECTBROWSER system variable specifies the name of the Object Browser application—by default it is set to "ObjectBrowser.APP" located in the Visual FoxPro 7 home directory. To specify a different Object Browser, you can select Tools | Options from the menu and modify the Object Browser selection in the File Locations tab.

Opening type libraries

You can launch the Object Browser by selecting Tools | Object Browser from the menu. To open a type library, click the Open Type Library button (located in the upper left corner of the Object Browser), which launches the Open dialog shown in **Figure 3**. If you click on the "down arrow" button next to the Open Type Library button, it displays a list of most recently used type libraries from which you can select.

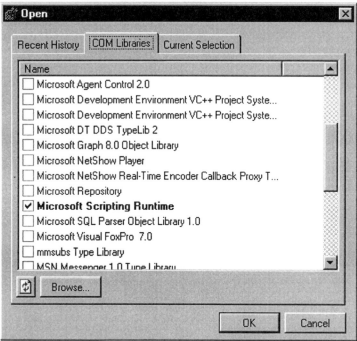

Figure 3. You can easily open type libraries by selecting from a list of all type libraries registered on your computer.

The Recent History tab lists the most recently opened type libraries. The COM Libraries tab displays a list of COM server type libraries registered on your computer. Click the Browse button to find one that's not in the list, or click the Reload System Component From Registry button to refresh the list from your system Registry. The Current Selection tab lists all type libraries that are currently open in the Object Browser.

Viewing type libraries

As shown in Figure 1, you can open multiple type libraries in the Object Browser at the same time. When you select a type library, the Description pane in the lower portion of the Object Browser displays information on the selected type library. If a server has an associated Help file, a hyperlink from which you can launch the Help file is displayed in the Description pane.

Viewing class details

You can drill down into a type library and view details of classes in a COM server. (**Figure 4** shows an example.) When you select a class in the Classes & Members left pane, its Events, Methods, and Properties are displayed in the Members pane on the right side.

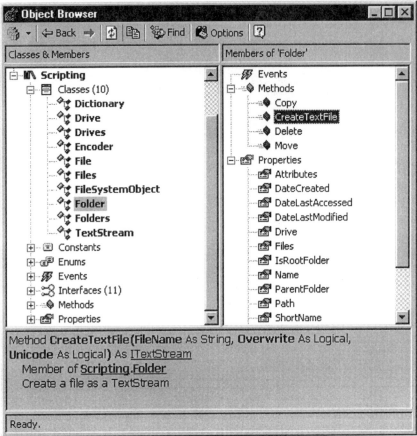

Figure 4. *Class events, methods, and properties details can be viewed in the Object Browser.*

In addition, you can click hyperlinks in the Description pane to go directly to an item for more information. Protected members in the left pane are shown with a lock icon.

Object Browser caching

To improve the speed of loading class details, VFP 7's Object Browser provides intelligent type library caching. When you open a type library for the first time, the Object Browser adds a "history" record to its ObjectBrowser.DBF table. History records in this table are used to data drive the Recent History tab of the Object Browser's Open dialog—however, this is history, not caching.

The real caching takes place when you open a type library in the browser and expand the Constants, Enums, Events, Methods, or Properties nodes in the Classes & Members pane. The Object Browser creates a separate record in the ObjectBrowser.DBF table for each one of these nodes that you expand. The cached information is stored as XML in the Properties memo field of the ObjectBrowser.DBF table. You can clear the cache for a type library by right-clicking on the type library in the Classes & Members pane and selecting Clear Cache from the context menu.

The Object Browser's caching is intelligent in that it only caches type libraries that are 60 days or older. This means the browser won't cache type libraries where the dust hasn't settled yet!

Understanding constants and enums

The Object Browser allows you to see the constants and enums associated with a type library. Constants are similar to a numeric #DEFINE in Visual FoxPro. An enum is a set of named integer constants. For example:

```
Jan=1, Feb=2, Mar=3, Apr=4...
```

Unfortunately, even though the Object Browser can display a COM server's constants and enums, you can't create and expose constants and enums in the servers you create using Visual FoxPro 7.

A *very* cool feature of the Object Browser is the ability to create a set of #DEFINE statements for all constants in a type library by dragging and dropping the Constants node from the Object Browser onto an editor window (see **Figure 5**).

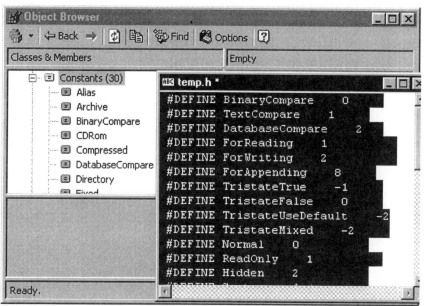

Figure 5. You can drag the Constants node from the Object Browser to an editor window to automatically create #DEFINE statements.

> The Object Browser also displays interface information for your
> COM server classes. COM interfaces are discussed in Chapter 13,
> "Implementing Interfaces."

Searching type libraries

If you click the Object Browser's Find button, it displays a Find pane at the top of the browser
as shown in **Figure 6**.

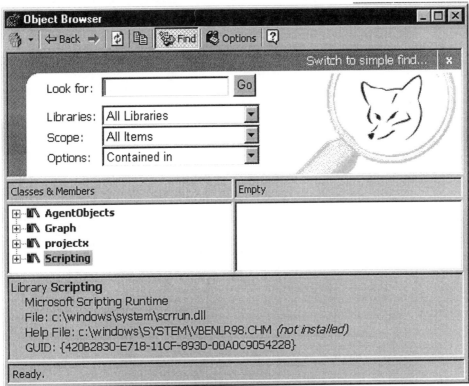

Figure 6. *The Object Browser's Find pane allows you to perform searches for text
in a type library.*

You can switch between the simple and advanced find panes to easily search for text in a
type library. The advanced find allows you to narrow your search to a particular library or an
element in a library (classes, constants, enums, interfaces, methods and events, properties). See
the Visual FoxPro 7 Help topic "Object Browser Window" for details on the Find features of
the Object Browser.

Setting Object Browser options

The Object Browser's Options button launches a dialog that allows you to set a variety of
display options. As shown in **Figure 7**, the options are a powerful tool for personalizing the

Object Browser display to your liking. See the Visual FoxPro 7 Help topic "Object Browser Window" for details on each of these options.

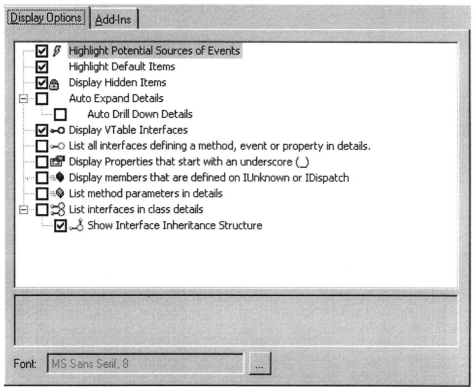

Figure 7. *The Object Browser's Options dialog allows you to set a variety of display options.*

Installing add-ins for the Object Browser
The Fox team has made it easy to extend the functionality of the Object Browser by means of add-ins. An Add-Ins Setup Wizard is provided for registering custom add-ins with the Object Browser. Check the Visual FoxPro 7 Help file topic "Using the Object Browser" for details.

The FoxRuntime Registry key identifier
When you register a Visual FoxPro 7 COM server in the system Registry, the entry contains a new Registry key named "FoxRuntime." This new key, shown in **Figure 8**, allows you to easily determine the Visual FoxPro run-time library used by the server.

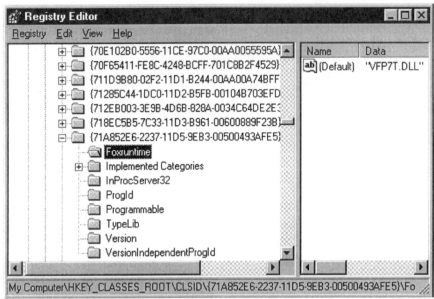

Figure 8. *The new FoxRuntime Registry key specifies which Visual FoxPro runtime is used by your COM server.*

Method and property visibility

In addition to the ability to specify which classes in your COM server are accessible by the outside world, you can also specify which properties, events, and methods (PEMs) of these classes are *visible* (publicly accessible). Almost all of the COM objects you create should have some portion of their functionality hidden, or protected.

The biggest reasons to limit access to your components are to prevent developers from:

- Doing something dangerous: Providing access to certain COM object methods has the potential for generating application errors or possibly corrupting your application's data.

- Doing something illogical: It doesn't make sense to call some class methods directly. For example, in the example code for this chapter, the KBizObj class defined in the KBizness.PRG file has a method called CreateDataSession(). This method instantiates a private data session for the business object. This only needs to be run once when the object is first instantiated and should never be run again. To prevent developers from running this method, it is marked as PROTECTED.

- Doing something illegal: There are many functions a business object can perform that, if exposed for public consumption, would break the security and rules of your application. For example, if you allowed developers to bypass methods that validate business rules and directly call methods that save data to the back end, your application's integrity would be violated.

Specifying visibility in Visual FoxPro 6

Visual FoxPro 6 provided the ability to specify the visibility of properties and methods as either public, protected, or hidden.

- Public: Unless you specify otherwise, properties and methods are public by default. This means that they are visible to other objects within a COM server and to external clients using your server.

- Protected: When a property or method of a class is marked as protected, it is visible to methods and events within that class or its subclasses. It is not visible at all outside of the COM server.

- Hidden: Hidden properties and methods cannot be accessed outside of the class definition—even by subclasses.

However, there are cases where you may want finer control than what these three settings have to offer. For example, the KBizness class in this chapter's example code (shown in **Figure 9**) has an associated data services class that contains the "rubber meets the road" data manipulation code. Both the KBizness class and the data services class have an Error event. When an error occurs in the data services class, it needs to pass the error up to the business object's Error event. Surfacing errors allows clients using your components to see errors that occur deeper in the containership hierarchy.

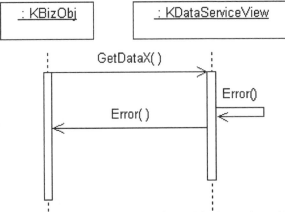

Figure 9. *The KDataServiceView object needs public access to KBizObj's GetDataX() method so it can surface errors to the business object.*

However, here's the catch—in order for the data service object (KDataServiceView) to call the business object's Error event, that Error event must be marked as public. However, if it's marked as public, it means that clients using your COM server will *also* have access to this method. Although this may not be dangerous, it certainly doesn't make sense to expose it in the COM interface. This is where Visual FoxPro 7's enhanced COM abilities come the rescue.

Specifying visibility in Visual FoxPro 7

VFP 7's DEFINE CLASS command has a new _COMATTRIB flags setting that allows you to specify that a PEM is restricted, hidden, or non-browsable. In the case of the Error event, you can use the new hidden setting, which specifies that a PEM is hidden from the object model—it's not displayed in Object Browsers, but it is still public. Since it's not shown in Object Browsers, clients don't know it exists! Here is the code from the example project's KBizness.PRG file that uses the new _COMATTRIB setting:

```
FUNCTION Error
ENDFUNC
Error_COMATTRIB = COMATTRIB_HIDDEN
```

 The CustomX class located in Common\Libs\KBizness.PRG in the Developer Downloads at *www.hentzenwerke.com* demonstrates the use of the new _COMATTRIB flags.

The _COMATTRIB flags can be added together to specify multiple property and method attributes. Check the Visual FoxPro 7 Help topic "DEFINE CLASS Command" for details on the other _COMATTRIB visibility settings.

Before distributing a COM server, open it in the Object Browser to make sure you've set the visibility correctly on all properties, events, and methods!

Specifying read-only and write-only properties

In addition to setting visibility for PEMs, the _COMATTRIB setting also allows you to specify that a property is READONLY or WRITEONLY. Note that this is for properties only, not for methods.

To understand how the READONLY and WRITEONLY features work, you need to know that there really are no true properties in a COM interface. In COM, properties are actually implemented as two methods—a PropertyGet() method and a PropertyLet() method. If you use the COMATTRIB_READONLY setting to specify that a property is read-only, you are really specifying that the PropertySet() method is not implemented for that property. Likewise, if you use the COMATTRIB_WRITEONLY setting to specify that a property is write-only, you are really specifying that the PropertyGet() method is not implemented for that property.

Specifying property and method attributes

Visual FoxPro 7 provides new capabilities for specifying attributes of methods and properties. A mix of COMATTRIB arrays and new parameters of the DEFINE CLASS command can be used to achieve control over property and method attributes in your type libraries.

Using COMATTRIB arrays to specify attributes

In addition to using a single COMATTRIB statement to specify attribute flags for a PEM, you can also create COMATTRIB *arrays* to set additional attributes—specifically help string, capitalization, property type, and number of parameters. In the example code, the KBizness.PRG file's KBizObj class definition contains the following COMATTRIB array used to set the attributes of the lError property:

```
lError = .F.

DIMENSION lError_COMATTRIB[5]
lError_COMATTRIB[1] = COMATTRIB_READONLY
lError_COMATTRIB[2] = "Specifies whether an error has occurred"
lError_COMATTRIB[3] = "lError"
lError_COMATTRIB[4] = "Boolean"
lError_COMATTRIB[5] = 0
```

 *The KBizObj class located in Common\Libs\KBizness.PRG in the Developer Downloads at **www.hentzenwerke.com** demonstrates the use of the _COMATTRIB array.*

As you can see, the naming convention for the _COMATTRIB array consists of the name of the property, an underscore, and "COMATTRIB" (for example, MyProperty_ COMATTRIB).

The first line of this code defines the lError public property and its default value. The second line dimensions a COMATTRIB array containing five rows for specifying attributes of the lError property (**Table 1** describes the function of each COMATTRIB array element).

Table 1. *The COMATTRIB array allows you to specify attributes for both properties and methods.*

Element #	Description
1	Attribute flags. Bit flags used to specify that a method or property is restricted, hidden, or non-browsable. Also used to specify properties as read-only or write-only. Multiple flags can be set simultaneously by adding bit values together.
2	Help string.
3	Method/Property name capitalization.
4	Property type (currency, date, variant, and so on).
5	Number of required parameters. If you specify a number less than the actual number of parameters, the additional parameters are declared optional.

Regardless of whether or not you need to specify all five attributes in a COMATTRIB array, Visual FoxPro still requires that a COMATTRIB array have all five rows with a default value of the proper type for each row. For example, here is a COMATTRIB array that specifies the default setting for each attribute for a property named "MyProperty":

```
MyProperty_COMATTRIB[1] = 0
MyProperty_COMATTRIB[2] = ""
MyProperty_COMATTRIB[3] = ""
```

```
MyProperty_COMATTRIB[4] = ""
MyProperty_COMATTRIB[5] = 0
```

Specifying method attributes

Although COMATTRIB arrays can be used to set attributes of both properties and methods, VFP 7 provides an additional (and easier) method for setting some attributes of methods. For example, to specify the capitalization of a method name, all you need to do is type the method as you would like it to appear in the type library and VFP 7 writes it to the type library as is.

If you want to specify the help string for a method, you can use the new HELPSTRING parameter:

```
PROCEDURE GetError(tnError) AS String ;
  HELPSTRING "Returns the nth error from the business object"
ENDPROC
```

In addition, you can also specify the type of a method's return value and parameters within the DEFINE CLASS command.

Strong typing

Visual FoxPro is a weakly typed language—all variables are *variants*. This means that you can create a variable without specifying its type and you can store a value of any type in the variable. For example:

```
LOCAL luVariable

luVariable = "Weak typing is fun!"
? luVariable
luVariable = DATE()
? luVariable
luVariable = 777
? luVariable + 5
luVariable = .T.
? luVariable
```

In a strongly typed language, you must declare variables as a certain data type and you can only store values of that type in the variable. Strong typing helps enforce good programming practices and helps catch bugs at compile time. Here is an example of strong typing in Visual Basic:

```
Dim MyMessage AS String
MyMessage = "Strong typing enforces good programming"
```

Although you might argue the merits of weak typing, when it comes to creating type libraries, weak typing is definitely not desirable. What's the issue? When developers who are using strongly typed languages use your COM servers, they want to know:

- What each method does.

- What parameters (including their types) are passed to each method.

- What return value (including type) is returned from each method.

Figure 10 shows a type library of a COM server created using Visual FoxPro 6.

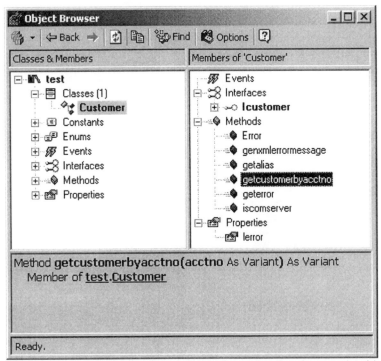

Figure 10*. Type libraries created by Visual FoxPro 6 are only able to show method parameters and return values as variants.*

Notice in the bottom pane of the Object Browser that the acctno parameter and the return value of the method are both variants.

Visual FoxPro 7 now has strong typing support. Although strong typing is *not* enforced within the Visual FoxPro language, you can specify the types of parameters and return values in the DEFINE CLASS command by means of the new AS clause. For example, here's the portion of the DEFINE CLASS function needed to specify the types of the parameters and return value of the GetCustomerByAcctNo shown in Figure 10:

```
PROCEDURE GetCustomerByAcctNo(AcctNo AS String) AS String ;
```

This method declaration specifies that the AcctNo parameter and the return value of the method are both strings. **Figure 11** shows how the type library created by Visual FoxPro looks using strong typing for the GetCustomerByAcctNo() method.

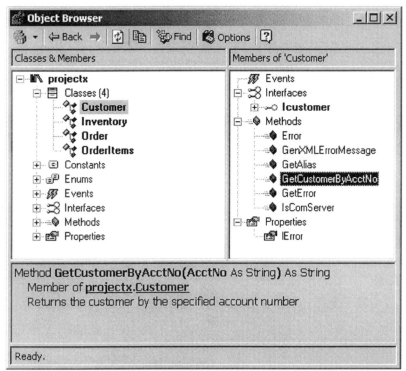

Figure 11. *Type libraries created in Visual FoxPro 7 can specify the type of method parameters and return values.*

Notice in the bottom panel of the Object Browser that the AcctNo parameter and the method return value are both strings. This makes it much easier to determine how to use a Visual FoxPro COM server. Check the Visual FoxPro 7 Help topic "DEFINE CLASS Command" for a table showing how Visual FoxPro's data types are mapped to COM data types.

Returning VOID from methods

Certain technologies such as COM+ Queued Components require that a method does not return anything. To specify that a VFP 7 method does not return anything, set its return value to VOID. For example:

```
PROCEDURE MyMethod() AS VOID
    RETURN
ENDPROC
```

It's good to note that this is really just for the benefit of building the type library. In the preceding code, MyMethod() still returns True. However, the fact that the type library says it returns nothing is good enough for COM+.

Passing strongly typed parameters by reference

In Visual FoxPro 7, the new @ token can be used to specify that a parameter passed to a COM server must be passed by reference. For example:

```
PROCEDURE GetDate(DateParm AS Date @)
  DateParm = DATE()
  RETURN
ENDPROC
```

In this class definition, the @ token specifies that the DateParm parameter should be passed by reference. Late binding clients do not encounter an error when passing a parameter by value if it is specified to be passed by reference. Early binding clients, however, will receive an error. For an explanation of early binding vs. late binding, see Chapter 13, "Implementing Interfaces."

Using the Session class in COM servers

The Visual FoxPro 7 Help file recommends that you use the Session class to create your COM server business objects. This is because using the Session class automatically provides your business objects with their own private data session. This prevents multiple instances of business objects from stepping on each other's data. As an added bonus, VFP 7 automatically excludes the intrinsic Session class PEMs and only writes your custom properties and methods to the type library.

However, if you plan to use your business objects in both desktop *and* Web environments, you may want to take a different approach. Although it's desirable for a business object in a COM server to have its own private data session, when the same business object is used in a desktop application, it's desirable for the business object to use the default data session of the form that instantiated it. Since the Session object's DataSession property is read-only at run time, there's no way to dynamically switch between a private and default data session dynamically.

However, if you use an approach similar to that taken with the business objects in the example code for this chapter, you can get the best of both worlds. The KBizObj class (located in KBizness.PRG) is based on VFP's Custom class. Instead of *being* a Session object, KBizObj *has* a Session object that's automatically instantiated at run time only when the business object is created from a COM server. The business object uses its IsCOMServer() method to determine how it was instantiated.

Passing arrays to COM servers

At times it's useful to pass arrays to COM servers as method parameters. In Visual FoxPro 6, the COMARRAY() function allowed you to pass an array by reference or by value. It also let you specify whether the array was zero-based (the first element, row, and column are referenced with 0).

Visual FoxPro 7 extends COMARRAY() by specifying an additional setting for the nNewValue parameter. The new, additive setting (100) specifies that the array passed to the COM server is a fixed size and cannot be redimensioned.

Returning information about a COM object

In some cases, you may want to programmatically determine Registry settings for a COM object at run time. In Visual FoxPro 6, the COMCLASSINFO command returned a COM object's:

- Programmatic identifier (ProgID)

- VersionIndependentProgID

- Friendly name

- Class ID (CLSID)

In Visual FoxPro 7, if you issue the COMCLASSINFO command passing 5 as the nInfoType parameter, it returns the type of the COM object passed (Visual FoxPro object, ActiveX control, COM component, or OLEBound object). See the Visual FoxPro 7 Help topic "COMCLASSINFO() Function" for details.

Accessing COM components from .NET

As mentioned in the section "The .NET component standard" in Chapter 11, "Building Component-Based Software," the .NET Framework introduces a new binary component standard that is different from the "classic" COM binary standard.

Microsoft has provided tools that allow .NET and COM components to work with each other. Before describing these tools, you first need to learn about .NET *assemblies* and *manifests*.

.NET assemblies and manifests

.NET components are referred to as "assemblies." A .NET assembly is similar in function to a COM component, but does not need to be added to the system Registry. The simple act of copying a .NET assembly to the appropriate folder on a computer makes it ready for use.

.NET assemblies have "manifests," which are similar to COM component type libraries. Manifests contain metadata describing the classes in the assembly. This metadata is stored in binary format, but can be exported to an XML schema or to a COM type library.

.NET early and late binding

Amazingly enough, if you want to access your COM components via late binding in products such as ASP.NET, you don't need to do anything special. You can simply use either the Server.CreateObject or the CreateObject() method to instantiate objects from your COM server.

Although it's *possible* to access your COM components this way via late binding, you should use early binding whenever possible. This is because late-bound code runs much more slowly than early-bound code.

Using the Type Library Importer to achieve early binding

The .NET Framework has a utility called the Type Library Importer (TblImp.EXE). This utility converts a COM type library into an equivalent .NET manifest. It encapsulates the manifest into a proxy assembly called a *Runtime Callable Wrapper* (RCW). This RCW is the key that allows your COM component to be accessed by means of early binding from .NET code. As **Figure 12** indicates, the RCW consumes the interfaces exposed by your COM component and in turn re-exposes them as .NET component interfaces.

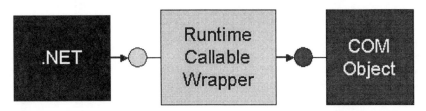

Figure 12. The Runtime Callable Wrapper allows .NET components to access your COM objects.

You can run the Type Library Importer (located in the Microsoft Visual Studio.NET\Common7\Tools directory) from the command prompt. The syntax for calling TblImp is:

```
TblImp cTypeLibrary /out:cRCW
```

where cTypeLibrary is the path and name of your COM server type library and cRCW specifies the path and name you want to give your Runtime Callable Wrapper. For example:

```
"c:\program files\microsoft visual studio.net\common7\tools\tlbimp.exe" ;
  ProjectX.dll /out:RCWProjectX.dll
```

Using the IL Disassembler tool

After running the Type Library Importer, you can view the contents of your new Runtime Callable Wrapper using VS.NET's IL Disassembler tool (ILDASM.EXE). You can run the IL Disassembler (located in the Microsoft Visual Studio.NET\Common7\Tools directory) from the command prompt. For example:

```
"c:\program files\microsoft visual studio.net\common7\tools\ildasm.exe"
```

After launching the Disassembler (shown in **Figure 13**), choose File | Open from the menu and select your new Runtime Callable Wrapper. The Disassembler allows you to see the public classes and methods referenced in your COM component's RCW. Directly under the word "MANIFEST," you'll see a "namespace" with the same name as your COM server DLL. In the .NET Framework, a namespace is a logical grouping of related classes, interfaces, and structures.

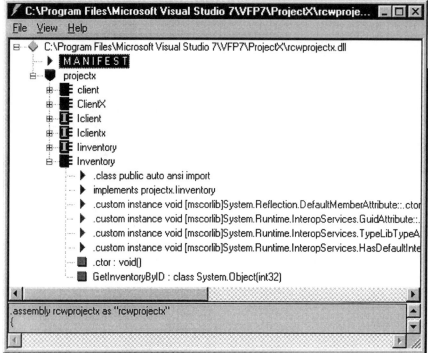

Figure 13. The .NET Framework's IL Disassembler allows you to view the contents of your COM component's Runtime Callable Wrapper.

Your RCW can be added to a Visual Studio.NET project by means of VS.NET's Solution Explorer. Just launch the Add Reference dialog by right-clicking on the References node. From the .NET Framework tab, browse and select your RCW and a reference to it is added to the project.

Accessing your COM server from ASP.NET

If you want to access your COM server from ASP.NET, the first step is to copy your server's RCW into the Bin directory of an ASP.NET application.

To easily reference your component from an ASP.NET page, just add the following line at the top of your ASP page:

```
<%Import namespace="COMServerNameSpace" %>
```

where COMServerNameSpace is the namespace of your COM server assigned within your RCW (see Figure 13). For example:

```
<%Import namespace="projectx" %>
```

After importing your server's namespace, you can easily instantiate and use objects from the server, as shown in this Visual Basic.NET code sample:

```
DIM oInventory AS Inventory
DIM cXML AS String

' Instantiate the Inventory object using the New command
oInventory = new Inventory

' Call the Inventory object's GetInventoryByID method
cXML = oInventory.GetInventoryByID("A123-45")
```

Advanced server capabilities

There are several miscellaneous commands that provide advanced capabilities for working with COM objects. These settings are specifically designed for advanced users and should be implemented with caution.

Using the new COMPROP() function

The new COMPROP() function changes the behavior of a COM server in two ways based on the specified property parameter.

If you specify "UTF8" as the second parameter, COMPROP() prevents a COM server from converting passed strings from Unicode to ANSI. Specifying this setting can, for example, prevent the display of multi-byte characters as question marks. For a good example of this use of COMPROP(), see the Visual FoxPro 7 Help topic "COMPROP() Function."

Specifying "PUTREF" as the second parameter allows you to work with ActiveX controls and COM objects that require object assignments as PROPERTY_PUTREF (Visual FoxPro defaults to PROPERTY_PUT). If you use COMPROP() to set a COM object's PUTREF, Visual FoxPro first attempts object assignment as PROPERTY_PUTREF. If this doesn't work, it tries PROPERTY_PUT instead.

For each of the COMPROP() uses, setting the third parameter to 0 specifies the default behavior and setting it to something else specifies the alternate behavior. For example, if the second parameter in COMPROP() is "UTF8", passing 0 as the third parameter causes the COM object to convert strings returned from methods from Unicode to ANSI. Passing 1 as the third parameter prevents the conversion from Unicode to ANSI.

SYS(2336)—critical section support

The new SYS(2336) function allows you to call the EnterCriticalSection and LeaveCriticalSection Windows API functions when working with multi-threaded COM server DLLs. In an MTDLL, critical sections provide thread synchronization, allowing only one thread to enter an object method at a time. If there is code in your COM components that is not thread-safe (not safe to be run by multiple threads of execution), you can bracket the code with calls to SYS(2336) to block other threads from calling the unsafe code. For example:

```
SYS(2336,1)    && Enter critical section

*** Place your unsafe code here

SYS(2336,2)    && Leave critical section
```

As mentioned in the Visual FoxPro 7 Help topic "SYS(2336)—Critical Section Support," see MSDN for more information on critical sections.

SYS(2339)—clean up references to unused libraries

The new SYS(2339) is used to get and set the value of an internal Visual FoxPro variable called g_CallCoFreeOnRelease. This variable specifies whether Visual FoxPro automatically cleans up references to unused libraries when releasing other servers.

> *In Visual FoxPro 6, this variable was set to 1, which automatically freed up unused libraries. In Visual FoxPro 7, the default has been changed to 0, which does* not *free unused libraries when another instance of a COM server is released.*

SYS(2340)—specifying NT service support

The new SYS(2340) command is used to enable or disable Windows NT service support. It intercepts logoff messages from Windows NT (or Windows 2000) and allows you to specify whether a COM server should continue running or shut down. You may need to use this function to prevent your COM server from being shut down if it is running a critical process.

Summary

The COM server enhancements discussed in this chapter, such as strong typing and property attributes, go a long way toward helping you create COM servers that can be used from a wide variety of clients, including COM+.

The new Object Browser allows you to fine-tune and inspect the COM servers that you build as well as to view and understand type libraries of COM servers created by other developers.

In addition, Microsoft has made it easy to access your COM servers from the new .NET languages and next-generation Web technologies such as ASP.NET.

Chapter 13
Implementing Interfaces

Visual FoxPro 7 blows the doors off limitations in previous versions of VFP by allowing you to implement COM interfaces. This functionality is critical for supporting COM+ Services such as COM+ Events. This chapter explains what it means to implement an interface and shows you how to use this ability in your VFP 7 COM servers.

Starting with version 3.0, Visual FoxPro supported a brand of inheritance known as "implementation inheritance." This means a subclass inherits the properties, events, and methods of its parent class as well as the code (the implementation) contained within the parent's methods.

As shown in **Figure 1**, the ABizObj class inherits the Init(), CreateDataService(), CreateDataSession(), Cursor2XML(), and other methods from the KBizObj class. The Customer, Order, and Inventory classes in turn inherit these methods and their implementation code from ABizObj.

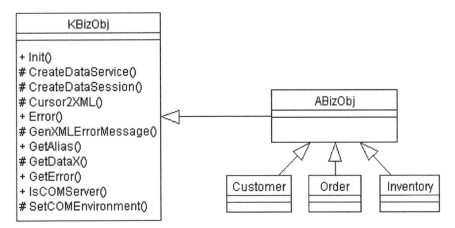

Figure 1. *Visual FoxPro's implementation inheritance allows subclasses to inherit methods and their corresponding implementation code.*

In contrast, Visual Basic, through version 6.0, does not have implementation inheritance. It has a different brand of inheritance known as *interface inheritance*. In version 7.0, Visual FoxPro also gains the ability to implement COM interfaces.

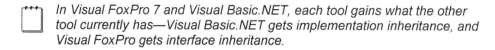

In Visual FoxPro 7 and Visual Basic.NET, each tool gains what the other tool currently has—Visual Basic.NET gets implementation inheritance, and Visual FoxPro gets interface inheritance.

What is interface inheritance and what does it mean for Visual FoxPro? In order to understand how to use this powerful feature, you need to first learn more about COM interfaces.

Understanding interfaces

In the world of object-oriented programming, the class is everything—classes are the foundation for your applications and are vehicles for reusing application logic. You can create a class, subclass it, and then extend its functionality by placing code in the methods of the subclass. Unlike Visual FoxPro, COM does not support implementation inheritance! For example, you cannot create a subclass of a COM Employee class that inherits the code contained within the Employee class methods.

In COM, the interface is everything. A COM interface is a set of related methods that define a particular type of behavior. However, it is more than just a casual grouping of related methods in a class. It conforms to a strict binary standard that defines how COM-enabled tools can communicate with COM objects. An interface is the only means by which a client can communicate with a COM component.

Every COM interface has a globally unique identifier (GUID) that uniquely identifies it. This GUID remains the same regardless of the machine on which a COM server is installed. In Visual FoxPro, this GUID is assigned when you compile a COM server.

Interfaces in Visual FoxPro COM servers

Visual FoxPro hides much of the complexity inherent in creating COM servers. When you build a COM server, Visual FoxPro automatically creates a *default* COM interface for each of your OLE Public classes. This interface is given the same name as your class plus an "I" prefix, and it contains all of your public class methods.

For example, if you create an OLE Public class named Customer, when you build your server, Visual FoxPro automatically creates a COM interface for your object named ICustomer (see **Figure 2**). It is through the ICustomer interface that all clients communicate with your Customer COM object.

*The source code for the examples used in this chapter is available in the Developer Download files at **www.hentzenwerke.com**.*

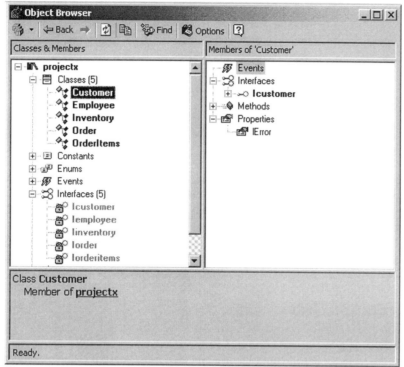

Figure 2. *Visual FoxPro automatically creates a default COM interface for your objects when you create a COM server.*

Understanding interface inheritance

Although COM does not support implementation inheritance, it does support interface inheritance. An interface is usually depicted as a "lollipop" in a class diagram using the UML notation. **Figure 3** shows Developer, ProjectManager, and ARClerk classes that implement the IEmployee interface, and an EventSink class that implements an IRecordSetEvents interface.

With interface inheritance, a class only inherits the public methods of a COM interface—it does not inherit any implementation code. So, if you don't inherit any code, how does interface inheritance benefit you?

First of all, interface inheritance gives you polymorphism—the ability to treat different objects in the same manner. If two components support the same interface, a client can use the same code to manipulate either component. Using the example from Figure 3, any place your application code expects an Employee object, you can use a Developer, ProjectManager, or ARClerk object because they all support the Employee interface.

An interface is similar in concept to an abstract class in Visual FoxPro. An abstract class usually contains no code, but simply exists to define an interface for a family of related classes.

However, one of the greatest benefits of implementing interfaces is the ability to use your Visual FoxPro COM objects in COM+ events. Only components that have the ability to implement interfaces can take advantage of the advanced capabilities of COM+. For details see Chapter 14, "Playing in the COM+ Sandbox."

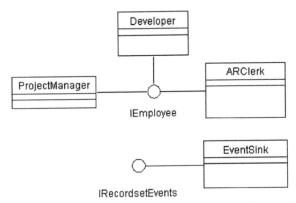

Figure 3. Classes can inherit the public methods of COM interfaces.

Supporting multiple interfaces

As mentioned earlier, Visual FoxPro automatically creates a default interface for each COM object when you compile a COM server. However, a single COM component can support more than one interface. In many cases, the client using a COM component may not even know all of the interfaces that a component supports.

The UML diagram in **Figure 4** shows the Developer class implementing both the IEmployee and the IUser interfaces. This models the real world—a developer can be both an employee and a system user. Implementing these interfaces allows the Developer object to be manipulated as an employee or as a system user.

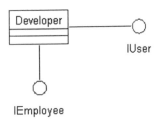

Figure 4. COM objects can implement one or more interfaces.

Creating new interfaces for new versions of COM components

One of the cardinal rules of COM is that once you have published a COM interface, it cannot change. If you change a COM interface, you will break all the client applications that use your COM objects and rely on the existing interface.

The key to avoiding this problem is the ability to support multiple interfaces. When you release new versions of your components, rather than changing an existing interface, you can create a new interface and add it to your component. This allows existing applications to continue functioning while allowing newer applications to take advantage of enhancements to your components.

Implementing interfaces in Visual FoxPro 7

Since Visual FoxPro automatically creates a default COM interface for you, how can you get your COM objects to support additional interfaces? In Visual FoxPro 7, the new IMPLEMENTS keyword of the DEFINE CLASS command allows you to specify that a COM class supports additional COM interfaces. For example:

```
DEFINE CLASS Developer AS ABizObj OLEPUBLIC

  IMPLEMENTS IEmployee IN "projectx.Employee"
  IMPLEMENTS IUser IN "projectx.User"
  ...
```

This specifies that the Developer class supports three interfaces: its own default IDeveloper interface, the IEmployee interface, and the IUser interface. **Figure 5** shows the Developer class in the Object Browser—notice that all three interfaces are listed.

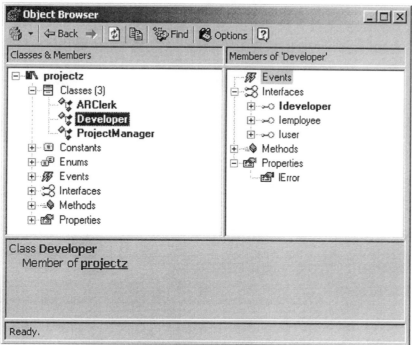

Figure 5. *The Object Browser displays all of the interfaces supported by a COM class.*

The syntax for the IMPLEMENTS declaration is:

```
IMPLEMENTS cInterfaceName [EXCLUDE] IN TypeLib | TypeLibGUID | ProgID
```

In this statement, cInterfaceName is the name of the interface to be implemented. You can either specify the name of the class that contains the default interface you want to implement (for example, Employee) or you can specify the actual interface name (for example, IEmployee).

The EXCLUDE keyword specifies that the implemented interface should be excluded from the type library. Although the interface is not displayed in the type library, clients can still access the interface if they know it exists in the class.

The IN clause is used to specify the location of the interface to be implemented. You can specify the interface location three different ways:

- By TypeLib (the type library that contains the interface). For example:

```
IMPLEMENTS IEmployee IN "c:\ProjectX\ProjectX.dll"
```

This is the least desirable option because it requires you to specify the path to the COM server, which is likely to change if you distribute your DLL.

- By the TypeLibGUID (the globally unique identifier of the type library that contains the COM object). For example:

```
IMPLEMENTS IEmployee IN {2C2392CE-3624-4CE6-ACB2-0C4FCA01B7BB}\1.0
```

You can determine the GUID of a type library by examining the VBR file that FoxPro creates when you compile your COM server. Notice that you must use the major and minor version designation when specifying the type library GUID.

- By the ProgID of the COM object containing the interface to be implemented. For example:

```
IMPLEMENTS IEmployee IN "ProjectX.Employee"
```

The ProgID is the name of the COM server ("ProjectX") and the name of the COM object ("Employee") separated by a period.

Supplying default implementations for interface members

When implementing an interface, you must supply a default implementation for each method in the implemented interface. For example:

```
DEFINE CLASS Developer AS ABizObj OLEPUBLIC

  IMPLEMENTS IUser IN "projectx.User"
  IMPLEMENTS IEmployee IN "projectx.Employee"

  PROTECTED PROCEDURE Iemployee_GetSalary(EmployeePK AS Number) AS Currency
  ENDPROC

  PROTECTED PROCEDURE Iemployee_GetHireDate(EmployeePK AS Number) AS DATE
  ENDPROC

  PROTECTED PROCEDURE Iemployee_GetStatus(EmployeePK AS Number) AS String
  ENDPROC

  PROTECTED PROCEDURE Iuser_GetUserGroups(UserPK AS Number) AS STRING
  ENDPROC

  PROTECTED PROCEDURE Iuser_GetUserID(UserPK AS Number) AS STRING
  ENDPROC

  PROTECTED PROCEDURE Iuser_GetUserPassword(UserPK AS Number) AS STRING
  ENDPROC

ENDDEFINE
```

Although it's not required that you add implementation code to the methods, you normally will since methods won't do very much without any code!

In addition, you must also provide a default implementation for any public properties in the interface you are implementing. Each property in a COM interface is actually implemented using two methods—a Get method and a Put method. You need to duplicate this structure in your class definition. For example, if the interface you're implementing contains a public UserName property, you would put the following implementation code in your class:

```
PROCEDURE Iuser_get_UserName() AS STRING;
  HELPSTRING "User Name"
ENDPROC

PROCEDURE Iuser_put_UserName(eValue AS STRING @);
  HELPSTRING "User Name"
ENDPROC
```

As you may have noticed, the default implementation methods you add to your class must be prefixed by the name of the associated interface. Why is this required? Since multiple interfaces can be implemented in a single class, it opens up the possibility that the interfaces you are implementing have methods with the same name. Adding the interface prefix avoids this interface naming collision.

Avoiding compiler errors

If you don't supply a default implementation for each method in an implemented interface, the Visual FoxPro compiler catches the error, displays a warning message similar to the one shown in **Figure 6**, and does not let you compile the server.

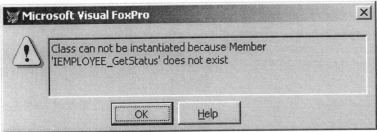

Figure 6. If you do not define a default implementation for all methods in an implemented interface, Visual FoxPro catches the error at compile time.

In addition, you must also specify the same number of parameters in an implemented method as specified in the original interface definition. If you do not specify the correct number of parameters, the compiler catches the error and displays a message similar to the one shown in **Figure 7**.

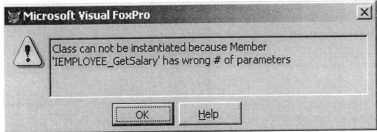

Figure 7. Visual FoxPro catches a mismatched number of parameters in implemented class methods at compile time.

Using the Object Browser to implement interfaces

Manually typing a default implementation for each property and method is time-consuming. Fortunately, Visual FoxPro 7's Object Browser makes creating default methods an easy task. You can drag an interface (by grabbing either the interface name or its associated icon) from the Object Browser onto a PRG file, and VFP 7 automatically generates all of the IMPLEMENTS code for you (see **Figure 8**).

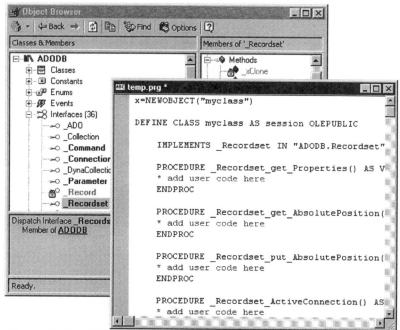

Figure 8. *The Object Browser makes implementing interfaces as easy as drag and drop!*

Protecting implemented interface methods

Typically, clients access your COM object's implemented interfaces by directly requesting a reference to the interface. Normally, you should mark implemented interface methods as PROTECTED so they are not visible in your COM object's default interface. **Figure 9** shows how unprotected methods appear in the Object Browser.

When you drag and drop an interface from the Object Browser, it makes all implemented methods public by default. This means you need to manually protect these methods yourself. To protect implemented interface methods, mark them as PROTECTED in the DEFINE CLASS command. For example:

```
DEFINE CLASS Developer AS Session OLEPUBLIC

  IMPLEMENTS Iemployee IN "projectx.Employee"

  PROTECTED PROCEDURE Iemployee_GetSalary(EmployeePK AS Number) AS Currency
  ENDPROC

  PROTECTED PROCEDURE Iemployee_GetHireDate(EmployeePK AS Number) AS DATE
  ENDPROC

  PROTECTED PROCEDURE Iemployee_GetStatus(EmployeePK AS Number) AS String
  ENDPROC
```

```
PROTECTED PROCEDURE Iuser_GetUserGroups(UserPK AS VARIANT @) AS VARIANT
ENDPROC

PROTECTED PROCEDURE Iuser_GetUserID(UserPK AS Number) AS STRING
ENDPROC

PROTECTED PROCEDURE Iuser_GetUserPassword(UserPK AS Number) AS STRING
ENDPROC

ENDDEFINE
```

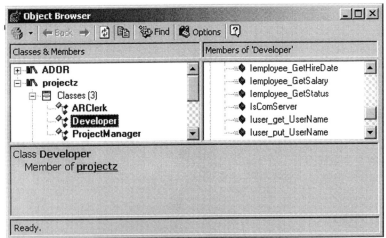

Figure 9. *Implemented interface methods should be hidden so they do not appear in Object Browsers.*

Creating interfaces in Visual FoxPro

Visual FoxPro makes it easy to define interfaces in your COM servers that can be implemented by other COM objects. It's as easy as creating a class definition and marking the class as OLE Public. For example:

```
*--------------------------------
*--- Define the Employee interface
*--------------------------------
DEFINE CLASS Employee AS Session OLEPublic
  PROCEDURE GetSalary(EmployeePK AS Integer) AS Currency
  ENDPROC
  PROCEDURE GetHireDate(EmployeePK AS Integer) AS Date
  ENDPROC
  PROCEDURE GetStatus(EmployeePK AS Integer) AS String
  ENDPROC
ENDDEFINE

*---------------------------------
*--- Define the User class interface
*---------------------------------
```

```
DEFINE CLASS User AS SESSION OLEPublic
  UserName = ""
  DIMENSION UserName_COMATTRIB[5]
  UserName_COMATTRIB[1]=0
  UserName_COMATTRIB[2]="User Name"
  UserName_COMATTRIB[3]="UserName"
  UserName_COMATTRIB[4]="String"
  UserName_COMATTRIB[5]=0

  PROCEDURE GetUserGroups(UserPK AS Integer) AS String
  ENDPROC
  PROCEDURE GetUserID(UserPK AS Integer) AS String
  ENDPROC
  PROCEDURE GetUserPassword(UserPK AS Integer) AS String
  ENDPROC
ENDDEFINE
```

Notice the methods defined in these classes contain no code, since interface inheritance does not include implementation code. Also, the Session class is a good choice for the base class when defining Visual FoxPro interfaces because its intrinsic properties are automatically hidden from the type library.

IUnknown, vtables, and early binding

Since a COM object can implement any number of interfaces, how can clients determine which interfaces a COM object supports? The answer is: with the *IUnknown* interface.

All COM interfaces inherit directly or indirectly from the IUnknown interface—a standard COM interface defined by Microsoft. For example, as shown in **Figure 10**, the ICustomer interface inherits from the IDispatch interface (discussed in the next section), which inherits from the IUnknown interface.

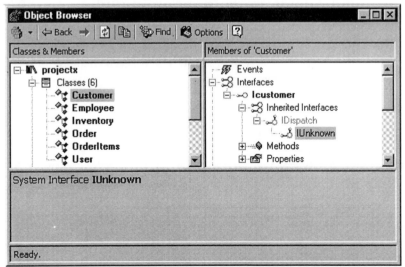

Figure 10. All COM interfaces inherit directly or indirectly from the IUnknown interface.

The COM standard specifies that a COM interface is, at a very low level, an array of function pointers. A *vtable*, or virtual table, is a list of all function pointers in a COM interface. The IUnknown interface contains only three methods—QueryInterface(), AddRef(), and Release() (see **Table 1**). Since IUnknown is the most fundamental COM interface, its methods are always the first three entries in the vtable of every COM interface.

Table 1. *The IUnknown interface contains only three methods.*

Method	Description
QueryInterface()	Used to determine the interfaces supported by an object.
AddRef()	Increments the reference count for an interface.
Release()	Decrements the reference count for an interface.

The QueryInterface() method allows clients to query a COM component to determine whether it supports a particular interface. If it does, QueryInterface() returns a pointer to the interface.

Accessing a COM interface using a vtable is known as *early binding*. Early binding is the fastest way to access a COM interface. Microsoft compares calling a method by means of early binding to using speed dial to call a telephone number.

IDispatch and late binding

Not all languages have the ability to access a COM interface by means of early binding. Typically, languages that have weak typing (scripting languages and previous versions of Visual FoxPro, for example) cannot use early binding. Microsoft created the IDispatch interface to address this problem.

The main purpose of IDispatch is to act as a portal to a component's functionality. Accessing a COM interface using IDispatch is known as *late binding*. Late binding is slower than early binding because a client has to perform a lookup on a COM object's methods and properties each time it accesses the interface of the object. Microsoft compares late binding to looking up a phone number each time you need to make a call.

Some COM objects do not support late binding by means of IDispatch. You must use early vtable binding in order to access their interfaces. Interfaces that support both early and late binding are known as *dual interfaces*. Visual FoxPro's COM interfaces are dual interfaces.

Visual FoxPro as an early-binding client

Earlier versions of Visual FoxPro allowed clients to access its COM interfaces by means of early binding, but it couldn't access other COM interfaces as an early-bound client. In version 7, Visual FoxPro finally gives us this ability.

Early binding with CREATEOBJECTEX()

CREATEOBJECTEX() has a new third parameter, cIID. The syntax is:

```
CREATEOBJECTEX(cCLSID | cPROGID, cComputerName [, cIID])
```

This parameter allows you to pass an interface GUID of a COM object. For example:

```
x = CREATEOBJECTEX("excel.application","",;
    "{000208D5-0000-0000-C000-000000000046}")
```

The CREATEOBJECTEX() command supports early, vtable binding when you pass the cIID parameter, thus improving performance. Unlike conventional early binding, which occurs at compile time, this brand of early binding takes place at run time.

Early binding with GETINTERFACE()

Visual FoxPro 7 has a brand-new function called GETINTERFACE() that provides early binding access to COM interfaces. The syntax of GETINTERFACE() is:

```
GETINTERFACE(oObject [, cIID | cInterface [, cTypelib | cProgID ] ])
```

The first parameter, oObject, is a reference to a COM object. The second parameter can be either cIID or cInterface. cIID specifies the GUID of the COM object's interface to which you want a reference. For example:

```
o = GETINTERFACE(oDeveloper, "{7EA33A7A-2DFD-11D5-9EB5-00500493AFE5}")
```

Alternately, you can use cInterface to simply specify the name of the interface in which you are interested:

```
o = GETINTERFACE(oPerson, "IEmployee")
```

The third parameter can either be cTypelib or cProgID. cTypelib specifies the name of the type library containing the desired interface, whereas cProgID specifies the ProgID of the class that defines the interface.

Here is an example of using GETINTERFACE() to get an early-bound reference to a COM interface:

```
oDeveloper = CREATEOBJECT("projectz.developer")
oEmployee = GETINTERFACE(oDeveloper, "IEmployee", "ProjectZ.dll")
```

GETINTERFACE() allows you to access interfaces that were not accessible before Visual FoxPro 7. The GETINTERFACE() topic of the VFP 7 Help file contains a great example of this. It shows how you can use GETINTERFACE() to get a reference to the IContextState interface. This interface gives you finer control over COM+ transactions.

Advanced COM server commands

VFP 7 adds a few commands intended for advanced developers needing fine control over their COM objects.

SYS(3095)—IDispatch pointer

The new SYS(3095) function is used to return an IDispatch pointer for a COM object. The integer returned from this function can be used in API routines that require this information.

SYS(3097)—add reference to object
SYS(3098)—release object reference

This pair of new SYS() functions is used to increment and decrement a COM interface's reference counter. For example:

```
oDeveloper = CREATEOBJECT("ProjectZ.Developer")
? SYS(3097, oDeveloper)    && Returns 2
? SYS(3098, oDeveloper)    && Returns 1
```

For an example showing the use of these new SYS() functions, check out the Accessibility Browser form (AccBrow.SCX) in the Visual FoxPro 7 Tools\MSAA folder.

Summary

The new features discussed in this chapter blow the doors off many limitations found when working with COM components under Visual FoxPro 6. The ability to implement interfaces allows Visual FoxPro to be a player in the COM+ arena. In addition, the new GETINTERFACE() and the enhanced CREATEOBJECTEX() functions provide early binding access to interfaces that open up a new world of speed and functionality for Visual FoxPro 7.

Chapter 14
Playing in the COM+ Sandbox

This chapter provides an overview of COM+ services and shows you which services you can take advantage of in Visual FoxPro 7.0 (not all are available). In the final analysis, VFP 7 makes great strides in enabling your COM servers to work with COM+. This chapter also discusses event binding, which is a precursor to Windows 2000 COM+ Events.

With its release of Windows 2000, Microsoft has married the Microsoft Transaction Server (MTS) and COM technologies to produce COM+. Rather than being an add-on (as was MTS), COM+ is tightly integrated into the Windows 2000 operating system. Before jumping into COM+, this chapter first discusses VFP's new COM event binding abilities.

COM event binding
Event binding is the ability to bind Visual FoxPro objects to events raised by COM servers. This functionality was first introduced in Visual FoxPro 6 by means of the VFPCOM utility. In Visual FoxPro 7, event binding is built right into the product. To understand how COM event binding works, you first need to understand the basics of outgoing interfaces and Connectable Objects.

Incoming and outgoing interfaces
The most common interaction between a client and a COM object involves the client calling a method of the COM object's interface; the COM object performs the requested service and returns a result to the client. COM interfaces supporting this type of client-to-object communication are called *incoming interfaces*.

However, there are times when communication needs to go the other way—a COM object needs to raise an event or "call back" the client to alert them that something interesting has happened. This requires an *outgoing interface*.

Connectable Objects
A standard COM technology called *Connectable Objects* (also called *connection points*) allows COM objects to raise events through outgoing interfaces and for clients to connect, or bind, to these events. A client that binds to a connectable object is known as an *event sink* because it receives the events raised by the connectable object (you can bind one or more event sinks to a connectable object). There are four COM interfaces in the Connectable Objects architecture:

- IConnectionPointContainer
- IConnectionPoint

- IEnumConnectionPoints

- IEnumConnections

A COM object indicates to clients that it supports the Connectable Objects technology by implementing the IConnectionPointContainer interface. The actual binding between client and connectable object occurs using the IConnectionPoint interface (see **Figure 1**).

For a client to bind to a connectable object and receive callbacks, it must implement one of the object's outgoing interfaces (for details see Chapter 13, "Implementing Interfaces").

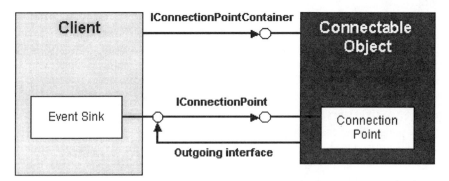

***Figure 1**. The Connectable Object architecture allows COM objects to make callbacks to clients, providing two-way communication.*

How can you tell whether a particular COM object supports raising events through outgoing interfaces? Visual FoxPro 7's Object Browser can help you determine this. As shown in **Figure 2**, the Object Browser shows any outgoing interfaces for a COM object.

Different types of interfaces are depicted differently in the Object Browser. Default interfaces are shown in bold and hidden interfaces in gray. Some interfaces may be bold and gray (usually event interfaces). Interfaces that have a lightning bolt icon may be used as an event interface. In addition, if the icon is blue it indicates an IDispatch or dual interface. A red icon indicates a vtable interface.

If you select an event in the Events node, the right pane of the Object Browser displays a list of all classes and interfaces that contain the event.

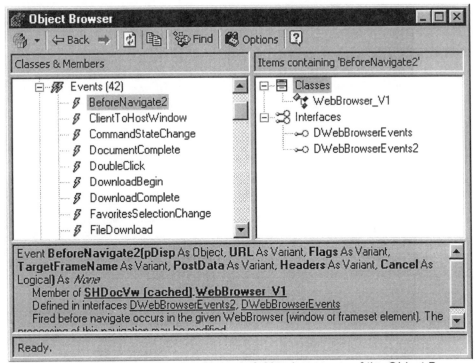

Figure 2. The Events node in the Classes & Members pane of the Object Browser displays a list of all events in outgoing interfaces of the type library's classes.

Outgoing interfaces and Visual FoxPro

COM objects created with Visual FoxPro 7 do not support the ability to raise events through the IConnectionPoint interface. This means that Visual FoxPro COM objects do not have outgoing interfaces and therefore cannot be Connectable Objects. However, this isn't as bad as it sounds. See the section "COM+ Events" later in this chapter for details.

Event binding with EventHandler()

In Visual FoxPro 7, the new EventHandler() function is used to bind a COM server's events to the implemented interface methods of a VFP object.

After you have identified a COM outgoing interface to which you want to bind, your next step is to create an event sink by implementing the outgoing interface in a Visual FoxPro class. As described in Chapter 13, "Implementing Interfaces," this is easily accomplished by following these steps:

1. Open the COM object's type library in the VFP 7 Object Browser.

2. Open a program file.

3. Drag and drop the outgoing interface from the Object Browser into the program file.

The following example code shows a partial definition of an event sink for Internet Explorer's DWebBrowserEvents outgoing interface.

> 📝 *The DWebBrowserEvents is an older Internet Explorer event interface that has been superseded by the new DWebBrowserEvents2 interface. (Notice that the new interface does not replace the older one, but is in addition to the older interface as explained in Chapter 13, "Implementing Interfaces.")*

```
Define Class IEEventSink As Session OlePublic

    Implements DWebBrowserEvents In "c:\winnt\system32\shdocvw.dll"

    Procedure DWebBrowserEvents_BeforeNavigate(URL As String, Flags As Number, ;
      TargetFrameName As String, PostData As VARIANT, Headers As String, ;
      Cancel As LOGICAL @) As VOID;
        HELPSTRING "Fired when a new hyperlink is being navigated to."
        * add user code here
    Endproc

    Procedure DWebBrowserEvents_NavigateComplete(URL As String) As VOID;
        HELPSTRING "Fired when the document being navigated to becomes " + ;
        "visible and enters the navigation stack."
        STRTOFILE("* " + Ttoc(Datetime())+"*"+Chr(10)+Chr(13)+;
           URL+Chr(10)+Chr(13),'IEEvents.log',.T.)
        * add user code here
    Endproc

    && Other interface events are implemented, but not shown here!

Enddefine
```

The DWebBrowserEvents_NavigateComplete() method contains implementation code that creates a rudimentary navigation log. This method is fired when a user successfully navigates to a URL. The current DATETIME() and the URL to which the user navigates are written to a text file named IEEvents.LOG.

Here is the code from this chapter's IEBind.PRG example file (located in the ProjectX folder) that demonstrates how to bind the Visual FoxPro IEEventSink object to Internet Explorer's outgoing interface:

```
Local loIE, loEventSink

loIE = Createobject("InternetExplorer.Application")
loEventSink = Createobject("IEEventSink")

EVENTHANDLER(loIE, loEventSink)

loIE.Visible = .T.

Read Events
```

*The program IEBind.PRG located in the ProjectX directory of the Developer Downloads for this chapter at **www.hentzenwerke.com** demonstrates binding events with Internet Explorer.*

The first line of code (after the variable declarations) instantiates Internet Explorer, and the second line of code instantiates the IEEventSink object. The third line of code runs the EVENTHANDLER() command, which binds Internet Explorer's DWebBrowserEvents outgoing interface to the implemented interface of the IEEventSink object. Afterwards, the code makes Internet Explorer visible and issues a READ EVENTS.

When you run this example, navigate to multiple Web sites from Internet Explorer. When you're finished, close Internet Explorer, and then open the IEEvents.LOG file to see the results.

There are many other interesting COM servers to which you can bind events such as Microsoft Office applications. The samples that ship with Visual FoxPro 7 include an example of binding events with ADO record sets.

EVENTHANDLER() allows you to bind a single COM object to several Visual FoxPro event sink objects. You can also bind several COM objects to a single Visual FoxPro event sink object.

If either object is released, event handling is automatically released. However, if you want to release event handling while both objects remain in scope, you can call EVENTHANDLER() with the optional third parameter, lUnbind, set to .T.

The downside of event binding
Although event binding works well in some situations, it has a downside. First, it requires that both the event source and the event sink objects be running at the same time through the entire cycle of raising and responding to events.

In addition, the client event sink objects cannot pick and choose which events in an event interface they want to receive—it's an all or nothing deal. If a client is only interested in one event out of an entire interface, it still receives notification when any other event in the interface is raised.

A client may also want even finer control over when it is notified of an event. For example, a client object may only be interested in specific stocks, and it may only wish to be notified if a stock drops below a particular price—not every time a stock price changes.

Introducing COM+ services
Microsoft's COM/DCOM technology allows you to seamlessly distribute your COM components to different computers across your network. Microsoft Transaction Server (MTS) and its successor, COM+, were created to provide that "something more"—a run-time environment for your distributed COM components.

MTS was created as an add-on for Windows NT. COM+ is tightly integrated into the Windows 2000 operating system and provides a wide variety of component services. The rest of this chapter discusses the services that are most relevant to Visual FoxPro 7.0: COM+

Events and Queued Components. You can also check out the Visual FoxPro 7.0 samples for information on COM+ Transactions and Compensating Resource Managers.

COM+ applications

In order to use these COM+ services, you must build your COM server as an in-process DLL and then configure it to run in the COM+ run-time environment.

The first step in configuring your server is to create a *COM+ application*. An application is the primary unit of administration and security for Component Services. After creating a COM+ application, you can add one or more COM components to the application (a COM+ application can contain components from one or more DLLs). All components in a COM+ application are administered as a unit and run in the same process.

Creating a COM+ application

To create a COM+ application, you need to use the Windows 2000 Component Services Explorer (you can also create an application programmatically using the COM+ Administrative interfaces). To launch the Windows 2000 Component Services Explorer, click the Windows Start button, and then select Programs | Administrative Tools | Component Services. If you don't find Component Services in the Administrative Tools menu, you can find it in Control Panel under Administrative Tools. To create a new COM+ application:

1. Expand the Component Services | Computers | My Computer node. Right-click on the COM+ Applications node and select New | Application from the context menu (see **Figure 3**). This launches the COM Application Install Wizard.

2. On the first page of the COM Application Install Wizard, click the Next button.

3. On the second page of the wizard, click the Create an empty application button. This launches the Create Empty Application dialog (see **Figure 4**).

4. In the Enter a name for the new application text box, enter the name you want to give your new application. Afterwards, accept the Server application default selection, and then click the Next button.

5. Under the Set Application Identity step, accept the Interactive user default and click the Next button.

6. On the last page of the wizard, click Finish.

When the wizard finishes, it creates the new COM+ application and displays it in the right-hand COM+ Applications pane of the Component Services Explorer.

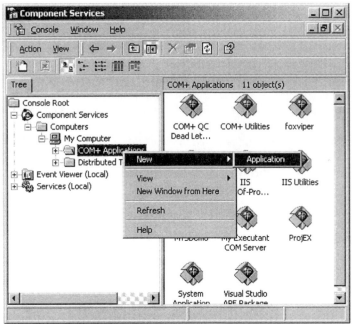

Figure 3. *Windows 2000 Component Services allows you to create and administer COM+ applications.*

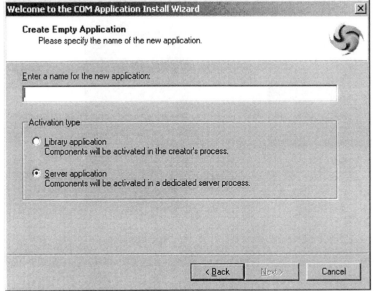

Figure 4. *The COM Application Install Wizard allows you to easily create new COM applications.*

COM+ Events

COM+ Events were created to address the problems associated with Connectable Objects and binding events. COM+ Events use a "publish and subscribe" model for communication between objects. Rather than having the Publisher and Subscriber directly bound to each other (as in event binding), an intermediary *Event class* is used to manage communication between a Publisher and one or more Subscribers. This decouples Publishers from Subscribers so they do not need to be running at the same time, and, in many cases, Publishers do not even know who the Subscribers are.

Information regarding events and Subscribers is stored in the COM+ catalog. The COM+ catalog stores information in two places—the Windows Registry and the COM+ Registration Database. The COM+ catalog provides a unified view of these two stores.

To generate COM+ Events you need three things:

1. An Event class that contains one or more event interfaces.

2. One or more Subscriber objects that implement at least one of the Event class's interfaces.

3. A Publisher that fires the event.

The sequence of a COM+ Event is shown in **Figure 5**. When a Publisher wants to raise an event, it instantiates an Event class and calls a method of one of the event interfaces. Next, a list of Subscribers is retrieved from the COM+ catalog and the event is passed on to each Subscriber.

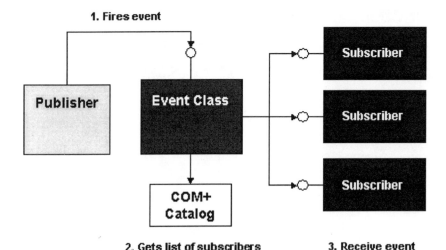

Figure 5. A COM+ Event involves a Publisher, an Event class, and one or more Subscribers.

> Since COM+ is part of the Windows 2000 operating system, you must be running Windows 2000 (any version) to run this chapter's example code.

A COM+ Events example

Visual FoxPro 7.0 includes sample code that demonstrates how to use COM+ Events from VFP. The sample code is located in the Samples\COM+\Events folder below the main Visual FoxPro program folder. Although the Readme.HTM file located in the COM+ folder contains some information regarding the example, the following sections provide additional insight to clarify the examples and help explain what's going on under the hood.

There are two event examples that use a form named Books to add new books to a table called Books.DBF and to change the prices of existing books (see **Figure 6**).

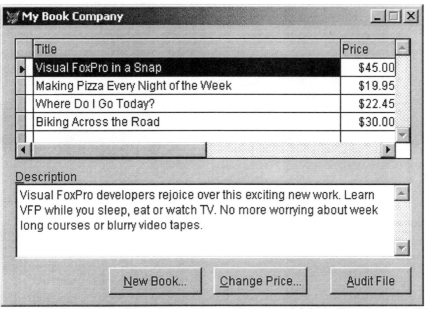

Figure 6. The Books form demonstrates the use of COM+ Events with VFP 7.

As new books are added or as prices are changed, the associated New Book and Change Price forms publish COM+ Events. Subscriber objects respond to the events by writing transactions into an audit file.

Persistent and Transient Subscriptions

There are two types of COM+ Subscriptions—Persistent and Transient.

Persistent Subscriptions are stored in the COM+ catalog and survive system shutdowns. With Persistent Subscriptions, when an event is published, a list of all applicable Subscriber classes is retrieved from the COM+ catalog and an object is created from each Subscriber class. Afterwards, the Event and Subscriber objects are released.

Persistent Subscriptions can be created using the Component Services Explorer. The first Event example discussed in this chapter uses Persistent Subscriptions.

In contrast, Transient Subscriptions are stored temporarily in the COM+ catalog and do not survive a system shutdown. Rather than being tied to classes, Transient Subscriptions work with existing objects. Transient Subscriptions cannot be created using the Component Services Explorer—you create them programmatically using the COM+ Administrative Interfaces (for details, see the section "The Transient Subscriber COM+ Events example"). The second Event example in this chapter uses Transient Subscriptions.

Transient Subscriptions are well-suited for applications that want to be alerted to events while they are running, but don't want to be alerted when they are not.

The Persistent Subscriber COM+ Events example

There are three main elements in this example (see **Figure 7**)—the Publishers (NewBook and PriceChange forms), the Event class (BookPub), and the Subscriber (BookSub1).

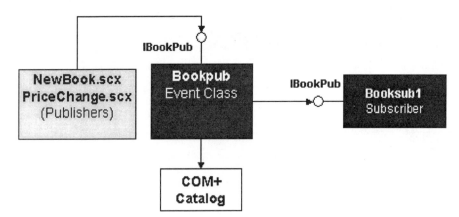

Figure 7. The example forms publish events by calling methods in the BookPub class. COM+ looks up any Subscribers for the specific event and passes the call on to them.

When the NewBook form saves a record, it sets off a whole series of actions:

1. The NewBook form instantiates the BookPub Event class and calls the NewBook event in BookPub's IBookPub interface passing the book title and price.

2. When the event is called, COM+ looks in the COM+ catalog to get a list of Subscribers who have registered interest in the NewBook event.

3. The BookSub1 Subscriber is found and instantiated. A call is made to the NewBook event in the object's IBookPub interface. By default, the implementation code in the BookSub1.NewBook() method writes out the book title and price to the c:\booksub1.txt audit file.

Looking under the hood

The BookPub Event class
The BookPub Event class is stored in the book_pub.PRG file in the Samples\COM+\Events folder. The class definition for BookPub is:

```
DEFINE CLASS bookpub AS SESSION OLEPUBLIC

    PROCEDURE NewBook(cBookName AS STRING, nPrice AS CURRENCY)
    ENDPROC

    PROCEDURE PriceChange(cBookName AS STRING, nPrice AS CURRENCY)
    ENDPROC

ENDDEFINE
```

BookPub is an OLE public class (located in the FoxBook_Pub project) that contains two empty methods—NewBook() and PriceChange(). These methods do not contain any implementation code because they are simply used for defining a COM interface. When the BookPub class is compiled, Visual FoxPro automatically creates an IBookPub default COM interface for the class.

The BookSub1 Subscriber class
The BookSub1 Subscriber class is stored in the book_sub1.PRG file. The class definition for BookSub1 is:

```
#INCLUDE EVENTS.h

DEFINE CLASS booksub1 AS SESSION OLEPUBLIC

    * Declare the interface
    IMPLEMENT Ibookpub IN foxbook_pub.bookpub

    * Notice that the method declarations are preceded by
    * the interface's name and have the same parameters
    * as their counterparts in the IbookPub class.

    PROCEDURE Ibookpub_NewBook(cBookName AS STRING, nPrice AS CURRENCY)
    STRTOFILE(TRANS(DATETIME()) + " (" + PROGRAM() + ") - ";
       + cBookName + ", ";
       + TRANSFORM(nPrice) + CRLF,;
       LOGFILE,.T.)
    ENDPROC

    PROCEDURE Ibookpub_PriceChange(cBookName AS STRING, nPrice AS CURRENCY)
    STRTOFILE(TRANS(DATETIME()) + " (" + PROGRAM() + ") - ";
       + cBookName + ", ";
       + TRANSFORM(nPrice) + CRLF,;
       LOGFILE,.T.)
    ENDPROC

ENDDEFINE
```

BookSub1 is an OLE public class that implements the IBookPub interface of the BookPub COM class. Notice that it contains implementation code in its methods. When an event is fired, this code writes out the "new book" or "price change" transaction to an audit file. LOGFILE is a constant defined in the Events.H include file that is defined as "c:\booksub1.txt".

The publisher forms

The publisher forms (NewBook.SCX and PriceChange.SCX) are launched from the main Books.SCX form when adding new books or changing existing book prices. These forms contain code that instantiates the BookPub Event class and publishes an event. For example, the NewBook form's **OK** button Click event contains the following code:

```
LOCAL oPublisher
oPublisher = CREATEOBJECT("foxbook_pub.bookpub")
oPublisher.NewBook(ALLTRIM(THISFORM.txtTitle.Value), THISFORM.txtPrice.Value)
RELEASE oPublisher
```

> *As shown in this code, the VFP 7 sample code and documentation refers to the Event object as the "publisher," but it's not—the form itself acts as the publisher by calling the Event object's NewBook event.*

This code instantiates the BookPub Event object and calls its NewBook event passing the book title and price. This is when the event publishing takes place.

Registering Event and Subscriber classes

How does COM+ know about the BookPub Event class and BookSub1 Subscriber class? Both of these classes must be registered with COM+. The next section shows you how to do this.

Creating and configuring the BookPub Event class

To create and configure the BookPub Event class for COM+:

1. Open the FoxBook_Pub.PJX project (located in \Samples\COM+\Events) and build a multi-threaded COM server DLL.

2. Create a new COM+ application named FoxBookPub (see the section "Creating a COM+ application").

3. From the Component Services Explorer, expand the FoxBookPub node and then select the Components node. Right-click on the Components node and select New | Component from the context menu. This launches the COM Component Install Wizard.

4. Click the **Next** button. Select the **Install new Event class(es)** button.

5. In the Select Files to Install dialog, navigate to the Samples\COM+\Events directory, select FoxBook_Pub.DLL, and then click **Open**.

6. Click the **Next** button, and then click the **Finish** button.

After the wizard is finished, the FoxBook_Pub.BookPub class is displayed in the Component Services Explorer as shown in **Figure 8**.

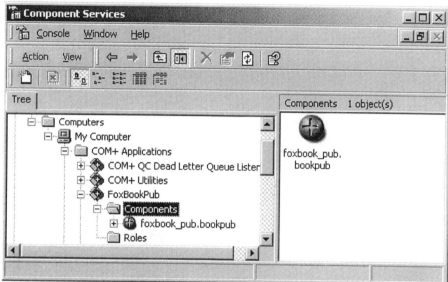

Figure 8. *The Component Services Explorer allows you to register COM+ Event classes.*

Creating and configuring a BookSub1 Subscriber

To create and configure the BookSub1 Subscriber class for COM+:

1. Open the FoxBook_Sub.PJX project (located in \Samples\COM+\Events) and build a multi-threaded COM server DLL.

2. Create a new COM+ application named FoxBookSub (see the section "Creating a COM+ application").

3. From the Component Services Explorer, expand the FoxBookSub node and then select the Components node. Right-click on the Components node and select New | Component from the context menu. This launches the COM Component Install Wizard.

4. Click on the Next button. This time, select the Install new component button.

5. In the Select Files to Install dialog, select FoxBook_Sub.dll and then click Open.

6. Click the Next button, and then click the Finish button.

After the wizard is finished, the FoxBook_Sub.BookSub1 class is displayed in the Component Services Explorer as shown in **Figure 9**.

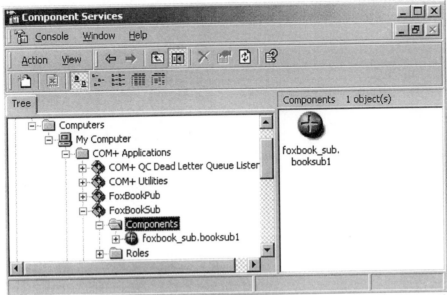

Figure 9. *COM+ components can be configured by means of the Component Services Explorer.*

Next, the BookSub1 component must be configured as a Subscriber to the BookPub events:

1. In the Component Services Explorer, expand the Computers | My Computer | COM+ Applications | FoxBookSub | Components node.

2. Expand the foxbook_sub.booksub1 node, and then select the Subscriptions node. Right-click on the Subscriptions node and select New | Subscription from the context menu. This launches the COM New Subscription Wizard.

3. Click the Next button. On the second page, select the Use all interfaces for this component check box, and then click the Next button.

4. After a few moments, the Select Event class page displays foxbook_pub.bookpub in the list box. Select the class and click the Next button.

5. In the Subscription Options page, enter a name for the new Subscription (for example, Fox Subscription 1). Next, select the Enable this Subscription immediately check box and then click the Next button.

6. Click the Finish button.

After the wizard is finished, the new Subscription is displayed in the Component Services Explorer as shown in **Figure 10**.

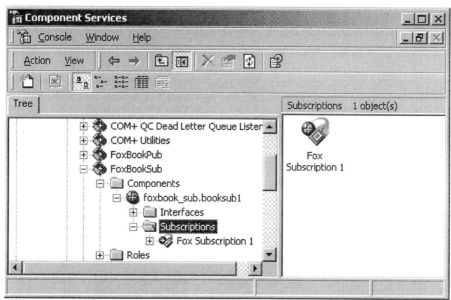

Figure 10. COM+ components can be configured as Subscribers using the Component Services Explorer.

At this point, you can set up additional Subscribers. However, it doesn't make sense for this particular example because they would all do the same thing—write out the same transaction to the audit file.

Running the Persistent Subscriber example

To run the example, enter "DO FORM Books" in the Visual FoxPro Command Window (make sure you're in the \Samples\COM+\Events folder). Click the New Book and Change Price buttons to add a new book or change the price of an existing book. As you save records, the forms publish a COM+ Event behind the scenes and Publishers respond by writing out a corresponding record to the audit file. The first time you save the record it takes a bit longer since it's the first time the DLLs are loaded. Subsequent records are saved more quickly.

To see the audit file containing transactions written out by Subscriber objects, click the Audit File button (see **Figure 11**).

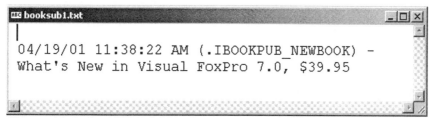

Figure 11. In the VFP 7 COM+ Events example, Subscriber objects write transactions to an audit log.

Filtering events

COM+ provides finer control over events by means of *filtering*. This mechanism allows you to filter out certain events for Subscribers. The filtering can be done either at the Publisher level (publish filtering) or at the Subscriber level (parameter filtering).

The best approach for setting up Publisher filtering requires creating a Publisher Filter COM object that sits between the event object and the Subscribers. However, configuring a Publisher filter is not supported in the Component Services Explorer and must be done programmatically.

It is far easier to use parameter filtering at the Subscriber level. Using the book-publishing example, you can set a filter by doing the following:

1. Launch the Component Services Explorer and right-click on the Fox Subscription 1 Subscription of the FoxBookSub application. Select Properties from the context menu. This launches the Subscription properties dialog.

2. Select the Options tab and enter the desired filter in the Filter criteria box. For example: cBookName = "What's New in Visual FoxPro 7.0".

3. Click the OK button to save the filter.

Now when you run the sample again, an event is only sent to Fox Subscription 1 if a change is made to the "What's New in Visual FoxPro 7.0" record.

The Transient Subscriber COM+ Events example

Transient Subscriptions work with existing objects rather than with class information stored in the COM+ catalog. Since Transient Subscribers are created dynamically at run time, the Transient Subscriber example has a form called TCE_Events that creates Publisher, Event, and Subscriber objects for you (see **Figure 12**).

> *The term TCE stands for "tightly coupled events" and is actually a misnomer that is used throughout the VFP 7 sample code. All COM+ Events are loosely coupled since there is an event object that sits between the Publisher and Subscriber. The sample code also tends to blur the line between the Publisher and the Event.*

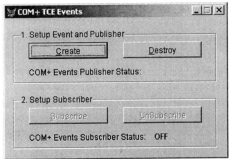

Figure 12. The VFP 7 Transient Subscriber COM+ Event example form dynamically creates Event, Publisher, and Subscriber objects.

Setting up the Event and Publisher

If you click the Create button, the TCE_Events form sets up the Event and Publisher objects. Here is a breakdown of the code that it executes in the form's CreatePublisher() method, shown in **Listing 1**.

The first line of code instantiates something interesting—a Type Library Information object. The Type Library Information (TLI) object library (stored in TlbInf32.DLL) is a set of COM objects that make it easy to programmatically examine a type library. The TLIApplication object is the top-level TLI application object.

> *For a complete description of the Type Library Information object library, download the HTML Help file contained in TlbInf32.EXE from Microsoft's Web site at the following URL:*
> **http://support.microsoft.com/support/kb/articles/Q224/3/31.ASP.**

After the TLI application object is instantiated, the fully qualified path to foxbook_pub.DLL is passed to its TypeLibInfoFromFile() method, which returns a TypeLibInfo object (a TypeLibInfo object represents a type library and, in this case, contains information about the foxbook_pub type library).

In the second block of code, the first line gets the globally unique identifier (GUID) of the BookPub COM+ Event class and the second line gets the name of its default interface (IBookPub). The next two lines of code are used to get an Interface Information object for the IBookPub interface.

Listing 1. This code demonstrates how to set up the Publisher and Event for a Transient Subscription.

```
typlibobj = CreateObject("TLI.TLIApplication")
cTypelibName = THIS.cthispath + BOOKTYPELIB
IF !FILE(cTypelibName)
  * File doesn't exist. Return an error to the user.
  MessageBox(NODLL_LOC)
  RETURN
ENDIF
typelib = typlibobj.TypeLibInfoFromFile(cTypelibName)

cPublishID = typelib.CoClasses(1).GUID
cPubInterface = typelib.Interfaces(1).Name
ifs = typelib.Interfaces
ifo = ifs.NamedItem(cPubInterface)

* create System and Event Objects
oEventSys = CreateObject("EventSystem.EventSystem")
oEventPub = CreateObject("EventSystem.EventPublisher")

* Define CLSID and ProgID from Event
oEventPub.PublisherID = cPublishID
oEventPub.PublisherName = PUBPROGID

* Store the Event into the Event system
oEventSys.Store("EventSystem.EventPublisher", oEventPub)
```

```
oEventClass = CreateObject("EventSystem.EventClass")
oEventClass.EventClassID = EVENTCLSID

* Store the classname.  This is the PROGID
oEventClass.EventClassName = PUBPROGID

oEventClass.FiringInterfaceID = ifo.Guid
oEventSys.Store("EventSystem.EventClass", oEventClass)
```

The rest of the code in the CreatePublisher() method (which should really be named CreateEvent) creates an Event and stores it into the event system.

> Although this code works fine for the example, MSDN recommends a different approach to creating Transient Subscriptions using the COM+ Administrative interfaces. For details, see the MSDN topic "Transient Subscriptions" at: *http://msdn.microsoft.com/library/default.asp?URL= /library/psdk/cossdk/pgservices_events_6yyb.htm*.

Setting up the Subscriber

To set up the Transient Subscriber, click the Subscribe button of the TCE_Events form (see Figure 12). This runs the form's CreateSubscriber() method, which instantiates a new Subscription object from the MyBooks class defined in the book_tce.PRG file.

Next, the IntallSubscription() method of the MyBooks class is run, which uses the COM+ Event system object library to add the Subscriber to the COM+ Event system.

Running the Transient Subscriber example

You test Transient Subscribers the same way you tested Persistent Subscribers—using the Books form. However, the example code is only set up to allow you to test Transient Subscribers by changing an existing price.

To do this, leave the TCE_Events form open, run the Books form, and click the Price Change button. In the Price Change form, select the Use TCE Events check box as shown in **Figure 13**.

Figure 13. Select the Use TCE Events *check box to test COM+ Transient Subscribers.*

After changing the price, click the OK button. When the Use TCE Events check box is selected, the Price Change form instantiates the Transient Event class created by the TCE_Events form rather than the BookPub Event class (stored in Book_pub.PRG) used when the box is unchecked. The Transient Subscriber object receives the published event and writes a record out to the audit log (**see Figure 14**).

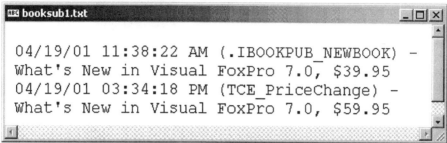

Figure 14. *Transactions written to the audit log by Transient Subscribers are marked with a TCE_PriceChange designation.*

To remove the Transient Subscription and Event from the COM+ Event system, click the UnSubscribe and Destroy buttons of the TCE_Events form, and then close the form.

Queued Components

Queued Components (often abbreviated as QC) is a COM+ service that uses Microsoft Message Queue (MSMQ) to provide both synchronous and asynchronous communication between components.

The telephone and voice mail present a good analogy of how synchronous and asynchronous communication works. If you call someone on the phone and he's available, he picks up the phone and the two of you can talk. This is an example of synchronous communication. If you call someone and he's not available, you can usually record a message on his voice mail. When the person becomes available again, he can listen to your recorded message. This is an example of asynchronous communication.

The word "available" in this telephone communication scenario is also a key issue with components. When a component on one machine is trying to communicate with a component on another machine, you can't guarantee that the other component is always available (for example, that machine may be down).

The Queued Components service fills this gap by acting as intermediary between components and providing a mechanism for storing messages that can be retrieved at a later date by the called components—similar to voice mail.

When you configure a component to use Queued Component Services, a number of other objects get involved in the client-to-object communication path (see **Figure 15**).

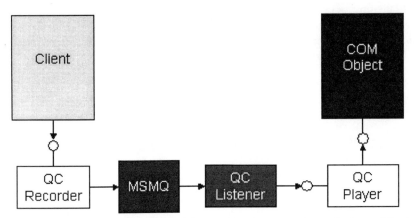

Figure 15. *When using Queued Components, a number of other objects are used in the communication path between client and COM object.*

When you instantiate a COM object that has been configured to use QC, you don't actually get an instance of the object. Instead, COM+ steps in and creates a QC Recorder object that possesses the same interface as the target COM object. As far as the client is concerned, the Recorder is the "real" COM object. When you call methods of the QC Recorder object, it turns the set of calls into a single MSMQ message. When you release the QC Recorder object, it sends the message to MSMQ where it is stored.

COM+ provides a QC Listener that constantly checks for messages that have been added to MSMQ. When the Listener sees a message waiting in the queue, it retrieves the message and activates a QC Player component. The QC Player instantiates the real COM object and plays back the original message into it.

Queued Component interfaces

One of the restrictions of Queued Components is that no method called through QC can return a value (otherwise, if the called COM component is unavailable, the client may go into limbo waiting for the value). In VFP 7, this means you need to use the new VOID keyword when specifying the type of the value a method returns. For example:

```
PROCEDURE OrderPizza(cCustomer AS string, nOrdAmount AS long) AS VOID
LOCAL lcStr
TEXT TO lcStr TEXTMERGE NOSHOW
Thank you for your Pizza Order!
  Order: <<THIS.Toppings>>
  Customer: <<cCustomer>>
  Ammount: <<TRANSFORM(nOrdAmount,"@$99.99")>>
ENDTEXT
THIS.cOutputString = lcStr
ENDPROC
```

When compiling a COM server, the VOID keyword is a signal to the VFP 7 compiler to specify that a method's return value should be set to "None" in the type library. In actual practice, the OrderPizza() method still returns True (VFP's default)—however, from the perspective of COM+, the fact that the type library specifies there is no return value is good enough, and the True that's returned is ignored.

This restriction actually makes sense—if you're using Queued Components, it's probably because you can't guarantee that the component you are calling is available; and if the component isn't available, you can't count on having it return a value to you.

A Queued Components example

Visual FoxPro 7.0 ships with sample code that demonstrates how to use Queued Components with VFP. The sample code is located in the \Samples\COM+\QC folder off of the main Visual FoxPro program folder.

The example is a simple pizza ordering system. A form is provided for entering a customer name and pizza toppings (see **Figure 16**).

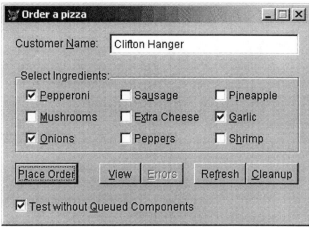

Figure 16. The Pizza form provides an interface for testing Queued Components with VFP 7.

As orders are taken, they are sent to a VFP COM server running as a Queued Component.

Setting up the Queued Components example

Before running the example, you must perform the steps outlined in the following sections to prepare your system.

Checking for MSMQ

The example requires that you have Message Queuing Services (MSMQ) installed on your computer. To verify this, click the Windows Start button and select Start | Programs | Administrative Tools | Computer Management (or go to the Control Panel under Administrative Tools) to launch the Computer Management Explorer. Next, expand the Services and Applications node. If MSMQ is installed, you will see a Message Queuing node.

If you do not have MSMQ installed, check out the following URL for MSMQ installation instructions: **http://support.microsoft.com/support/kb/articles/Q256/0/96.ASP**.

Building the FoxQC COM server

1. Go to the \Samples\COM+\QC folder and open the FoxQC project.

2. If you want to test the server portion of the example on your local computer, skip to step 3. If you want to test it on a remote server, select the Other tab and open the Foxqc include file. Change the QC_MACHINE constant definition from an empty string to the name of your remote computer. Afterwards, close the file and save changes.

3. Build a multi-threaded COM server.

Creating a COM+ application that supports queuing

1. Create a new COM+ application named QC1 (see the section "Creating a COM+ application").

2. Right-click on the new QC1 application and select Properties from the context menu. This launches the QC1 Properties dialog.

3. Select the Security tab and make sure the Enforce access checks for this application check box is not selected. Change the Authentication level for calls to None.

4. In the Queuing tab, check the Queued and Listen check boxes (see **Figure 17**).

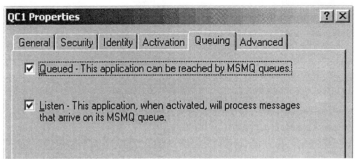

Figure 17. The COM+ Application Properties dialog allows you to configure an application to support Queuing.

5. Click OK to close the QC1 Properties dialog.

After closing the dialog, COM+ creates message queues for the new QC1 application. If you'd like to view these queues, launch the Computer Services Explorer, and then open the

Message Queuing node. Finally, open the Public Queues folder (if your server is set up to use work groups rather than domains, open the Private Queues folder instead).

If everything worked properly, you should see a QC1 message queue along with several other related queues with a "QC1_" prefix (see **Figure 18**).

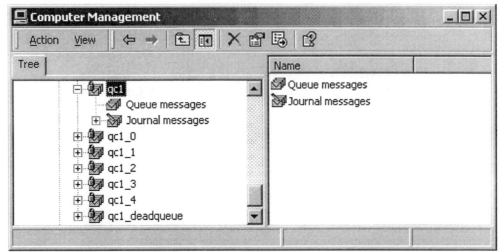

Figure 18. When you configure a COM+ application to support queuing, a series of queues are automatically created for the application.

COM+ uses a series of message queues when trying to deliver a message. On the first try, the message is stored in the qc1 queue. If the message is not successfully delivered after several attempts, it gets bumped to the next queue (qc1_0). This process of moving messages continues for each subsequent queue. If the message cannot be delivered from any of the other queues, it ends up in the "dead" queue where it stays until it is manually moved to another queue or removed completely using the Computer Management Explorer.

Adding a component to the application
Now that the application is set up, you need to add a component to the application.

1. In the Component Services Explorer, expand the QC1 node and select the Components subnode. Right-click on the Components node and select New | Component from the context menu.

2. Click the Next button and then click the Install new components button on page 2. In the Select Files to Install dialog, select Samples\COM+\QC\FoxQC.DLL, and then click Open.

3. Click the Next button, and then click the Finish button to close the wizard.

4. When the wizard is finished, the new FoxQC.pizza component appears in the right pane of the Component Services Explorer.

5.   Expand the Components node under QC1, right-click on FoxQC.pizza, and select Properties from the context menu. This launches the FoxQC.pizza Properties dialog. Select the Security tab and uncheck Enforce component level access checks. Click OK to close the dialog.

Specifying queued interfaces

After adding the component to the application, you need to specify which interfaces in the component are to be queued.

1.   Expand the Interfaces node under FoxQC.pizza, right-click on the Ipizza interface, and select Properties from the context menu. This launches the Ipizza Properties dialog.

2.   Select the Queuing tab, and then check the Queued check box. Click OK to close the dialog.

Running the Queued Components example

Make sure you are in the Samples\COM+\QC directory, and then issue DO FORM Pizza in the Command Window.

To make sure everything is set up properly, check the Test without Queued Components box at the bottom of the form as shown in Figure 16, and then click the Place Order button. If it's working correctly, your pizza order should be displayed in a text file (see **Figure 19**).

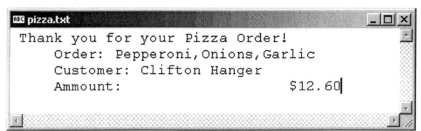

```
Thank you for your Pizza Order!
    Order: Pepperoni,Onions,Garlic
    Customer: Clifton Hanger
    Ammount:                 $12.60
```

Figure 19. The Pizza.TXT file holds information regarding pizza orders. (The misspelling of "amount" here is an error in the sample application.)

Now, for the real test, uncheck the Test without Queued Components box, and then click the Cleanup button. Enter a new customer and ingredients information, and then click the Place Order button. If everything is working properly, you will see your new order in the displayed text file.

Looking under the hood

Although the results of the example may not be exciting from a user interface perspective, a look under the hood can help you appreciate the "magic" that's happening behind the scenes.

Using the Component Services Administration Library

When you click the Place Order button (with Test without Queued Components unchecked), the following code in cmdOrder.Click() is run:

```
loCat = CreateObject("COMAdmin.COMAdminCatalog")
loCat.Connect(QC_MACHINE)
loCat.StartApplication(FOXQC_APP)
loOrder = GetObject("queue:/new:FoxQC.Pizza")
loOrder.Toppings = lcIngredients
loOrder.OrderPizza(ALLTRIM(THISFORM.txtCust.Value),lnCost)
loOrder.OutputTxtFile()
loCat.ShutdownApplication(FOXQC_APP)
```

The first line of code instantiates the COMAdminCatalog object from the COMAdmin (Component Services Administration Library) server. COMAdmin is an extremely useful library containing objects that automate administration of all COM+ applications and services. See the MSDN topic "Automating COM+ Administration" for details.

In line 2, the COMAdminCatalog object is used to connect to the server (QC_MACHINE is set to an empty string by default, indicating your local computer). The catalog object is used in the third line to launch the QC1 COM+ application and again in the last line to shut down the QC1 application. Normally, you don't need to include this code to start and shut down a COM+ application. The application can be started using the Component Services Explorer and left running.

Instantiating Queued Components with GETOBJECT()

The real excitement occurs in line 4 where the Pizza object gets instantiated. Notice that GETOBJECT() is used rather than CREATEOBJECT() to instantiate the server.

You can use CREATEOBJECT() to instantiate the Pizza object, but if you do, the object will not use Queued Component Services. In order to use QC, you must instantiate the Pizza object using the GETOBJECT() function and pass the *Queue Moniker* as the first parameter.

Understanding Queue Monikers

A moniker is a COM object that implements the IMoniker interface. Monikers are a COM mechanism used to find and activate other objects. COM has a number of different types of monikers that perform specific functions. For example, the File Moniker allows you to create an object from the contents of a file; the URL Moniker allows you to download and activate ActiveX controls from a specified URL. The Queue Moniker is used to locate and activate Queued Components.

In Visual FoxPro 7, the GETOBJECT() function has been enhanced to accept a moniker name as the first parameter. The syntax of the Queue Moniker is:

```
Queue:[options]/New:CLSID
```

Line 4 of the code sample provides an example of using the Queue Moniker:

```
loOrder = GetObject("queue:/new:FoxQC.Pizza")
```

The first portion of the string (queue:) specifies the Queue Moniker; the forward slash is a separator for the Queue Moniker options (the example code doesn't include any options); the next portion of the string (new:) specifies the New Moniker (another standard Microsoft Moniker used to instantiate objects); and the final portion (FoxQC.Pizza) specifies the CLSID of the Queued Component. For details on the Queue Moniker, see the MSDN topic "Using the Queue Moniker to Activate Queued Components."

Running the Queued Components example with Listener off

In the previous example, the Queued Component Listener was active. As soon as you placed an order, a message was sent to MSMQ, the Listener saw the message and created a QC Player that instantiated the Pizza object, which, in turn, wrote out the order to the text file. In this next example, you will turn the Listener off and see what happens when you place an order.

To turn the Listener off:

1. Close Visual FoxPro.

2. In the Component Services Explorer, right-click on the QC1 application and select Shutdown from the context menu (see **Figure 20**).

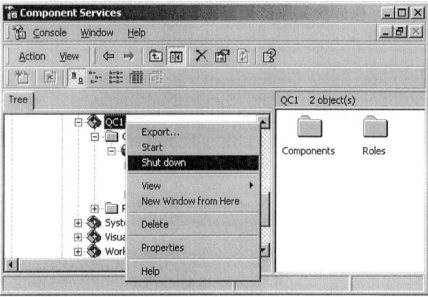

Figure 20. *The Component Explorer can be used to shut down COM+ applications.*

3. Next, launch the Properties dialog for the QC1 application by right-clicking on QC1 and selecting Properties from the context menu. Select the Queuing tab and uncheck the Listen check box. This displays a warning dialog that you can ignore. Click the OK button to close the Properties dialog.

4. Restart VFP 7, go back to the Samples\COM+\QC directory, and run the Pizza form again. Click the Cleanup button to delete any existing order file.

5. Enter a new Customer Name, select new ingredients, and then click the Place Order button. Since the Listener is turned off, an order text file is not displayed.

With the COM+ application Listener turned off, you can launch the Computer Management Explorer and look at the "qc1" message queue to see the message that's waiting to be delivered (see **Figure 21**).

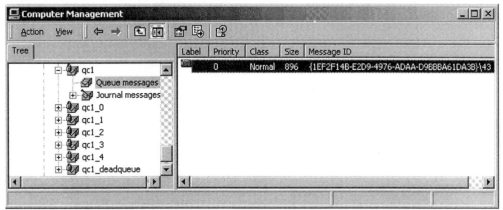

Figure 21. With a COM+ application's Listener turned off, you can easily use the Computer Management Explorer to see queued messages sent from the sample application.

Turning the Listener back on
In order to deliver the Pizza order message that's waiting in the queue, you need to turn the listener back on:

1. Close Visual FoxPro again.

2. In the Component Services Explorer, right-click on the QC1 application and select Shutdown from the context menu.

3. Launch the Properties dialog for the QC1 application and select the Queuing tab. Select the Listen check box, and then click OK to close the Properties dialog.

4. Restart Visual FoxPro and run the Pizza form. The View button is disabled because an Order text file doesn't exist. If you look in the Computer Management Explorer, you will see the message still waiting in the queue.

5. Go back to the Component Services Explorer and start the QC1 application by right-clicking on QC1 and selecting Start from the context menu. As soon as the QC1 application restarts, it receives the queued order and writes it out to the Order text file.

6. Go back to Visual FoxPro and click the Refresh button on the Pizza form—the View button should now be enabled. Click the View button to see the text file, and then go to the Computer Management Explorer to see that the message is gone from the queue.

Summary

Visual FoxPro's enhanced COM capabilities allow you to create enterprise-level distributed applications that are able to use a wide range of COM+ services. This means that you can let the operating system do the work and concentrate on your application-specific business logic.

Chapter 15
Working with Web Services

The next generation of Web applications involves the use of Web Services. Visual FoxPro 7's new built-in XML capabilities and Web Services extensions make it easy to create Web Services that can be accessed from anywhere on the Internet.

Before jumping into the topic of Web Services, it's best to first understand the basics of XML, how it has been integrated into VFP 7, and where you can use it in your applications.

Introducing XML

In a nutshell, XML is a (relatively) new text-based data format. So what's all the hubbub about? Primarily it's because XML has been universally accepted by all major platform vendors, paving the way for a universal cross-platform standard for sharing data.

XML bears a strong resemblance to HTML, and with good reason—they are both related to a parent language definition standard called Standard Generalized Markup Language (SGML). XML contains tags (words in angled brackets) surrounding blocks of text. However, unlike HTML where each tag has a specific meaning, XML is extensible—its tags have no predefined meaning. You can assign your own meaning to the tags.

For example, in HTML, the <TABLE> tag has a specific meaning. Based on this, any browser that understands the HTML specification can render tables correctly. In contrast, the <TABLE> tag can mean anything in XML. For example, in the following XML fragment, the <TABLE> tag refers to different kinds of furniture—a dining room, coffee, or card table:

```
<FURNITURE>
  <TABLE>"Dining Room"</TABLE>
  <TABLE>"Coffee"</TABLE>
  <TABLE>"Card"</TABLE>
</FURNITURE>
```

> *For a more detailed explanation of XML, see the MSDN topic "XML Tutorial."*

The structure of an XML document

Here is an example of an XML document:

```
<?xml version = "1.0" encoding="Windows-1252" standalone="yes"?>
<VFPData>
  <customer>
    <iid>1</iid>
    <cacctno>001000</cacctno>
    <cname>Journey Communications</cname>
    <caddress1>101 Main St.</caddress1>
```

```
    <ccity>Richmond</ccity>
    <cstate region="1">VA</cstate>
    <czip>22901</czip>
    <ctype/>
  </customer>
  <customer>
    <iid>4</iid>
    <cacctno>001003</cacctno>
    <cname>Sergio Vargas, Attorney at Law</cname>
    <caddress1>115 Pacific Coast Highway</caddress1>
    <ccity>Malibu</ccity>
    <cstate region="5">CA</cstate>
    <czip>80766</czip>
    <ctype/>
  </customer>
</VFPData>
```

The first line in the document is the *XML declaration*:

```
<?xml version = "1.0" encoding="Windows-1252" standalone="yes"?>
```

This declaration is not required, but it's recommended that you place it at the top of all of your XML documents. It identifies the document as an XML document and specifies the version of XML used to create it. Optionally, it can contain the character encoding used. The "standalone" instruction specifies whether the XML document stands alone or needs additional definitions declared in other files. Note that the word "xml" must be in lowercase. XML tags (unlike HTML) are case-sensitive.

The next line in the document is the start tag of the root element:

```
<VFPData>
```

The XML specification requires that all XML documents contain a single root element that encompasses all other elements in the document.

Within the root element are two <customer> elements, each representing an individual customer record. Within the customer element there are nine other elements, each representing a field in a record.

Elements

Elements are the most common form of markup found in an XML document. They consist of an opening and closing tag, content between the tags (also referred to as "data"), and optionally attributes with associated values (see the next section). For example:

```
<cname>Sergio Vargas, Attorney at Law</cname>
```

If a particular element does not have any content, you can use a single tag element to represent it. For example, the ctype tag in the previous section contains no data and is represented as:

```
<ctype/>
```

This contains both the start and end tag information in a single tag element.

Attributes

An attribute is a name-value pair enclosed within the opening tag of an element. For example:

```
<cstate region="5">CA</cstate>
```

In this element, region="5" is the name-value pair that comprises the attribute. Attributes can be used to provide additional information regarding a particular element.

Comments

In an XML document, comments take the form:

```
<!-- This is a comment -->
```

Comments are ignored by XML parsers.

Well-formed XML

XML documents are *well-formed*, if they adhere to the basic rules of XML. For example, the XML specification dictates that XML documents must contain a unique root node. Another rule of well-formed XML is that start and end tags match—including their capitalization. For example, these are valid XML tags:

```
<cacctno>001003</cacctno>
```

But these are not, since the case doesn't match:

```
<cacctno>001003</cAcctNo>
```

With HTML, you can be somewhat lax about ending tags. Browsers rendering HTML can be very forgiving—if you leave off an ending tag, the browser can compensate and render the HTML in a presentable fashion. In contrast, XML parsers are not at all forgiving. For each start tag, there must be a corresponding end tag.

Reserved characters

There are special reserved characters in XML that cannot be used "as is" in the data portion of an element because they have an alternate meaning in the XML specification. For example, the left angle bracket < is used in XML to mark the beginning of a tag; so if you want to use this character in the data portion of an XML element, you need to replace it with: <.

The reserved characters and their replacement character sequence (entity encoding) are shown in **Table 1**.

Table 1. *This table shows commonly used special reserved characters that must be replaced by corresponding entity encoding.*

Reserved character	Entity encoding replacement
& (ampersand)	&amp;
< (less than)	&lt;
> (greater than)	&gt;
" (double quote)	&quot;
' (apostrophe)	&apos;

For example, in XML, the text "Liederbach & Associates" must be changed to:

```
<cname>Liederbach &amp; Associates</cname>
```

Element-centric and attribute-centric XML

Visual FoxPro 7 can produce XML data in three different formats:

- Element-centric

- Attribute-centric

- Raw

The following sections show how a Customer table with the structure shown in **Table 2** is represented by VFP 7 in each of these formats.

Table 2. *This table shows the structure of a Customer table used in the XML examples for this chapter.*

Name	Type	Width
iID	Integer	4
cAcctNo	Character	6
cName	Character	50
cAddress1	Character	40
cCity	Character	25
cState	Character	2
cZip	Character	10

Element-centric XML

Records formatted in element-centric XML look like this:

```
<?xml version = "1.0" encoding="Windows-1252" standalone="yes"?>
<VFPData>
  <customer>
    <iid>1</iid>
    <cacctno>001000</cacctno>
    <cname>Journey Communications</cname>
    <caddress1>101 Main St.</caddress1>
```

```
      <ccity>Richmond</ccity>
      <cstate>VA</cstate>
      <czip>22901</czip>
   </customer>
   <customer>
      <iid>4</iid>
      <cacctno>001003</cacctno>
      <cname>Sergio Vargas, Attorney at Law</cname>
      <caddress1>115 Pacific Coast Hwy</caddress1>
      <ccity>Malibu</ccity>
      <cstate>CA</cstate>
      <czip>80766</czip>
   </customer>
</VFPData>
```

In this format, each record is represented as an individual element. Each field is also represented as an element, but nested within a record element.

Attribute-centric XML
Records formatted in attribute-centric XML look like this:

```
<?xml version = "1.0" encoding="Windows-1252" standalone="yes"?>
<VFPData>
   <customer iid="1" cacctno="001000" cname="Journey Communications"
      caddress1="101 Main St." ccity="Richmond" cstate="VA" czip="22901"/>
   <customer iid="4" cacctno="001003" cname="Sergio Vargas, Attorney at Law"
      caddress1="115 Pacific Coast Hwy" ccity="Malibu" cstate="CA" czip="80766"/>
</VFPData>
```

In this format, each record is represented as a single-tag element (each element is given the same name as the associated cursor). All field values are represented as an attribute of a record element. All field values are represented as strings regardless of their original type. As you can see, attribute-centric XML is more concise than element-centric.

Raw XML
Records formatted in raw XML look like this:

```
<?xml version = "1.0" encoding="Windows-1252" standalone="yes"?>
<VFPData>
   <row iid="1" cacctno="001000" cname="Journey Communications" caddress1="101
      Main St." ccity="Richmond" cstate="VA" czip="22901"/>
   <row iid="4" cacctno="001003" cname="Sergio Vargas, Attorney at Law"
      caddress1="115 Pacific Coast Hwy" ccity="Malibu" cstate="CA" czip="80766"/>
</VFPData>
```

This format is the same as attribute-centric, except each record element is named "row."

Schemas and valid XML
As described in the section "Well-formed XML," in order for an XML document to be interpreted properly by a parser, it must be well-formed. In addition to being well-formed, an XML document can also be *valid*—if it adheres to a specified *schema*.

A schema defines the structure and meaning of an XML document including element names and data types and attributes. You can use a schema to specify the format you expect for an XML document.

Schemas can be stored in a separate file, or included in an XML document. Here is an example of an in-line schema:

```
<?xml version = "1.0" encoding="Windows-1252" standalone="yes"?>
<VFPData>
    <xsd:schema id="VFPSchema" xmlns:xsd=http://www.w3.org/2000/10/XMLSchema
xmlns:msdata="urn:schemas-microsoft-com:xml-msdata">
        <xsd:element name="customer" minOccurs="1" maxOccurs="unbounded">
            <xsd:complexType>
                <xsd:attribute name="iid" use="required" type="xsd:int"/>
                <xsd:attribute name="cacctno" use="required">
                    <xsd:simpleType>
                        <xsd:restriction base="xsd:string">
                            <xsd:maxLength value="6"/>
                        </xsd:restriction>
                    </xsd:simpleType>
                </xsd:attribute>
                <xsd:attribute name="cname" use="required">
                    <xsd:simpleType>
                        <xsd:restriction base="xsd:string">
                            <xsd:maxLength value="50"/>
                        </xsd:restriction>
                    </xsd:simpleType>
                </xsd:attribute>
                <xsd:attribute name="caddress1" use="required">
                    <xsd:simpleType>
                        <xsd:restriction base="xsd:string">
                            <xsd:maxLength value="40"/>
                        </xsd:restriction>
                    </xsd:simpleType>
                </xsd:attribute>
                <xsd:attribute name="ccity" use="required">
                    <xsd:simpleType>
                        <xsd:restriction base="xsd:string">
                            <xsd:maxLength value="25"/>
                        </xsd:restriction>
                    </xsd:simpleType>
                </xsd:attribute>
                <xsd:attribute name="cstate" use="required">
                    <xsd:simpleType>
                        <xsd:restriction base="xsd:string">
                            <xsd:maxLength value="2"/>
                        </xsd:restriction>
                    </xsd:simpleType>
                </xsd:attribute>
                <xsd:attribute name="czip" use="required">
                    <xsd:simpleType>
                        <xsd:restriction base="xsd:string">
                            <xsd:maxLength value="10"/>
                        </xsd:restriction>
                    </xsd:simpleType>
                </xsd:attribute>
            </xsd:complexType>
        </xsd:element>
```

```
    <xsd:element name="VFPData" msdata:lsDataSet="true">
       <xsd:complexType>
          <xsd:choice maxOccurs="unbounded">
             <xsd:element ref="customer"/>
          </xsd:choice>
       </xsd:complexType>
    </xsd:element>
 </xsd:schema>
 <customer iid="1" cacctno="001000" cname="Journey Communications"
   caddress1="101 Main St." ccity="Richmond" cstate="VA" czip="22901"/>
 <customer cacctno="001003" cname="Sergio Vargas, Attorney at Law"
   caddress1="115 Pacific Coast Hwy" ccity="Malibu" cstate="CA" czip="80766"/>
</VFPData>
```

If you look closely at the in-line schema, you can see it specifies the name of elements, whether they are required, their length, and their type. Visual FoxPro 7 supports the W3C XML Schema standard (XSD). For details, see **http://www.w3.org/TR/2000/CR-xmlschema-0-20001024/**.

For a table that shows you how Visual FoxPro data types map to XSD types, see the VFP 7 Help file topic "XML Functions."

XML namespaces
Namespaces are a way to uniquely identify elements in an XML document. This is important because the author of an XML document defines its XML tags, and if you merge documents from multiple authors, you run the chance of a collision occurring between tag names.

You can define one or more namespaces for a document with the xmlns attribute in an opening XML element tag. The namespace applies to all the contents of an element. Since a namespace is used to uniquely identify tags, the namespace itself must be unique. Often, XML document authors choose the URL of their company as a namespace since it's guaranteed to be unique. For example:

```
<VFPData xmlns="www.oakleafsd.com">
  <customer iid="1" cacctno="001000" cname="Journey Communications"
    caddress1="101 Main St." ccity="Richmond" cstate="VA" czip="22901"/>
  <customer iid="4" cacctno="001003" cname="Sergio Vargas, Attorney at Law"
    caddress1="115 Pacific Coast Hwy" ccity="Malibu" cstate="CA" czip="80766"/>
</VFPData>
```

XML functions in Visual FoxPro 7
Although you could write your own custom functions that converted a cursor to XML and vice versa, VFP 6 knew nothing about XML. Visual FoxPro 7 changes that with the introduction of three new functions: CursorToXML(), XMLToCursor(), and XMLUpdateGram().

CursorToXML()
The new CursorToXML() function does just what its name says—converts a Visual FoxPro cursor to XML. This command can be used by business objects to convert internal cursors to XML that can be consumed by clients.

The syntax of CursorToXML() is:

```
CursorToXML(nWorkArea | cTableAlias, cOutput [, nOutputFormat [, nFlags [,
nRecords [, cSchemaName [, cSchemaLocation [, cNameSpace ]]]]]])
```

The first parameter allows you to specify either the work area or the alias of the cursor to be converted. The cOutput parameter specifies the name of a memory variable or file to which the resulting XML is stored. By default, cOutput specifies a variable name. To specify a file name, you must set the corresponding bit in the nFlags parameter (see the VFP 7 Help topic "CURSORTOXML() Function" for details).

The nOutputFormat parameter specifies the output format of the XML (1=Element-centric, 2=Attribute-centric, and 3=Raw).

The cSchemaName, cSchemaLocation, and cNameSpace parameters allow you to specify information regarding schemas and namespaces. The nFlags parameter allows you to specify additional output options such as preserving white space, output encoding, and how to format empty elements.

The following command converts the contents of the Customer table to element-centric XML and stores the result in a memory variable named lcXML:

```
CursorToXML("Customer", "lcXML")
```

This next command converts the contents of the Customer table to attribute-centric XML, stores the results in a file named Results.XML, and generates an inline schema with a "www.microsoft.com" namespace:

```
CURSORTOXML("customer","Results.xml", 2, 512, 0,"1", "", "www.microsoft.com")
```

XMLToCursor()

The new XMLToCursor() function converts an XML string to a Visual FoxPro cursor. This function can be used by business objects to convert XML input received by clients into an internal cursor format.

The syntax of XMLToCursor() is:

```
XMLToCursor(cXMLExpression | cXMLFile [, cCursorName [, nFlags]])
```

The cXMLExpression parameter specifies either XML text or an expression that evaluates to XML data. This can be any one of the following:

- A memory variable.

- A memo field.

- The return from an HTTP request.

- The return from a SOAP method call (see the section "Simple Object Access Protocol (SOAP)" later in this chapter).

- XML from the XML DOM (Document Object Model). The XML DOM is a programming interface for XML documents that allows you to access an XML document as a tree view with nodes.

- An ADO stream.

Alternately, you can specify the name of an XML file in the cXMLFile parameter. The nFlags parameter specifies how to handle the first parameter. For details, see the table in the VFP 7 Help topic "XMLToCursor()."

The cCursorName parameter specifies the name of the cursor to store the results. If this cursor is in use, VFP generates an error. XMLToCursor() can convert XML with or without a schema.

The following command converts the Results.xml file to a cursor named "MyCursor":

```
XMLTOCURSOR("Results.xml", "MyCursor", 512)
```

XMLUpdateGram()

The new XMLUpdateGram() function returns an XML string listing all the changes in a buffered table or cursor. You must enable table buffering and SET MULTILOCKS ON before running XMLUpdateGram().

The syntax of XMLUpdateGram() is:

```
XMLUpdateGram([cAliasList [, nFlags]])
```

The cAliasList parameter specifies a comma-delimited list of open tables or cursors to be included in the updategram. If cAliasList is empty, XMLUpdateGram() includes all open tables and cursors in the current data session.

The nFlags parameter contains a list of additive flags that specify how the XML output is formatted (if at all). See the VFP 7 Help file topic "XMLUPDATEGRAM() Function" for a table describing these flags.

Updating records

To demonstrate how XMLUpdateGram() works when updating records, launch Visual FoxPro, go to this chapter's ProjectX\Data directory, and enter the following in the Command Window:

```
USE Customer
SET MULTILOCKS ON
CURSORSETPROP("Buffering", 5, "Customer")    && Enable table buffering
REPLACE caddress1 with "500 Water St." IN Customer    && Make a change
lcUpdateXML = XMLUpdateGram("Customer")    && Generate the Update Gram
STRTOFILE(lcUpdateXML, "UpdateGram.xml")
MODIFY FILE UpdateGram.xml
```

*The Developer Download files at **www.hentzenwerke.com** include the Customer table referenced in this chapter.*

The UpdateGram.xml file should contain the following:

```
<?xml version = "1.0" encoding="Windows-1252" standalone="yes"?>
<root xmlns:updg="urn:schemas-microsoft-com:xml-updategram">
   <updg:sync>
      <updg:before>
         <customer>
            <iid>1</iid>
            <cacctno>001000</cacctno>
            <cname>Journey Communications</cname>
            <caddress1>101 Main St.</caddress1>
            <ccity>Richmond</ccity>
            <cstate>VA</cstate>
            <czip>22901</czip>
         </customer>
      </updg:before>
      <updg:after>
         <customer>
            <iid>1</iid>
            <cacctno>001000</cacctno>
            <cname>Journey Communications</cname>
            <caddress1>500 Water St.</caddress1>
            <ccity>Richmond</ccity>
            <cstate>VA</cstate>
            <czip>22901</czip>
         </customer>
      </updg:after>
   </updg:sync>
</root>
```

The updategram has a single "root" node containing a single <updg:sync> element. Nested within this element are the <updg:before> and <updg:after> elements. The <updg:before> element contains a list of the record's original values for *all* fields. The <updg:after> element contains a list of all current values. Notice the <caddress1> element contains the new "500 Water St." value.

If you use CURSORSETPROP() to set the key field list for the table before running XMLUpdateGram(), the resulting updategram contains only the key and changed fields. You can try this by entering the following in the Command Window:

```
TABLEREVERT(.T., "Customer")   && Revert the changes to the table
CURSORSETPROP("KeyFieldList", "iid", "Customer")   && Set the key field list
REPLACE caddress1 with "500 Water St." IN Customer   && Make a change
lcUpdateXML = XMLUpdateGram("Customer")   && Generate the Update Gram
STRTOFILE(lcUpdateXML, "UpdateGram1.xml")
MODIFY FILE UpdateGram1.xml
```

The UpdateGram1.xml file should contain the following:

```
<?xml version = "1.0" encoding="Windows-1252" standalone="yes"?>
<root xmlns:updg="urn:schemas-microsoft-com:xml-updategram">
```

```
<updg:sync>
   <updg:before>
      <customer>
         <iid>1</iid>
         <caddress1>101 Main St.</caddress1>
      </customer>
   </updg:before>
   <updg:after>
      <customer>
         <iid>1</iid>
         <caddress1>500 Water St.</caddress1>
      </customer>
   </updg:after>
</updg:sync>
</root>
```

Notice the updategram contains only information regarding two fields—the specified key field (iid) and the changed field (caddress1).

Adding records

To demonstrate how XMLUpdateGram() works when adding records, enter the following in the Command Window:

```
TABLEREVERT(.T., "Customer")   && Revert the changes to the table
INSERT INTO Customer (cacctno, cname, caddress1, ccity, cstate, czip);
   VALUES ("001004", "The Fox", "952 Market St.", "Reston", "VA", "22903")
lcUpdateXML = XMLUpdateGram("Customer")   && Generate the Update Gram
STRTOFILE(lcUpdateXML, "UpdateGram2.xml")
MODIFY FILE UpdateGram2.xml
```

The UpdateGram2.xml file should contain the following:

```
<?xml version = "1.0" encoding="Windows-1252" standalone="yes"?>
<root xmlns:updg="urn:schemas-microsoft-com:xml-updategram">
   <updg:sync>
      <updg:before/>
      <updg:after>
         <customer>
            <iid>6</iid>
            <cacctno>001004</cacctno>
            <cname>The Fox</cname>
            <caddress1>952 Market St.</caddress1>
            <ccity>Reston</ccity>
            <cstate>VA</cstate>
            <czip>22903</czip>
         </customer>
      </updg:after>
   </updg:sync>
</root>
```

Notice the <updg:before/> element is an empty single-tag element—since this is a new record, there is no "before" data. The <updg:after> element contains all the values for the new record.

Deleting records

To demonstrate how XMLUpdateGram() works when deleting records, enter the following in the Command Window:

```
TABLEREVERT(.T., "Customer")    && Revert the changes to the table
LOCATE    && Move the record pointer to the first record
DELETE    && Delete the first record
lcUpdateXML = XMLUpdateGram("Customer")    && Generate the Update Gram
STRTOFILE(lcUpdateXML, "UpdateGram3.xml")
MODIFY FILE UpdateGram3.xml
```

The UpdateGram3.xml file should contain the following:

```
<?xml version = "1.0" encoding="Windows-1252" standalone="yes"?>
<root xmlns:updg="urn:schemas-microsoft-com:xml-updategram">
    <updg:sync>
        <updg:before>
            <customer>
                <iid>1</iid>
                <cacctno>001000</cacctno>
                <cname>Journey Communications</cname>
                <caddress1>101 Main St.</caddress1>
                <ccity>Richmond</ccity>
                <cstate>VA</cstate>
                <czip>22901</czip>
            </customer>
        </updg:before>
        <updg:after/>
    </updg:sync>
</root>
```

Notice the <updg:before> element contains the original values of the deleted record and <updg:after/> is an empty single-tag element.

Multi-user contention checking

Why does the XMLUpdateGram() function include original values when generating an updategram? This allows you to verify that no other user has changed a record that is being updated or deleted.

Using updategrams in SQL Server 2000

Where can you use updategrams? First of all, updategrams are a new feature of SQL Server 2000 that allows SQL Server database updates to be defined as XML. Notice in the root node of the generated updategrams, the namespace is specified as:

```
<root xmlns:updg="urn:schemas-microsoft-com:xml-updategram">
```

The format used for VFP 7 updategrams is the standard format used by SQL Server 2000.

Using updategrams in distributed applications

Even if you're not using SQL Server 2000 as your back-end database, updategrams can be very useful in n-tier architectures. The Windows Distributed Internet Architecture (Windows DNA) specifies that business objects should be composed of two pieces—an emissary and an executant. In a distributed desktop system, the emissary portion of the business object resides on the workstation, and the executant portion resides on an application server elsewhere on the network.

When the workstation needs data, it sends a request to the emissary portion of the business object. Rather than retrieving the data directly, the business object passes the request to an executant object. The executant retrieves the data from the back end and passes it to the emissary. What transport mechanism can the executant use to send the data to the emissary? The most common choices are ADO and XML, but given VFP 7's new XML capabilities coupled with VFP 7's lightning fast string-manipulation abilities, there are compelling reasons to favor XML.

When the business object on the workstation receives the requested data as an XML string, it can convert it to a VFP cursor to be consumed by the desktop application. The application can manipulate the cursor—editing, adding, and deleting records. When the user saves changes, the emissary can run XMLUpdateGram() against the VFP cursor and pass the resulting updategram to the executant, which then applies the changes to the back-end database.

VFPXMLProgID

The new _VFP.VFPXMLProgID property allows you to specify a COM component that can be used instead of the built-in VFP 7 XML functions (CursorToXML(), XMLToCursor(), XMLUpdateGram()).

This property specifies the programmatic identifier (ProgID) of the surrogate COM component. The COM component you specify must implement VFP 7's IVFPXML interface. The VFP 7 Help topic "VFPXMLProgID Property" gives an example creating a COM object that implements this interface.

Introducing Web Services

Web Services are the next generation of Web applications. They are modular, self-describing applications that can be published and invoked across the Web. Web Services can range from simple functions to complex business processes.

A simple way to understand what Web Services are is to look at the way current generation Web applications work. At present, if you book a hotel room online, you usually need to go to a different Web site to determine what the weather will be during your stay (as long as the trip is not too far into the future). Wouldn't it be better if the hotel's Web site could provide this information for you? This requires the Web site to be able to communicate with a weather Web site—to pass it information regarding the weather based on the location of the hotel and your arrival date.

In actuality, this type of functionality has been available for some time. There are hotel Web sites that display the current weather; however, they're typically not using Web Services to accomplish this—they're using more of a "hard-coded" model. Usually, a weather service Web site posts a GIF file on their Web server, and hotel (or other) Web sites simply contain a pointer to the location of the GIF file. However, this approach is inflexible because it forces the weather information to be shown in a particular display format (size, shape, color, and so on). Using Web Services to retrieve the current weather allows consumers of this service to display the weather information in any format they choose.

Real, live Web Services!

How can you know what kind of Web Services are available on the Web? There are a number of Web Service resources that you can search. One of these is the Web site **http://www.xmethods.net/**, which provides a list of available Web Services (see **Table 3**).

Just looking through this list can help you visualize how Web Services can revolutionize Web applications. Web Services does for Web applications what ActiveX controls did for Win32 applications. Rather than reinventing the wheel, you can use services of existing Web sites to enhance your Web applications.

Table 3. *Some of the more interesting Web Services available on the Internet.*

Name	Description	Schema location
FedEx Tracker	Access to FedEx tracking information	http://www.xmethods.net/sd/FedExTrackerService.wsdl
Babel Fish Service	Babel Fish Language Translation	http://www.xmethods.net/sd/BabelFishService.wsdl
Headline News	Latest news coverage from various sources	http://www.SoapClient.com/xml/SQLDataSoap.wsdl
Who Is	A SOAP version of the standard "who is" service that returns info on a specified Internet domain	http://soap.4s4c.com/whois/soap.asp?WSDL
Soap Web Search	SOAP interface to major search engines	http://www.soapclient.com/xml/SQLDataSoap.WSDL
SMS Messaging	Send a text message to a mobile phone	http://sal006.salnetwork.com:83/lucin/smsmessaging/process.xml
Currency Converter	Converts values from one international currency to another	http://sal006.salnetwork.com:83/lucin/currencyconvertor/ccurrencyc.xml

In addition to using the Web Services provided by other sites, you can also publish your own VFP 7 COM servers as Web Services that others can access.

Simple Object Access Protocol (SOAP)

Thinking about the example of hotel Web site to weather Web site communication raises some important questions—how does the hotel site know the capabilities of the weather Web site? How does it know the format of the request to be sent and the response it receives?

The answer to these questions is SOAP—Simple Object Access Protocol. SOAP leverages the existing HTTP and XML standards to provide a standard way to pass commands and parameters between clients and servers. Clients send requests to a server in XML format and the server sends the results back as XML. These messages are encapsulated in HTTP protocol messages.

> *For more information on SOAP-related topics, check Microsoft's SOAP Developer Resources Web site (**http://msdn.microsoft.com/soap/**).*

Using the SOAP Toolkit 2.0

To make it easier to publish Web Services and create applications that invoke Web Services using SOAP, Microsoft has created the SOAP Toolkit (version 2.0 at the time of this writing).

> *The SOAP Toolkit 2.0 comes with an excellent Help file (Soap.CHM) located in the MSSOAP/Documentation folder. Rather than duplicate that information, this chapter touches on the highlights of the Toolkit. Refer to the Help file and samples for details.*

Installing the SOAP Toolkit

You can download the SOAP Toolkit from Microsoft's SOAP Developer Resources Web site (**http://msdn.microsoft.com/soap/**). The download consists of two files: the SOAP Toolkit 2.0 Gold Release (SoapToolkit20.EXE) and Gold Release samples (SoapToolkit20Samples.EXE).

After downloading the Toolkit, double-click the EXE files and follow the instructions in the Install Wizard. By default, the SOAP Toolkit files are installed in the Program Files\MSSOAP directory.

The Toolkit contains the following components and tools:

- A component that makes it easier for clients to call a Web Service.

- A component that resides on the Web server and maps Web Service operations to COM object method calls.

- Additional components that construct, transmit, read, and process SOAP messages.

- A tool that generates Web Services Description Language (WSDL) documents and Web Services Meta Language (WSML) files (see the corresponding sections that follow).

- The SOAP Messaging Object (SMO) Framework, which provides an alternative to the XML DOM for processing XML in SOAP messages.

Web Services Description Language (WSDL)

The Web Services Description Language (WSDL) file can be likened to an XML type library for Web Services. This file identifies the services and sets of operations provided by a server. The WSDL file is placed on a Web server. Any client that wants to invoke the services of that server must first download a copy of the WSDL file to determine how to format a SOAP request for the provider.

Document-oriented and RPC-oriented operations

There are two main types of operations defined in a WSDL file—*document-oriented operations* and *RPC-oriented operations* (Remote Procedure Call). With document-oriented operations, request and response messages contain XML documents. The SOAP Messaging Object (SMO) Framework makes it easy to process the XML documents in a SOAP message.

RPC-oriented operations expect input parameters for input messages, and output messages contain return values.

Web Services Meta Language (WSML)

A Web Services Meta Language (WSML) file contains information that maps the operations of a service described in the WSDL file to a method in a COM object.

SOAP Listeners

A Listener is the entity that handles incoming SOAP messages on the server side. There are two types of Listeners you can choose from:

- An Internet Server API (ISAPI) Listener

- An Active Server Pages (ASP) Listener

From a sheer performance perspective, an ISAPI Listener is the best choice. Some developers have reported speeds of up to four times faster for an ISAPI Listener. However, if you want to do some processing between the request received from the client and the call to a method on a COM object, you may want to implement an ASP Listener instead. You can place code in an ASP page surrounding the call to the object. See the SOAP Toolkit 2.0 Help topics "Specifying an ASP Listener" and "Specifying an ISAPI Listener" for details.

Visual FoxPro 7.0 Web Services extensions

Although you can use the Microsoft SOAP Toolkit 2.0 directly, Visual FoxPro 7 provides a set of extensions to the Toolkit that make it easy to register a Web Service for use by a client (if you need finer control over publishing and consuming Web Services, you should use the SOAP Toolkit directly). The extensions also make it easy to publish Web Services, and can produce WSDL and WSML files for your COM servers.

> *For details on using the SOAP Toolkit with Visual FoxPro, check out Rick Strahl's white paper "Using Microsoft SOAP Toolkit for remote object access" at **http://www.west-wind.com/presentations/soap/**.*

Registering a Web Service

To register a Web Service for use by a client:

1. From the Tools menu, select IntelliSense Manager.

2. Select the Types tab and click the Web Services button (see **Figure 1**).

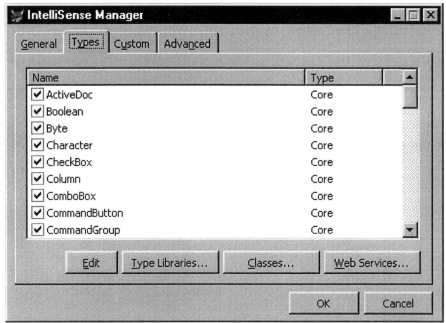

Figure 1. The IntelliSense Manager's Web Services *button launches the Web Services Registration dialog.*

3. In the Web Services Registration dialog's Web Service Name box, specify a friendly name for the Web Service (see **Figure 2**). The name can include spaces (for example, "Language Translation"). A history of all Web Service names you've entered is stored and displayed in the Web Service Name combo box.

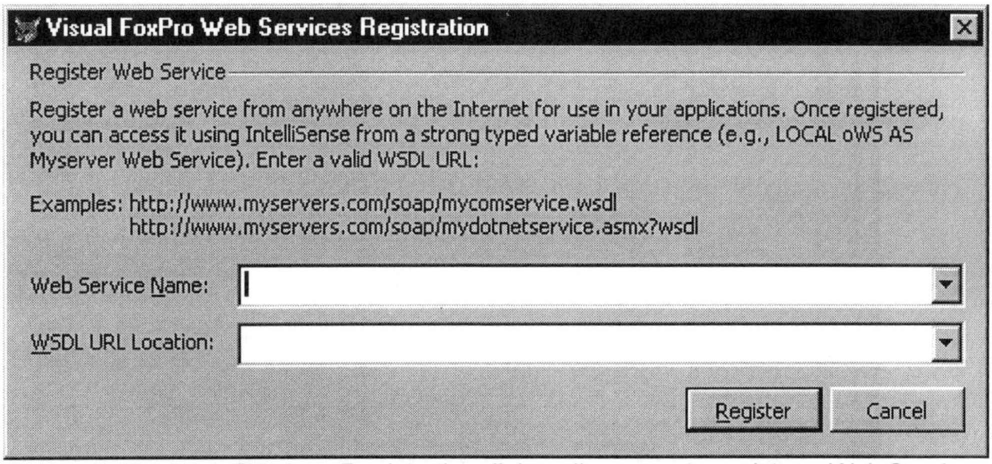

Figure 2. The Web Services Registration dialog allows you to register a Web Service located anywhere on the Internet for use in your applications.

4. In the WSDL URL Location box, enter the WSDL URL of the Web Service you are registering. For example: **http://www.xmethods.net/sd/BabelFishService.wsdl**.

5. Click the Register button.

At this point, the dialog generates IntelliSense scripts based on the information you have entered. Note that this may take several seconds with no visual cue that any processing is going on! When the process is complete, you will see the dialog shown in **Figure 3**.

Figure 3. This dialog displays when your Web Service registration has successfully completed. Note that it may take quite a while for this dialog to appear.

Click the OK button to close this dialog. Your new Web Service is added to the list in the Types tab of the IntelliSense Manager. The next section discusses how you can access the new Web Service.

> *It is not required that you register a Web Service using the IntelliSense Manager. However, if you do, VFP provides IntelliSense for Web Service methods and parameters.*

Calling Web Services

To programmatically call a Web Service that you have set up, do the following:

1. In code, declare a strong-typed variable. For example:

```
LOCAL loTranslate AS
```

2. In the dropdown list of IntelliSense types, select a Web Service. For example:

```
LOCAL loTranslate AS Language Translation
```

3. When you press the Enter key, Web Service proxy code is automatically added to your source file. For example:

```
LOCAL loTranslate AS Language Translation
LOCAL loWS
loWS = NEWOBJECT("Wsclient",HOME()+"ffc\_webservices.vcx")
```

```
loTranslate =
loWS.SetupClient("http://www.xmethods.net/sd/BabelFishService.wsdl",
"BabelFish", "BabelFishPort")
```

This code instantiates the VFP 7 WSClient base class (loWS) and then creates a
SOAP client object (loTranslate).

4. To use this service, add the following code:

```
?loWS.BabelFish("en_es","fox")
```

This code tells the Babel Fish Web Service to translate the word "fox" from English
to Spanish ("en_es") and display it on the VFP desktop.

Publishing Web Services

In addition to calling Web Services, the VFP 7 Web Services extensions allow you to publish
VFP COM servers as Web Services.

> *In order to publish Web Services, you must have Internet Information
> Server installed.*

To publish a Web Service:

1. Create a COM server project, containing at least one OLE Public class, and then build
    an in-process VFP COM server DLL (usually a multi-threaded COM server DLL)
    from the project.

2. Right-click your VFP COM server project and select Builder from the context menu
    (see **Figure 4**). This launches the Wizard Selection dialog. In the Wizard Selection
    dialog, select Web Services Publisher and click OK.

3. If this is the first time you have published a Web Service, the dialog in **Figure 5** is
    displayed recommending that you select a default URL for your Web Service support
    files such as ASP Listeners and WSDL and WSML files. Specifying a default
    directory is not mandatory, but if you don't specify one, you are prompted for a
    location each time you publish a Web Service. Click OK to launch the Web Service
    Location dialog.

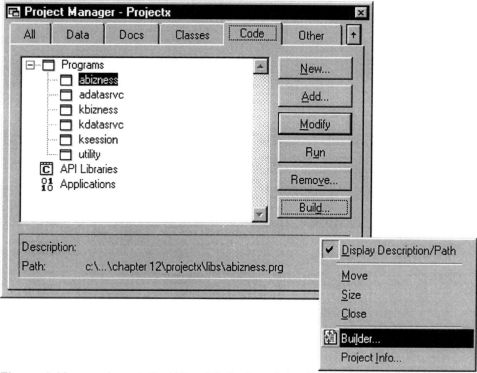

Figure 4. You can launch the Wizard Selection dialog from the Project Manager context menu. You can also launch it by selecting Tools | Wizards | All Wizards from the VFP 7 menu, and selecting Web Services Publisher in the Wizard Selection dialog.

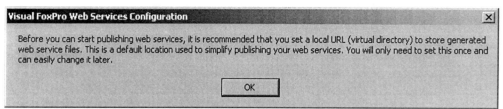

Figure 5. The first time you publish a Web Service, the Web Services Configuration dialog displays recommending that you select a default URL for your Web Service files.

4. In the Web Service Location dialog, select an existing virtual directory for your Web Services support files or create a new one (see **Figure 6**).

You can select an existing virtual directory by clicking the Existing option and selecting a directory from the Select Virtual Directory combo box.

You can select a new directory by clicking the **New** option and entering a directory name in the **New Virtual Directory Name** box. Next, click the **Path** command button and specify the physical path for the new virtual directory. Typically, you should create a new directory under your c:\inetpub\wwwroot directory.

Figure 6. *The Web Service Location dialog allows you to specify a default virtual directory for your Web Services support files.*

The information entered in this dialog gets saved to a table named FoxWS.DBF located in your Visual FoxPro 7 program directory.

5. Click the **Select** button to continue. This launches the Web Services Publisher dialog (see **Figure 7**). By default, the **COM Server** combo box contains a list of all COM servers associated with open projects as well as previously published COM servers. Select a COM server from the combo box or click the ellipsis button to select a COM server that is not in the list.

6. The **Select Class** combo box displays a list of OLE public classes in the selected COM server. Select the class you want to publish. If the COM server you choose has only one class, the combo box is disabled.

    If the class you choose contains Currency or Variant parameter or return value types, an "information" image is displayed next to the **Select Class** combo box (see Figure 7). If you click on this image, a dialog displays telling you to specify strong typing for these; otherwise, an invalid WSDL file may be generated.

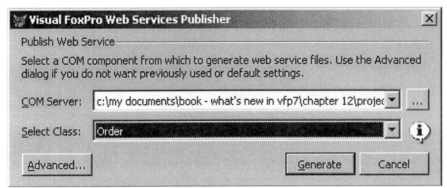

Figure 7. The Web Services Publisher dialog allows you to generate Web Service files for a VFP 7 COM component.

> *One of the downsides of using the VFP 7 Web Services extensions is that you cannot pick and choose which methods in a COM server are published—it's an all or nothing proposition. If you need finer control, you can use the SOAP Toolkit directly.*

7. If you click the **Advanced** button, it launches the Web Services Publisher dialog shown in **Figure 8**. This dialog allows you to specify additional information such as:

   - The URL and name of the WSDL files

   - The type of Listener (ISAPI or ASP)

   - If using an ASP Listener, information regarding the ASP files

   - IntelliSense scripts

   For details on these settings, see the VFP 7 Help topic "Web Service Publishing."

8. Click the **Generate** button to generate the Web Service files.

If the Web Services Publisher is successful, it displays a dialog similar to the one shown in **Figure 9**.

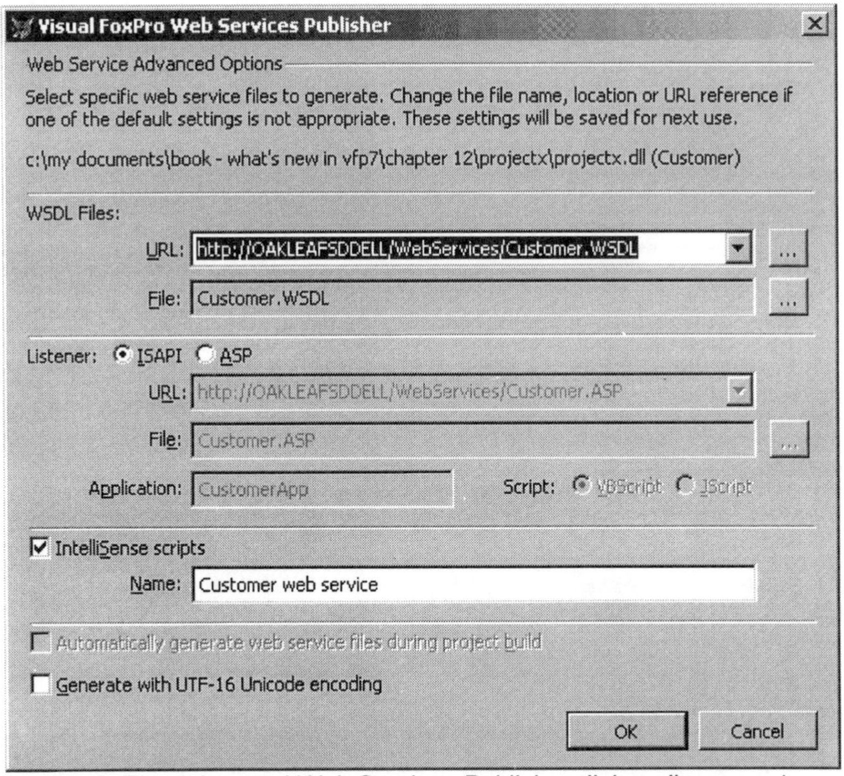

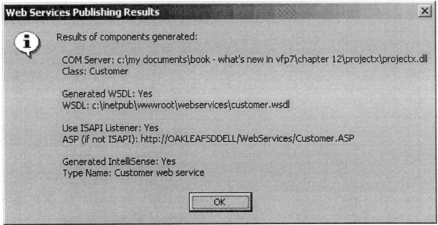

Figure 8. *The Advanced Web Services Publisher dialog allows you to specify additional information regarding the generated Web Service files.*

Figure 9. *The Web Services Publisher displays the Results dialog if it successfully publishes Web Services for your COM component.*

The primary by-products of the publishing process are the WSDL and WSML files. These files are stored in the directory you specified in the Web Services Publisher dialog. Here is a partial listing of a WSDL file generated from the example ProjectX Customer class (all methods have been protected except GetCustomerByAcctNo):

```xml
<?xml version='1.0' encoding='UTF-8' ?>
 <!-- Generated 04/27/01 by Microsoft SOAP Toolkit WSDL File Generator, Version
1.00.623.0 -->
<definitions  name ='customer'  targetNamespace = 'http://tempuri.org/wsdl/'
    ...
  <message name='Customer.GetCustomerByAcctNo'>
    <part name='AcctNo' type='xsd:string'/>
  </message>
  <message name='Customer.GetCustomerByAcctNoResponse'>
    <part name='Result' type='xsd:string'/>
  </message>
  <portType name='CustomerSoapPort'>
    <operation name='GetCustomerByAcctNo' parameterOrder='AcctNo'>
      <input message='wsdlns:Customer.GetCustomerByAcctNo' />
      <output message='wsdlns:Customer.GetCustomerByAcctNoResponse' />
    </operation>
  </portType>
  <binding name='CustomerSoapBinding' type='wsdlns:CustomerSoapPort' >
    <stk:binding preferredEncoding='UTF-8'/>
    <soap:binding style='rpc' transport='http://schemas.xmlsoap.org/soap/http'
/>
    <operation name='GetCustomerByAcctNo' >
      <soap:operation
soapAction='http://tempuri.org/action/Customer.GetCustomerByAcctNo' />
      <input>
        <soap:body use='encoded' namespace='http://tempuri.org/message/'
        encodingStyle='http://schemas.xmlsoap.org/soap/encoding/' />
      </input>
      <output>
        <soap:body use='encoded' namespace='http://tempuri.org/message/'
        encodingStyle='http://schemas.xmlsoap.org/soap/encoding/' />
      </output>
    </operation>
  </binding>
  <service name='customer' >
    <port name='CustomerSoapPort' binding='wsdlns:CustomerSoapBinding' >
      <soap:address location='http://OAKLEAFSDDELL/WebServices/customer.wsdl'
/>
    </port>
  </service>
</definitions>
```

 *The Developer Download files at **www.hentzenwerke.com** include the Customer class referenced in this example.*

Here is the associated WSML file generated by the Web Services Publisher:

```
<?xml version='1.0' encoding='UTF-8' ?>
 <!-- Generated 04/27/01 by Microsoft SOAP Toolkit WSDL File Generator, Version
1.00.623.0 -->
<servicemapping name='customer'>
  <service name='customer'>
    <using PROGID='projectx.Customer' cachable='0' ID='CustomerObject' />
    <port name='CustomerSoapPort'>
      <operation name='GetCustomerByAcctNo'>
        <execute uses='CustomerObject' method='GetCustomerByAcctNo' dispID='0'>
          <parameter callIndex='1' name='AcctNo' elementName='AcctNo' />
          <parameter callIndex='-1' name='retval' elementName='Result' />
        </execute>
      </operation>
    </port>
  </service>
</servicemapping>
```

For an explanation of the contents of these files, check the SOAP Toolkit 2.0 Help files.

If the Web Services Publisher encounters errors while mapping data types during generation of the Web Services files, you will see the dialog shown in **Figure 10**. You can examine the resulting WSDL file to determine the parameters and/or return values that could not be mapped.

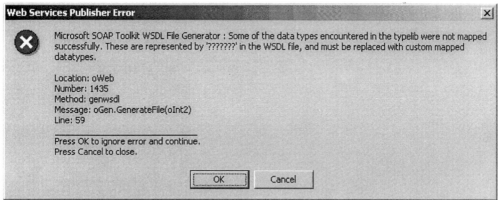

Figure 10. *The Web Services Publisher lets you know if errors are encountered when mapping data types of your COM component's methods.*

The Web Services project hook

The Web Services Publisher Advanced dialog (Figure 8) has a check box that allows you to automatically generate Web Service files during a project build. If you select this check box, it sets up a project hook for your project. This hook calls the Web Service engine to rebuild the support files whenever you build your project.

In addition, the Web Service project hook automatically terminates any IIS process that has a lock on your COM server. If you do not use the project hook, you must manually terminate the process using the Component Services Explorer.

Summary

Once again, the Fox team has done a great job of keeping Visual FoxPro in line with the future of software development. The enhancements to VFP 7 for XML and Web Services make it even easier to build distributed, Web-based, "next generation" applications.

Appendix

Appendix
New Installation Features

Installing VFP 7 is relatively straightforward, but there are a few new features you should be aware of.

Ironically, while the first thing you'll do with your new VFP 7 CD is install it, this appendix on installation appears at the end of the book. That's because installation isn't really a feature of the product, just how you get it on your computer so you can use it. However, there are a few new issues regarding installation.

Installing VFP 7

When you insert the VFP 7 CD, you'll see the dialog displayed in **Figure 1**. This allows you to view the Readme file on the CD, install VFP, and install several other components from the CD. Choose the "Install Visual FoxPro" link to install VFP.

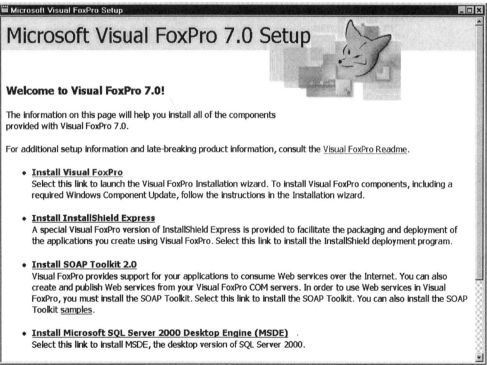

Figure 1. This dialog allows you to install VFP and several other components on the CD.

As with most applications, the installation program for VFP 7 is called Setup.EXE. This program uses the Windows Installer technology to install VFP 7. The Windows Installer requires that certain components be installed on your system, so after you choose to install VFP 7 from the Setup dialog, the first step performed is the Windows Component Update. This ensures that the latest copies of various operating system components, including Microsoft Internet Explorer 5.5, the Microsoft XML Parser (MSXML) 3.0, Microsoft Data Access Components (MDAC), and the Windows Installer itself, are installed on your system. This step is likely to involve at least one restart of your system. Fortunately, you can specify the user name and password so the process can automatically login after a restart to continue the installation process unattended.

After the Windows Component Update, the installation of VFP 7 is relatively simple. There are only a few dialogs (you can choose where VFP should be installed and which features, such as sample files, you want to install along with VFP), and the installation process is fairly quick. You should read the Readme.HTM file for installation issues, such as minimum hardware requirements and known issues.

Installing other components

In addition to installing VFP, you can also install the following from the VFP 7 CD:

- InstallShield Express Limited Edition, the replacement for the VFP Setup Wizard (see Chapter 3, "New and Better Tools").

- SOAP Toolkit 2.0, required for Web Services (see Chapter 15, "Working with Web Services").

- Microsoft SQL Server 2000 Desktop Engine (MSDE), a personal version of SQL Server you can use to create client/server applications without having to purchase and install the full SQL Server. You can even distribute it-freely to your clients.

- Technical articles discussing topics such as using the Application Wizard and other tools to create applications, working with Web Services, and deploying applications with InstallShield Express.

- Microsoft Developer Network (MSDN) Library, the most recent quarterly release of this huge developer resource of Help files, technical articles, and sample source code.

Other installation issues

Some of these issues have been discussed in the appropriate chapters in this book, but they are briefly mentioned here because they relate to installation.

As mentioned in Chapter 8, "Resource Management," VFP 7 now installs resource files for other languages with the English version of VFP 7. Also, VFP no longer installs its run time files (VFP7R.DLL, VFP7T.DLL, and the VFP7Rxxx.DLL language resource files) in the Windows System directory. Instead, they're installed in C:\Program Files\Common Files\Microsoft Shared\VFP.

Chapter 4, "More IDE Changes," points out that to meet Windows 2000 logo requirements, VFP 7 stores user-specific files, such as the resource and FoxCode tables, in a user application data directory (for example, on Windows 2000, it's C:\Documents and Settings\<user name>\Application Data\Microsoft\Visual FoxPro by default). This directory is created as part of the installation process.

The Start menu shortcut for VFP 7 is a special shortcut that points to a Windows Installer application rather than VFP7.EXE in the VFP home directory. Before launching VFP, this application checks that all required components are installed, and if anything is missing, it launches the Windows Installer. This makes VFP similar to Microsoft Office 2000 in that it can repair itself when components become corrupted or are deleted.

VFP6Strt.APP was the default startup program in VFP 6. It displayed a Welcome dialog offering to perform one of several tasks, such as opening the Component Gallery or opening an existing project. VFP 7 doesn't include a VFP7Strt.APP. However, it does include a new VFPClean.APP. This application cleans up any problems with file locations and Registry settings that may have been caused by beta versions of VFP 7. It doesn't run automatically, but you may want to run it the first time you launch VFP 7. The source code for VFPClean.APP is in the Tools\XSource directory (unzip XSource.ZIP to create a VFPSource\VFPClean subdirectory containing the source code). See the Readme file on the VFP 7 CD for more details.

Summary
The installation process for VFP 7 is pretty straightforward (although it may require a few system restarts due to the Windows Component Update) and starts you on your way to working with the latest version of our beloved development tool.

Index